Transforming U.S. Army Supply Chains

Transforming U.S. Army Supply Chains

Strategies for Management Innovation

Greg H. Parlier

Colonel, U.S. Army, Retired

Transforming U.S. Army Supply Chains: Strategies for Management Innovation
Copyright © Business Expert Press, LLC, 2011.
All rights reserved. No part of this publication may be reproduced, stored in a retrieval system, or transmitted in any form or by any means—electronic, mechanical, photocopy, recording, or any other except for brief quotations, not to exceed 400 words, without the prior permission of the publisher.

First published in 2011 by
Business Expert Press, LLC
222 East 46th Street, New York, NY 10017
www.businessexpertpress.com

ISBN-13: 978-1-60649-235-2 (paperback)

ISBN-13: 978-1-60649-236-9 (e-book)

DOI 10.4128/9781606492369

A publication in the Business Expert Press Supply and Operations Management collection

Collection ISSN: 2156-8189 (print)
Collection ISSN: 2156-8200 (electronic)

Cover design by Jonathan Pennell
Interior design by Scribe Inc.

First edition: February 2011

10 9 8 7 6 5 4 3 2 1

Printed in the United States of America.

Abstract

This text offers a practical approach for understanding the U.S. Army's extremely complex global logistics system, widely acknowledged as one of the largest in the world. The focus is on inventory management policy where prescriptions are illuminated through the prism of an enterprise supply chain analysis. Although Army aviation logistics examples are emphasized throughout, the fundamental issues and potential solutions are broadly applicable to other large-scale military and industrial supply chains as well. Following a summary of recent trends for background and context, a multistage conceptual model of the logistics structure is presented to segment and guide the effort. This multistage model is used to systematically analyze major organizational components of the supply chain, diagnose structural, disorders and prescribe solutions. Integration challenges are addressed using cost-benefit perspectives, which incorporate supply chain objectives of efficiency, resilience, and effectiveness. The design and evaluation section proposes an "analytical architecture" consisting of four complementary modeling approaches, collectively referred to as "dynamic strategic logistics planning," to enable a coordinated, enterprise approach for U.S. Army Logistics Transformation. An organizational construct is presented for an "engine for innovation" to accelerate and sustain continual improvement for Army logistics and supply chain management—a "Center for Innovation in Logistics Systems." Finally, strategic management challenges associated with enterprise integration and transformational change are addressed: organizational design; management information and decision support systems; strategic alignment for a learning organization; and workforce considerations including human capital investment needs. The text concludes with a relevant historical vignette and closes with a summary of expected benefits.

Features

Logically structured using an operations research (OR) approach with an enterprise analytical framework, the text introduces, describes, and applies the new concept of "management innovation as a strategic technology." Cutting-edge supply chain theory, powerful analytical methods, and innovative strategic planning and management concepts are applied to this seemingly intractable national security resource challenge which has remained on the U.S. Government Accountability Office's (GAO) "high-risk" list for two decades now.

Benefits

The text simplifies a very complex, "large-scale" system to enable clarity, provide insight, and guide understanding through analysis, synthesis (integration), design, and evaluation. In order to fully capitalize on advances in information technology (IT), the complementary power of modeling, simulation, and rigorous analysis for dramatic performance improvement is demonstrated. The text provides an "analytical architecture"—a comprehensive road map—to sustain continuous performance improvement, relate budget and investment levels to current and future capability outcomes, and create and sustain a learning organization for the U.S. Army's complex, global supply chain enterprise.

Keywords

Supply chain, demand forecasting, inventory policy, dynamic strategic planning, management innovation, systems integration, enterprise transformation

An army fights with its weapons but lives off its logistics.

—Military maxim

So now let us embark on our enquiry into what is true…we sometimes notice that our senses deceive us, and it is wise never to put too much trust in what has let us down.

—Rene Descartes

If we could first know where we are and whither we are tending,
We could better judge what to do, and how to do it.

—Abraham Lincoln, June 16, 1858

Nothing is more powerful than an idea whose time has come.

—Victor Hugo

Contents

List of Figures xiii

Preface xvii

Acknowledgments. xxix

PART I	**PROJECT OVERVIEW**. 1	
Chapter 1	Background. 3	
Chapter 2	The Immediate Problem 9	
Chapter 3	Current Logistics Structure 13	
Chapter 4	Supply Chain Concepts: Analytical Foundation for Improving Logistics System Effectiveness 17	
PART II	**MULTISTAGE ANALYSIS OF SYSTEMIC CHALLENGES** 27	
Chapter 5	Readiness Production Stage: Tactical Units 29	
Chapter 6	Operational Mission and Training Demand Stage 39	
Chapter 7	Retail Stage: Tactical Level. 51	
Chapter 8	Reverse Logistics Stage: Retrograde 59	
Chapter 9	Wholesale Stage: National Level 69	
Chapter 10	Acquisition Stage. 85	
Chapter 11	Summary. 95	
PART III	**MULTISTAGE INTEGRATION FOR EFFICIENCY, RESILIENCE, AND EFFECTIVENESS** 101	
Chapter 12	Achieving Efficiency: An Integrated Multiechelon Inventory Solution. 103	

Chapter 13 Designing for Resilience: Adaptive Logistics
            Network Concepts.......................... 111

Chapter 14 Improving Effectiveness: Pushing the Logistics
            Performance Envelope....................... 119

**PART IV   DESIGN AND EVALUATION: AN
            "ANALYTICAL ARCHITECTURE" TO GUIDE
            LOGISTICS TRANSFORMATION............ 125**

Chapter 15 Multistage Supply Chain Optimization........... 129

Chapter 16 System Dynamics Modeling and Dynamic
            Strategic Planning........................... 133

Chapter 17 Operational and Organizational Risk Evaluation.... 145

Chapter 18 Logistics System Readiness and
            Program Development........................ 151

Chapter 19 Accelerating Transformation: An
            "Engine for Innovation"...................... 157

**PART V   MANAGEMENT CONCEPTS FOR
            TRANSFORMATION........................ 167**

Chapter 20 Organizational Redesign for Army
            Force Generation............................ 171

Chapter 21 Contributions of (Transactional) Information System
            Technology and (Analytical) Operations Research.... 183

Chapter 22 Performance-Based Logistics and Capabilities-Based
            Planning for an Expeditionary Army............. 193

Chapter 23 Financial Management Challenges to "Business
            Modernization"............................. 201

Chapter 24 Human Capital Investment for a
            Collaborative Enterprise...................... 219

Chapter 25 Strategic Management Concepts for a Learning
            Organization............................... 233

Chapter 26 Final Thoughts 243

Appendix A Acronyms 251

Appendix B Additional Reading 257

Notes. 261

References 273

Index 287

Figures

1. AWCF Hardware (Aviation) Resource Trends 10
2. Assessment 11
3. Conceptual Approach: Multistage Logistics Model 14
4. Improving System Effectiveness: Integration and Optimization 15
5. Supply Chain Flows: Materiel, Information, and Financial. 18
6. Demand Volatility in Multistage Supply Chains: The "Bullwhip" Effect 20
7. Suppressing the "Bullwhip" 21
8. Supply Chain Strategies. 22
9. Tactical Unit Stage. 29
10. The "Production Function" for Readiness 31
11. "Production Function": Components of Readiness 33
12. "Connecting" Condition Based Maintenance (CBM) to the Supply Chain 37
13. Capacity, Inventory, and Knowledge 38
14. Mission Demand Stage 39
15. Enhanced Class IX Planning: Linking Operational Patterns, Demand Forecasting, and Supply Planning. 41
16. Part Demand: Relative Composition and Magnitude 45
17. MBF Compared to Current Methods: Part Breadth. 46
18. MBF Compared to Current Methods: Part Depth. 47

xiv FIGURES

19.	Retail Stage	51
20.	Readiness-Based Sparing at 101st Airborne—Blackhawk Parts	55
21.	Reverse Logistics Stage	59
22.	Reverse Logistics Structure	62
23.	Evaluating Retrograde Efficiency: Readiness Return on Net Assets	64
24.	Effects of Improved Retrograde Operations	67
25.	Wholesale Stage	69
26.	Six Sigma, Lean, and the Theory of Constraints: Contributions in the Cost-Performance Trade Space	72
27.	ICAAPS: Intelligent Collaborative Aging Aircraft Parts Support	75
28.	System Life-Cycle Failure Rate Pattern: The "Bathtub" Curve	78
29.	Availability Improvement Analysis	80
30.	Acquisition Stage	85
31.	The "Production Function" for Readiness	91
32.	Components of Operational Availability	92
33.	Improving System Efficiency: Across the System of Stages and Within Each Stage	98
34.	Multiechelon Integration	105
35.	Multistage Optimization Advantages	107–108
36.	Impact of Increasing Investment at Wholesale on Blackhawk Equipment Readiness at 101st Airborne	110
37.	Current Structure: Arborescence	112
38.	Readiness-Driven Supply Network (RDSN)	115

39.	Achieving "Efficiency" in the Cost-Availability Trade Space	120
40.	Increasing "Effectiveness" in the Cost-Availability Trade Space	121
41.	Pushing the Envelope: Innovation to Sustain Continual Improvement	121
42.	"Optimizing" the System: Applying a Dynamic (Multistage) Programming Model	131
43.	Stock Management Structure: System Dynamics Model	137
44.	Reducing Organizational Risk: Analytical Demos, Field Tests, and Experiments	148
45.	Reducing Organizational Risk: Systems Analysis, Management Information, and Decision Support	153
46.	Logistics Readiness and Early Warning System	154
47.	Center for Innovation in Logistics Systems	160
48.	Reduced Transformation Risk: Using Analysis to Disentangle Cause and Effect, Reduce Cost and Uncertainty	162
49.	Sustaining Innovation While Linking Execution to Strategy	164
50.	Logistics Transformation Framework: Linking Strategy to Measurable Results	168
51.	Officer ORSA Strength in Army Materiel Command (AMC)	173
52.	Civilian ORSA Strength in AMC	174
53.	ARFORGEN Synchronization Using RBS and MBF	177
54.	Linking Processes and Systems with Operational and Financial Performance	187
55.	The Evolution of Insight	190

56.	Management Innovation for Improved Decision-Making.	192
57.	PBL Scoring Regime Results	197
58.	The Fallacy of "Fill Rate" as an Incentive for Supply Chain Performance	198
59.	Common Expectations and the Reality of Change.	221
60.	Objective Hierarchy: Relating Outcomes (Results) to Goals and Objectives (Strategy).	237
61.	Aligning Execution and Strategy: Learning from Performance Variability	239
62.	Potential Project Impacts.	247–249
63.	Stratified Sampling	262

Preface

Fully engaged in the Global War on Terror during what has been characterized as "an era of persistent conflict," the U.S. Army is also committed to an ambitious "enterprise transformation." Fundamentally, however, without an enabling transformation in logistics there can be no genuine, comprehensive army-wide transformation. This book presents an analytical framework that has guided an ongoing project addressing major challenges confronting Logistics Transformation for the army's materiel enterprise. The focus here is on inventory management policy prescriptions illuminated through the prism of an enterprise-wide supply chain analysis. Since the project was initiated at the U.S. Army Aviation and Missile Command (AMCOM), Army aviation logistics examples are emphasized throughout the book. Nonetheless, the fundamental challenges and potential solutions are broadly applicable to other military and defense-related supply chains as well.

Project Summary

The genesis for the book is a multiyear, multiorganization research and development project initiated by AMCOM within a year after the attacks of September 11, 2001. The ongoing effort has been divided into three somewhat arbitrary and overlapping phases. Following the initial tasking, guidance, and problem formulation, Phase 1 focused on understanding the fundamental nature of the challenge, gaining an appreciation of the historical evolution and dynamics at play, and developing a clear understanding of the capabilities and limitations of various organizational sources of expertise, both within the army and externally. With this knowledge, a simplifying research model was designed, essential elements of analysis were developed, and a research task organization was established to link sources of expertise with the components of the research model. Several demonstrations, experiments, and field tests were also conducted. Initial efforts to understand newly emerging (certainly to the U.S. Army at that time) "supply chain theory and management concepts" and, more importantly, if and how they could potentially be *adapted—not* blindly *adopted*—to army logistics challenges were pursued. This initial phase took 15 months from summer 2002 to fall 2003 and concluded with a comprehensive project report that included a wide array of findings, observations, and conclusions with seven specific recommendations.

Phase 2, which lasted for about two years from late 2003 to 2005, included sufficient funding for four of the seven Phase 1 recommendations. The primary participating research agencies, identified in Phase 1, included the Army Materiel Command's Logistics Support Activity (LOGSA) and Army Materiel Systems Analysis Activity (AMSAA), RAND Corporation, Institute for Defense Analyses (IDA), and Logistics Management Institute (LMI). Expertise was also sought from the private sector and several academic institutions, including Stanford; the Wharton School at the University of Pennsylvania; and at the Massachusetts Institute of Technology, the Forum for Supply Chain Innovation, Center for Transportation and Logistics, and Lean Advancement Initiative. The emerging research results led to the identification of a few, absolutely crucial, enabling "catalysts for innovation" and growing recognition that dramatically improved supply performance was possible through analytically driven "management innovation." Furthermore, by combining these emerging catalysts it was increasingly apparent that resources could indeed be related to performance: Existing budgets could be correlated with current readiness, and programs (future investment levels) could be credibly related to future capabilities. The Phase 2 effort was funded by AMCOM and coordinated, led, and managed through the Research Institute at the University of Alabama in Huntsville.

The focus during Phase 3, ongoing since 2006, shifted from research and concept development toward implementation. The research program clearly revealed promising, analytically proven approaches that, for the most part, were technologically mature. The Phase 3 effort focused on acquiring and integrating the catalysts and analytical capabilities within an organizational construct. Properly designed and positioned within the army's materiel enterprise, this capability will provide an essential "engine for innovation" to spearhead transformational change and continuous performance improvement. Such a capacity is needed not only to provide the compelling arguments for improvements in policy, process, and systems but also to provide a source for innovation that the logistics communities and their respective cultures can embrace. Yet the organizational and cultural challenges associated with the transition from concept to implementation were, and have remained, significant. While the need for such a capability has been universally acknowledged at all levels, one of the impediments has been determining where to best locate and implement such an "engine" within the existing materiel enterprise bureaucracy. Funding to support Phase 3 has been provided by multiple agencies within Army Materiel Command (AMC).

The three project phases are summarized as follows. Phase 1 was devoted to understanding current operating methods and procedures, identifying specific problems, strategic outreach to identify sources of expertise, evaluating promising approaches and potential opportunities for improvement, and developing and refining a research model and associated task organization for analysis. Phase 2 focused on implementing research tasks and concept development. And Phase 3 has oriented on the design and engineering of technology innovation and management systems for organizational implementation.

Countless technical reports, briefings, seminars, and workshops were developed, conducted, and presented during these three project development phases. Many of these are referenced or mentioned and cited throughout the book. Additionally, each phase has been summarized with comprehensive presentations and formal publications. Nearly all of these documents are unclassified and most are available in the open literature.

Reasons for the Book

Five purposes motivate this book. The *first and foremost purpose* is to encourage and assist the U.S. Army in resurrecting and reintroducing traditional operations research as a management philosophy and problem-solving approach to current and future challenges. The book describes the application of this multidisciplinary approach to one particularly complex, multifaceted, persisting problem within the institutional army—supply management. Frankly, as a career Air Defense Artillery officer and former deputy commander for transformation at the AMCOM it has been professionally embarrassing to note the Government Accountability Office's (GAO) continued—two decades long now—indictment of army supply chain management. Surely we can do better, and the question of how was the essence of the challenge presented by my commanding general (CG) at AMCOM in the summer of 2002 when the project described previously was first conceived.

And so, from a military operations research analyst perspective, this book is my attempt to provide part of the answer—a response to our former CG's thoughtful question, "How can we do better?" Although it has certainly not been easy to write, I do feel obligated to offer it as a source of—for the most part, hopefully—good ideas for defining a way ahead. I deeply regret that I cannot present this book to him personally given his recent untimely death. As anyone who served with him instantly sensed, Lieutenant General Larry J. Dodgen was a superb, inspirational leader who always focused on what was best for soldiers. He was the only officer I worked for twice during my 30-year army career, and I am deeply grateful to him for that "second chance," which he created. Respectfully and thankfully, I dedicate this book to him.

Second, this endeavor should also be viewed from the perspective of our current national financial predicament and the ongoing quest for solvency in public policy. Despite our incredible advantage in global military power, we face enormous strategic resource challenges on a perilous cusp of history. Current trends within our federal budget, in both discretionary and "entitlement" programs, render current spending trajectories unsustainable and future programs unachievable. We are mortgaging not only our future but also increasingly our posterity's by imposing a great disservice on future generations. This condition in our national public policy is both strategically bankrupt and morally reprehensible. We must not continue along this path.

Now, after a decade of substantial, real Department of Defense (DoD) budget growth along with several years of wartime supplemental funding, the defense budget pendulum is swinging back. As Secretary of Defense Robert Gates observed,

> The attacks of September, 11th, 2001, opened a gusher of spending that nearly doubled the base budget over the last decade, not

counting the supplemental appropriations for the wars in Iraq and Afghanistan . . . But today we face a very different set of American economic and fiscal realities . . . The gusher has been turned off, and will stay off for a good period of time . . . The culture of endless money that has taken hold must be replaced by a culture of savings and restraint.

Major cutbacks in current and future programs will be needed to hold defense budgets within politically realistic limits. While operating and support (O&S) cost growth has always been difficult to contain, it has been expanding rapidly and outpacing the overall DoD growth rate. And since defense budgets likely to be in place over the next several years cannot accommodate higher force levels, sustain readiness, and support modernization, difficult trade-offs are inevitable. To the extent that immense and ever-growing O&S costs can be contained and tied to predictable readiness outcomes, these painful trade-offs can be better managed by defense policy officials, budget analysts, and future administrations.

Consequently, a *second purpose* for this book is to apply the "power of analysis"—operations research methods, innovative strategic planning and management concepts, and in this case, cutting-edge supply chain theory—to this persistent, seemingly intractable national security resource challenge. The potential for improvement appears to be dramatic. For example, as described in chapter 6, the potential for dramatically improved demand forecast accuracy has been demonstrated using a new method referred to as "mission-based forecasting." This new approach has consistently yielded an *order of magnitude* improvement over existing methods in forecast accuracy across a range of platforms, missions, and operational environments. Several billions of dollars in savings are likely, and for the first time, it actually becomes possible to relate resources to readiness—to accurately correlate investment levels to both current readiness and future capabilities.

Third, the book develops a practical approach for understanding the army's extremely complex materiel enterprise and logistics system and provides an "analytical architecture"—a comprehensive road map—to sustain continuous performance improvement, relate budget and investment levels to current and future capability outcomes, and create and sustain a "learning organization" for the owner of the world's largest, most complex, global supply chain enterprise: the U.S. Army. Since traditional operations research was originally defined by its multidisciplinary approach to assist decision makers with complex operational problems, an important *third purpose* for the book is to serve as a "connecting bridge" to link and encourage collaboration across the many logistics communities—operational, technical, educational, scientific and analytical—in academia, industry, federally funded research and development centers, and other government agencies, as well as DoD.

Fourth, the book demonstrates an application of "management innovation as a strategic technology." MIST, for short, is a new concept for transformational change in large-scale, complex, interdependent organizations that compose an extended enterprise. The three conceptual building blocks for MIST include (a) data-driven, operations research–based, decision support systems (also referred to as "business intelligence" or "analytics"); (b) a transformational, rather than incremental, approach to strategic planning that is guided by an "engine for innovation"; and (c) an "integrated" management science to increase the likelihood for successful transformative change by enabling, rather than impeding, organizational implementation. By describing the components of MIST and demonstrating their application to army materiel enterprise challenges, others will hopefully be encouraged to consider and, where appropriate, adapt and apply MIST to our many other daunting national security challenges. A *fourth purpose* of the book, then, is to develop an appreciation and understanding of MIST and its emphasis on analytical architectures as a strategic management means for improved performance in our public sector organizations and government institutions.

The *fifth and final, more pragmatic purpose* is to describe in narrative form the roads taken and paths pursued. In response to the CG's initial challenge "How can we do better?" the goal has been to identify and develop a prudent and principled strategy for a sensible, cost-effective way ahead to genuinely transform the army's materiel enterprise. Especially worthy of documentation are the contributions provided by so many exceptional, dedicated colleagues who span countless disciplines and professional skills across a wide range of public and private sector organizations. Their contributions are creative yet analytically rigorous and as individually insightful as they are collectively transformative. Important lessons have been both observed and (re)learned. Modest suggestions are offered in some cases and very strong recommendations in others.

Outline of the Book

Following a summary of recent trends and critical events for background and context, a multistage conceptual model of the army's logistics structure is presented to segment and guide the effort. Supply chain concepts are explained in terms relevant to Logistics Transformation. A systems approach is then used with major sections focusing on comprehension and analysis, synthesis and integration, design and evaluation, and finally change management for organizational implementation. The multistage model is used to systematically *analyze* major organizational components of the supply chain, diagnose structural disorders, and prescribe solutions. A summary of these disorders and their consequences is presented. *Integration* challenges are addressed using cost-benefit perspectives that incorporate supply chain objectives of efficiency, resilience, and effectiveness. The *design and evaluation* section proposes an "analytical architecture" consisting of four complementary modeling approaches, collectively referred to as "dynamic strategic logistics planning," to enable a coordinated, enterprise approach for Logistics Transformation. An organizational construct is presented for an "engine for innovation" to accelerate and sustain continual improvement for army logistics and supply chain management—a Center for Innovation in Logistics Systems. Finally, strategic *management* challenges associated with transformation are addressed: organizational design, management information and decision support systems, financial management, workforce considerations including human capital investment needs, and strategic alignment for a learning organization. The book then concludes with a relevant historical vignette and closes with a summary of expected benefits.

Thus as one advances through the book, major sections ("parts," with each part consisting of several chapters) focus progressively on understanding the *fundamental purpose and challenges* for supply management within the army's materiel enterprise (chapters 1–4 in part I), *analyses* (chapters 5–11 in part II), *integration* (chapters 12–14 in part III), *design and evaluation* (chapters 15–19 in part IV), and finally *management of change* challenges associated with transformation implementation (chapters 20–26 in part V).

Contributors

Necessarily, the book captures a relatively short snapshot in time for a very large part of the institutional army (the "generating force") that is undergoing considerable turbulence. New organizations have been established at the same time others are being reengineered and relocated in accordance with the latest congressional Base Realignment and Closure Act. Simultaneously, the "operating force" has substantially reorganized from a traditional division design to a modular brigade architecture. These combat units are now operating under a new force management concept known as Army Force Generation (ARFORGEN), which has transformed reserve component forces (U.S. Army Reserve and Army National Guard) from strategic reserves to operational forces that now routinely deploy worldwide alongside active component units. Simultaneously, ARFORGEN has replaced the Cold War–era "tiered" force readiness posture with an expeditionary "rotational" readiness concept—a cyclical process for units to repeatedly deploy, return to recover and reset, train and prepare, and then deploy again.

Synchronizing the institutional "generating force" army—which includes the materiel enterprise and logistics systems—with continually deploying "operating force" combat units continues to present an enormous coordination challenge for ARFORGEN. And amid all this change ongoing for a decade now, our U.S. Army has endured the longest period of sustained ground combat in American history.

Given all of the turmoil that has been occurring in both "forces," some characterizations herein will inevitably no longer be valid or accurate. Initiatives will have ebbed and flowed, been eliminated, morphed, merged, or combined into programs—and, of course, relabeled with new acronyms. For certain, however, many organizations have contributed to the endeavor described in this book. Although several colleagues in these organizations have since been promoted, changed positions or organizations, or retired, I have listed them in the assignments they held at the time they provided their valuable assistance and contributions to this project.

At AMCOM, thanks to Deputy Commander for systems Support John Johns; Wayne Bruno, Josh Kennedy, and especially project sponsor Frank Lawrence in the Command Analysis Directorate; Tom Ingram and Rick Turner in the Integrated Materiel Management Center; Bill Matthews, Director for Resource Management; special thanks to presentation specialist Jennifer Todd and "my" talented and wonderful executive assistants Pam Baird and Jenni Jerome in the headquarters.

Thanks to AMRDEC's Systems Simulation and Development Division for funding; the Army Aviation Program Executive Office and Project Management Offices for Cargo (CH-47) and Utility (UH-60), especially Ron Dalton, David Frey, and Lowell Bidwell; Bill Rutherford, John Hall, and Will Stratton, in LOGSA; and Meyer Kotkin, Jeff Landis, Eric Wehde, Art Hutchison, Mike Johnson, and Clark Fox at AMSAA's Logistics Analysis Directorate at Aberdeen Proving Ground. And at AMC Headquarters, thanks to Lauren Reyes, John LaFalce, General Paul Kern, and especially Dr. Benson Adams.

At Fort Lee, Colonel Howard Butler, Chief of Staff for Combined Arms Support Command (CASCOM), Joe Fortner, and analysts at TRADOC Analysis Command (TRAC-Lee). At White Sands Missile Range, Acting Director for TRAC-WSMR Colonel Greg Hoscheit; and at Fort Bliss, Brigadier General Bob Lennox, Assistant Commandant at the Air Defense Artillery School.

At Headquarters, Department of the Army, thanks to Lieutenant General Charles Charles Mahan, his G-4 staff, and the Logistics Transformation Agency; Wympie Pybus and Lieutenant General Ross Thompson in the office of the Assistant Secretary of the Army for Acquisition, Logistics, and Technology; Vern Bettencourt, Deputy Chief Information Officer; and Don Tison, Deputy Director for Program Analysis and Evaluation.

Other services and agencies provided critical knowledge, major contributions, and useful ideas: the Joint Staff J-4 and J-8; Roger Kallock, Randy Fowler, and Alan Estevez at the Logistics and Materiel Readiness, and Supply Chain Integration offices in OSD; Carmen Oeltjen and Greg Grindey at TRANSCOM's Joint Distribution Process Analysis Center;

and the Defense Logistics Agency. Thanks to Dean Golden at the Air Force Logistics Management Agency and Lorna Estep at the Air Force Global Supply Chain Center; Commander Walt DeGrange at the Naval Inventory Control Point's Operations Research Section and the Navy Fleet Readiness Center at Lemoore Naval Air Station; also to Brad Botwin, Director of Industrial Studies in the Office of Technology Evaluation, U.S. Department of Commerce; and especially to the Joint Council on Aging Aircraft (JCAA) and former fellow representatives from all the services, Coast Guard, FAA, and NASA, especially chairman Bob Ernst at NAVAIR.

Similarly, in the private sector, thanks to the Avraham Goldratt Institute near Yale University in New Haven and QualPro near Oak Ridge, Tennessee; Sean Connors and Roy Bryant at Clockwork Solutions; Professor Morris Cohen at MCA Solutions; Bob Butler, Craig Sherbrooke, John Millhouse, and Ron Cumings at TFD Group; Bill Braddy and Michelle Liddon at Westar Aerospace; Steve Geary at Supply Chain Visions; Kaizhi Tang at Intelligent Automation Inc.; B. J. Thornburg at MAT Inc.; and Scott Moss, Matt Gorevin, Bob O'Connell, Terry Reiman, Jan Chervenak, Rob Elich, John Scales, Paul Deason, and especially "maestro" Norm Myers at SAIC's Huntsville-based Engineering and Analysis Operation.

Several federally funded research and development centers have participated and contributed their respective expertise to the project. Thanks to Mark Wang, John Halladay, Eric Peltz, Keenan Yoho, Ken Giardini, and Tom Held at the RAND Corporation; Dan Levine, Bob Fabrie, Larry Goldberg, Chris Hanks, Karen Tyson, and Stan Horowitz at the Institute for Defense Analyses (IDA); Evelyn Harleston, Ron Durant, Sal Culosi, Rob Jordan, and George Kuhn at the Logistics Management Institute (LMI); and at two of our U.S. Department of Energy labs, Mark Robershotte and Dave Scharette at the Pacific Northwest National Laboratory (PNNL), and Dr. Bob Cranwell, manager for the Center for Systems Reliability at Sandia National Laboratories (SNL).

Staff and faculty members from over a dozen academic institutions, within and outside DoD, have contributed: the Army Force Management School, Army Logistics Management College, Defense Acquisition University, and Air Force Institute of Technology; special thanks to

Professor Jim Eagle, Operations Research Department Chair at the Naval Postgraduate School, and especially to my former teachers there, Professor Patricia Jacobs and Distinguished Professor Don Gaver.

At the University of Alabama in Huntsville (UAH), thanks to all my former colleagues in the Office of Economic Development, particularly Maruf Rahman, Greg Harris, Bill Killingsworth, and especially Allison Moore, and to professors Hau L. Lee in the Graduate School of Business and Warren Hausman in the Graduate School of Engineering at Stanford, Yacov Haimes and Kash Barker at the University of Virginia, and especially Jack Muckstadt at Cornell. Several organizations at MIT have contributed: Jim Rice and Yossi Sheffi in the Center for Transportation and Logistics; Deborah Nightingale, Kirk Bozdogan, and Doug Matty at the Lean Advancement Initiative; Richard de Neufville and David Simchi-Levi in the Engineering Systems Division; Arnoldo Hax, Rebecca Henderson, and George Westerman at the Sloan School of Management; and special thanks to both Shoumen Datta, Executive Director at the Forum for Supply Chain Innovation, and Professor Emeritus Jeremy Shapiro. In England, thanks to Helen Peck, Mike Bathe, and Martin Christopher at Cranfield University.

Acknowledgments

Early on during the "discovery" phase of this project, several senior officials were "recruited" as technical advisors and reviewers to assist in focusing initial efforts and guiding progress. I thank them all for their sincere interest, thoughtful suggestions, invaluable guidance, strong support, and encouragement.

Senior Technical Advisors

Dr. Benson D. Adams, Special Assistant to the Commanding General for Transformation Integration, U.S. Army Materiel Command

Dr. Robin B. Buckelew, Director, Weapons Integration and Development Directorate, U.S. Army Aviation Missile Research Development and Engineering Center (AMRDEC)

Dr. Robert M. Cranwell, Manager, Center for Systems Reliability, Sandia National Laboratories

Rear Admiral (Retired) Donald R. Eaton, Logistics Chair, Graduate School of Business and Public Policy, Naval Postgraduate School (NPS)

Dr. Bruce W. Fowler, Chief Scientist, AMRDEC

Brigadier General (Retired) James L. Kays, Dean, Graduate School of Engineering and Applied Sciences, NPS; and formerly Professor and Head, Department of Systems Engineering, USMA

Colonel (Retired) John L. Millhouse, Royal Australian Air Force; and Chief Scientist, TFD Group

Colonel Craig Naudain, Project Manager for Precision Fires, U.S. Army

Professor Emeritus Jeremy F. Shapiro, former Codirector of the Operations Research Center, Sloan School of Management, Massachusetts Institute of Technology (MIT)

Professor David Simchi-Levi, Professor of Engineering Systems, Engineering Systems Division, MIT

Senior Review Officials

Dr. David S. C. Chu, President, Institute for Defense Analyses; former Under Secretary of Defense (Personnel and Readiness)

Roger W. Kallock, former Deputy Under Secretary of Defense (Logistics and Materiel Readiness)

Michael Kirby, Deputy Under Secretary of the Army (Business Transformation)

Lieutenant General (Retired) Richard G. Trefry, Program Director, Army Force Management School; and former Inspector General, U.S. Army

General (Retired) William G. T. Tuttle Jr., Logistics Management Institute (LMI) Board of Trustees, former CEO and President, LMI; and Commanding General, U.S. Army Materiel Command

The project has tremendously benefitted from discussions, constructive criticism, and extended dialogue generated from countless briefings, presentations, classes, seminars, and workshops. These have been hosted by several professional societies and associations, including the Military Operations Research Society (MORS), Military Applications Society (MAS) of the Institute for Operations Research and the Management Sciences (INFORMS), American Helicopter Society (AHS), Huntsville Simulation Conference, International Society of Logistics (SOLE), and a Canadian-sponsored NATO Interoperability Conference. A course on "Supply Chain Concepts for Performance-Based Logistics" was developed and taught for the UAH continuing education program, and several workshops have been presented at conferences sponsored by the Institute for Defense and Government Advancement (IDGA).

Diplomatic and foreign exchange programs have also provided venues and opportunities to extend and present these concepts for consideration and possible application in other nations as well. So far, these have included training seminars for acquisition and logistics professionals in the Republic of the Philippines (RP), conducted at their National War College under the bilateral US-RP Defense Resource Management Project; in South Africa, as part of the People-to-People Ambassador Program (founded by former President Eisenhower), the first professional exchange delegation for Operations Research and Management Science that involved mutual exchanges with logistics and supply chain academics in five South African universities and defense professionals at two national research centers; and most recently, for the Iraq Training Advisory Mission in the Multi-National Security Transition Command (MNSTC-I) in Baghdad to support the transition of authority and responsibility for national security to the government of Iraq.

The transformational concepts in this book have also been presented and vetted at international professional conferences in Puerto Rico; Honolulu; Toronto; Buenos Aires; Taegu, South Korea; Melbourne, Australia; and at the International Symposium on Military Operational Research (ISMOR) at the Royal Military College of Science in Shrivenham, England.

I was fortunate to recently serve in an advisory capacity with U.S. forces in Iraq. Although my official duties were focused elsewhere, I am truly grateful for the considerable time I was able to spend with our superb logisticians at "the point of the spear" assigned to the AMC Logistics Support Element for Multi-National Division-Baghdad (1st Cavalry Division at that time) at Camp Liberty. Thanks to commanding officer CW5 Mary Czuhajewski, Deputy Lonnie Whitaker, and their professional band of Logistics Assistance Reps, Senior Systems Tech Reps, and Reset Liaison Officers including Lisette Rivers, Woody Sanders, Emmett Wayne, Jack Hernandez, and especially Bill Clemons. Also thanks to Colonel Paul Hurley, Deputy J-4, U.S. Forces-Iraq, for sharing his personal perspectives on the many strategic and operational logistics-planning challenges associated with theater-level support operations in a very demanding and dynamic environment.

Portions of this book were published previously by the Association of the United States Army's Institute of Land Warfare in *Transforming U.S. Army Logistics: A Strategic "Supply Chain" Approach for Inventory Management,* Land Warfare Paper 54, Arlington, Va., September 2005, and, more recently in the *Air Force Journal of Logistics,* 32(4), and Journal Annual, 33(1), "Transforming Army Supply Chains: An Analytical Architecture for Management Innovation." Permission to reproduce herein these earlier versions is gratefully acknowledged. And for their useful suggestions and constructive comments on them, I thank Bill Killingsworth at UAH; Cindy Young and Jim Rainey, editor and editor-in-chief for the *Air Force Journal of Logistics*; Sandra Daugherty and Eric Minton, program director and editor, respectively, at the Institute of Land Warfare, and Lieutenant

General Ted Stroup, Vice President for Education at the Association of the United States Army (AUSA).

The final draft was thoughtfully reviewed by Rick Makowski, Mike Johnson, Paul Varian, Walt DeGrange, George Kuhn, Professor James Ignizio, and General Paul Kern; and special thanks to David A. Grossman, fellow 82nd Airborne paratrooper who I have known and admired for over 35 years. At Business Expert Press, thanks to Cindy Durand, Sheri Allen, and Danny Constantino for your gracious assistance and guidance, to Steven Nahmias for encouraging the effort, and to CEO David Parker for the opportunity.

All U.S. Army commissioned officers recognize the key to unit cohesion, mission achievement, and operational success is our incomparably professional Noncommissioned Officer (NCO) corps. Our NCOs, universally acknowledged as the "backbone" of the Army, are not only held in high esteem within the army but also the envy of all other militaries today. Over the course of a full career, officers typically serve with many NCOs, and most of us would like to believe that we have in some way contributed to their success. Yet perhaps a handful of these same NCOs stand out among all others for what they taught us and for their contributions to our success as officers. I know I was the benefactor of more than my fair share of these great NCOs, among them Leroy McCullough, Don Wingrove, William Bosheers, Tim Lind, Carl Snyder, Stephen Miranda, and Roscoe Young.

Perhaps less well known, yet equally esteemed by those who have served with them, is the Army's Warrant Officer corps: our technical specialists including aviators and weapon systems, maintenance, and supply support experts. With their technical skills, creative prowess, detailed knowledge, and deep experience, they too have become indispensable as our systems have increased in complexity. For their professionalism, dedication, staunch support, and for being such great teachers and advisors, especially to me when we served together, thanks to John Sewell, Tim Davis, Ron Matthews, James Grant, Tony Caudle, Mark Eitreim, Paul Varian, and Travis Brown.

To my family, thanks for your support and encouragement throughout this endeavor, and especially to my wife Judy, for your patience tolerating incessant revisions to "final?" drafts. Although you have heard this before more than once, "I think I am done now . . . finally."

In Memoriam

Benson D. Adams, Special Assistant to the Commanding General for Transformation Integration, Army Materiel Command

Larry J. Dodgen, former Commanding General, U.S. Army Aviation and Missile Command

Robert L. Jordan, Research Fellow, Logistics Management Institute

Frank T. Lawrence, Director, Command Analysis Directorate, U.S. Army Aviation and Missile Command

Lauren L. Reyes, Chief, Asset Management and Distribution Division, Army Materiel Command G-3 Support Operations

Roscoe P. Young, former Command Sergeant Major, 5th Battalion, 2nd Air Defense Artillery Regiment

PART I

Project Overview

I am now convinced beyond a doubt that unless some great and capital change suddenly takes place in that line, this Army must inevitably be reduced to one or other of these three things: starve, dissolve, or disperse.

—General George Washington to the Continental Congress, December 23, 1777

You will not find it difficult to prove that battles, campaigns, and even wars have been won or lost primarily because of logistics.

—General Dwight Eisenhower

As an infantryman I used to be no more concerned with logistics than what you could stuff in a rucksack. . . . Now I know that although the tactics are not easy they are relatively simple when compared to the logistics.

—General David Petraeus

Chapters

1. Background
2. The Immediate Problem
3. Current Logistics Structure
4. Supply Chain Concepts: Analytical Foundation for Improving Logistics System Effectiveness

Now, fully engaged in the Global War on Terror, the U.S. Army is simultaneously committed to the most ambitious and comprehensive reengineering endeavor in its history. Universally known by the ubiquitous term "Army Transformation," the early intellectual stages of this effort clearly revealed a crucial need to transform logistics concepts, organization, technology, and culture to improve strategic responsiveness, force projection, and sustainment capabilities. Thus as the organization's then-top logistician noted, the army-wide "transformation of organizations, processes, doctrine and culture demands a corresponding transformation in sustaining those organizations."[1] Fundamentally, without a transformation in logistics there can be no successful Army Transformation.

These four initial chapters (part I) describe the fundamental nature of this challenge, present historical background, and explain several converging conditions and recent events that provide context and motivate the current, and increasingly compelling, need for transformational change. An analytical framework is then developed that adapts recent supply chain theory, management concepts, and design strategies to army logistics challenges. A supporting model of the materiel enterprise organizational structure is introduced and explained. This "model"—a highly simplified graphical representation of an enormously complex set of diverse organizations, processes, and information systems—is then subsequently used throughout the text as a "road map" for orientation and progress. More importantly, the model is intended to provide clarity, insight, and understanding as one advances through the book's major sections with chapters focused progressively on *analyses* (chapters 5–11 in part II), *integration* (chapters 12–14 in part III), *design and evaluation* (chapters 15–19 in part IV), and finally *change management* challenges for enterprise transformation (chapters 20-26 in part V). As a mental construct, the model has been consistently used as a focal point to allocate, align, and guide the respective efforts of our research teams and to convey results in understandable and meaningful ways to leaders, managers, operators, technicians, educators, and researchers alike.

CHAPTER 1

Background

We have a serious problem looking to the future . . . The way we are functioning today is not going to be satisfactory for the challenges we face in the future, and knowing that, we must change.
—General Peter Pace, chairman, Joint Chiefs of Staff, July 20, 2006

Persistent Challenges

In January 2005, the Government Accountability Office (GAO) identified Department of Defense (DoD) supply chain management as one of 25 activities across the entire federal government classified as "high risk" and in need of "broad-based transformation." This is not a new observation. Indeed, since 1990, the GAO has identified DoD inventory management as high risk because "management systems and procedures were ineffective and wasteful [and] the military services each lack strategic approaches and detailed plans that could help mitigate spare part shortages and guide their many initiatives aimed at improving inventory management."[2] This has clearly been a long-term persistent problem, especially for the army, and is directly attributed to an inability to link spare part inventory investment levels to weapon system readiness objectives.

Consequently, the army is not capable of reporting to the U.S. Congress how additional investments in spare parts would increase readiness. The army contends that it cannot do so because there is no direct correlation between spare parts investment levels and the resulting impact of those investments on system readiness due to other factors such as maintenance capacity and training requirements.[3] Furthermore, the army's ability to conduct coordinated, systemic improvements across the multiple organizations involved in the supply chain has been ineffective. This inability has been attributed to numerous complexities associated with separate, diverse, and independently operating organizations that are further compounded by a lack of accountability and authority for making improvements across the enterprise. Finally, previous efforts for transformation "strategies" have not provided a clear vision to guide, gauge, and synchronize future supply chain improvement efforts with specific performance goals, programs, milestones, and resources needed to achieve stated objectives.

This persistent inability to relate strategic resource investment inputs to fleet-wide readiness outcomes continues to have serious consequences for the tactical war-fighting army. Recent operational experience reinforces this assertion and further provides both urgency and a compelling, chronic need for improvement. After action reports (AARs) from Operation Enduring Freedom (OEF) and Operation Iraqi Freedom (OIF) indicate the hierarchical stovepipe supply system was too slow and inflexible to adequately support operations. Demand forecasts were determined by an inflexible and outdated requisition process that relied on World War II–era historical wartime and even current *peacetime* consumption rates. One army AAR stated that OIF success "stemmed more from luck than design." The Deputy Under Secretary of Defense responsible for logistics policy stated, "Whether push or pull, our current logistics are reactive. [We have] an industrial age vendor struggling to satisfy an information age customer. Reactive logistics—the old logistics—will never be able to keep up with warfare as we know it."[4] The army's chief logistician acknowledged, "We weren't as effective as we could be," while the GAO estimated at least $1.2 billion worth of supplies were lost during the deployment and follow-on operations.

The army, through its new Single Army Logistics Enterprise (SALE) project, is also investing heavily in an effort to fully capitalize on the enterprise-wide promise offered by information technology (IT). The scope of this enterprise resource planning (ERP) effort is believed to be the largest and most complex undertaken so far. Although enormous sums have been invested by the corporate world in IT-based ERP "solutions," these investments have had very mixed results.[5] Emerging evidence suggests dramatic improvements in performance and competitiveness can be achieved, but this success has been limited to those companies that have applied IT to an existing foundation of mature, efficient, and appropriate business processes. Simply procuring information systems alone, especially ERP "solutions," cannot substitute for lack of such a foundation. In fact, the evidence suggests that such attempts not only fail to increase performance—despite large and lengthy investment efforts—but also result in reduced performance for those companies pursuing such an IT-centric "strategy."[6]

Purpose

Countless ideas and technology initiatives have been offered to support Army Logistics Transformation.[7] However, the tasks for the analytical community supporting the army are to recognize and fully comprehend the fundamental nature of this challenge and then to develop, offer, and implement a strategic approach and supporting "analytical architecture" that will guide the army through this transformative period. This book addresses significant challenges confronting logistics transformation by introducing and summarizing a comprehensive systems approach that has guided this ongoing project.[8] Fundamentally, this project requires an investigation into the nature, causes, and consequences of supply chain variability within U.S. Army logistics policies, structures, and methods. Such an ambitious effort has not been previously undertaken through comprehensive and systematic analyses. Consequently, the means and methods by which variability and uncertainty might be recognized, better understood, reduced, and controlled have also remained largely undetermined. The project endeavors to produce these clarifying insights and provide innovative solutions using a supply chain framework adapted to army-specific challenges.

Several conditions motivate this endeavor:

1. The changed geopolitical landscape resulting in the army's transition from a static, "tiered readiness" force posture during the Cold War to an expeditionary, capabilities-based, globally deployable organization using a dynamic, "rotational readiness" Army Force Generation (ARFORGEN) concept
2. The opportunity to consider, adapt, and extend, where appropriate, integrating supply chain design, management, and analysis concepts and principles that have been driven by increasing competition in the corporate world
3. A clear understanding of the enabling potential offered by information systems technology and so-called IT solutions

4. The DoD mandate to adopt performance-based logistics (PBL), a major change in defense logistics management philosophy
5. An obvious and compelling need that presents a unique opportunity to develop and implement an "analytical architecture," in conjunction with a newly emerging strategic management paradigm, to guide Army Logistics Transformation within a "resources to readiness" framework

Scope

This project involves several supporting organizations both within and outside the army and DoD. Although the project was initially focused on aviation-specific spare part inventory management as a test bed, the goal has been to develop a prototype that will provide the foundational "analytical architecture" to support, guide, and accelerate the full spectrum of Army Logistics Transformation. The army's global logistics operation is a tremendously complex and dynamic system and a central component of even larger multiservice, joint, and, increasingly, interagency and international logistics operations. This system consists of a wide variety of highly variable product flows; extensive management information systems; considerable maintenance and supply infrastructure; globally dispersed transportation assets; several command and management agencies; countless vendors, suppliers, and original equipment manufacturers (OEMs); and supporting financial management processes that track tens of billions of dollars annually.

In terms of scope, magnitude, and complexity, the entire DoD supply chain includes over 30,000 specific "customers" (tactical units), 22 maintenance and repair depots, 14 national inventory control points, 22 regional (and international) distribution depots, over 80 major air and sea transportation ports, 5 million consumable and reparable items procured from more than 100,000 suppliers, and over 2,000 legacy information systems. According to an Office of the Secretary of Defense (OSD) senior logistics official, the logistics system consumed $140 billion of the FY2004 $450 billion annual DoD budget, with $80 billion spent on inventory and $60 billion on maintenance. And in FY2007, DoD estimated that it was then spending $178 billion on its supply chain. This DoD materiel enterprise—global in scope, enormous in scale, unsurpassed in complexity, and employing more than 1 million personnel—is the largest supply chain in the world.

Despite the initial euphoria over remarkably successful combat operations in OEF and OIF, symptoms of ailing and inadequate logistics support operations have since become increasingly apparent as ongoing operations place substantial stress on our complex logistics structure. This book does not dwell on these "symptoms," which are outlined and detailed in several official and public reports,[9] but rather endeavors to address, or "diagnose," underlying root causes and associated effects revealed as a consequence of the substantial stress placed upon this crucial, complex system. Finally, while there are numerous interacting dimensions to this challenge, the focus here will be primarily, although not exclusively, on inventory management policy "prescriptions" that are illuminated through the prism of a comprehensive enterprise-wide supply chain analysis.

Organization

This book is organized into five major sections consisting of 26 chapters. Part I provides some recent historical context and describes the genesis of this project from an army aviation logistics perspective. A multistage conceptual model of the logistics organizational structure is introduced, and major supply chain concepts that form the basis for subsequent analysis and synthesis are explained in terms relevant to Army Logistics Transformation. Part II then uses this multistage model to sequentially analyze each of the six stages using supply chain theory and principles to diagnose "disorders" and prescribe "remedies" within each stage. Part III endeavors to synthesize and integrate the components of this multistage enterprise model using three resource-to-readiness supply chain objectives: efficiency, resilience, and effectiveness. In part IV the design and evaluation aspects of the supply chain analyses culminate in the proposal of an analytical architecture to guide transformation using an "engine for innovation." Additionally, four supporting and complementary modeling approaches, collectively referred to as "dynamic strategic logistics planning," are presented. Finally, part V addresses six crucial management implementation challenges for transforming the army's materiel enterprise: organizational and force structure design, management information and decision support systems, PBL for a capabilities-based force, financial management challenges to business modernization, workforce challenges including the psychological effects of disruptive change and human capital investment needs, and aligning execution with strategy for a learning organization to successfully undertake this large-scale transformation. The book concludes with a relevant historical vignette and summary of expected benefits.

CHAPTER 2

The Immediate Problem

Why am I still throwing billions down this black hole called "spares"?
—General Eric Shinseki, Chief of Staff, Army, 1999–2003

Despite exponential growth in both spare parts requirements and investment over the preceding 5-year period, unfunded requirements (UFRs) and associated back orders had been growing dramatically. In fact, at the beginning of FY2003, prior to Operation Iraqi Freedom (OIF), the cumulative UFR for aviation spares alone was in excess of $1 billion (Figure 1). Readiness reports had been relatively steady though slowly declining at the same time. However, there was growing skepticism regarding the accuracy of these reports. For example, during FY2001 while randomly inspecting units reporting 90% readiness or better, the U.S. Army Forces Command (FORSCOM) inspector general found actual readiness in these units to be 30–50% lower than reported.[1]

Although tactical-level "workarounds" in the field were also known to be increasing as well, it was not clear what impact, in terms of an incremental increase in actual readiness, fully funding the growing spares budget shortfall might have. Long depot repair cycles and procurement lead times are associated with many of these components, and both obsolescence issues and diminishing sources of supply characterize increasingly aging army rotorcraft fleets. Nonetheless, Department of the Army level resource managers were not convinced that growing spare part requirements for aviation programs submitted by the logistics community were valid. And since relationships between investment levels and readiness outcomes did not exist, the gap between spare part resource requirements and the amount budgeted for them continued to grow as well.

At the same time, another worrisome pattern was emerging. Major weapon systems across the army were increasingly rated nonoperational due to relatively inexpensive spare parts. Since the army was engaged in

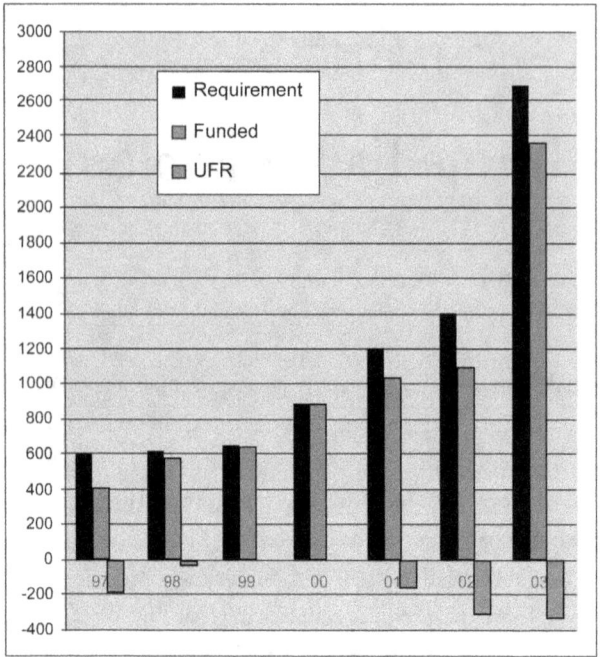

Source: AMCOM RMD

Figure 1. AWCF hardware (aviation) resource trends.

Operation Enduring Freedom (OEF) in Afghanistan at the time, the growing fear, just a few months prior to initiating OIF, was that significant additional stress on helicopter fleets could result in dramatic and sustained readiness deterioration in terms of aircraft operational availability.

The combined effect of these trends portrayed, at worst, an organization faced with the proverbial "death spiral"—decreasing performance in the face of rapidly escalating costs at a time of potentially devastating consequences. At best, the actual location in a conceptual investment versus performance trade space, defined in this case as "cost availability," was uncertain and, relative to an "efficient frontier," simply unknown (Figure 2).

Despite the uncertainty in the existing logistics operating environment, magnified by the anxiety of anticipated additional combat operations, there was certainly growing awareness that these trends could not be sustained. While logistics management officials were increasingly

Investment is increasing yet backorders are growing and UFRs are increasing
"Work-arounds" are increasing, readiness is slowly declining
Readiness reporting appears suspicious, lacks credibility
Systems are deadlined for relatively inexpensive parts

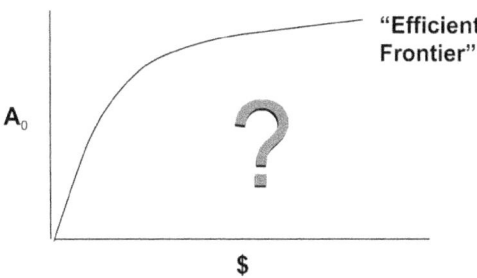

Figure 2. Assessment.

worried that resources would be inadequate to sustain future readiness at desired levels, those concerns were accompanied by perceptions of tremendous inefficiencies within the logistics support system. Major U.S. Army Aviation and Missile Command (AMCOM) concerns, expressed by the commanding general in fall 2002 when these conditions existed, were "How much should we be investing on spares at the wholesale level to meet army aviation fleet readiness goals?" and "Are we spending our resources on the right things?"

CHAPTER 3

Current Logistics Structure

> We want to change the logistics system. Logistics has always been central to the military. But it's also been a drag on what the military can do. And right now, it's a drag on transformation because so much money and so many people are absorbed in logistics processes, that we need to reach for new constructs.
> —Vice Admiral Arthur Cebrowski, director, Office of Force Transformation, Office of the Secretary of Defense, February 2004

This chapter presents a conceptual multistage logistics model, explains the functions and interdependencies of these particular stages, and summarizes emerging insights and supporting recommendations from organizations participating in the initial phase of this project. The materiel enterprise systems framework presented here continues to guide the overall project in subsequent phases.

This multistage model is a graphical simplification of the U.S. Army's very complex logistics structure (Figure 3) and consists of the following stages: a unit stage representing army tactical organizations where readiness "production" actually occurs; a demand stage representing training requirements and operational missions; a retail stage representing installation and tactical supply support activities providing direct or general support to specific units; a wholesale stage consisting of the aggregate continental United States (CONUS)-based repair and supply depots managed by Army Materiel Command and the Defense Logistics Agency; a reverse logistics stage representing the retrograde pipeline for depot-level reparables (DLRs) including, for example, turbine engines, transmissions, and rotor blades for aviation systems; and an acquisition stage representing original equipment manufacturers and suppliers responding to the procurement and sustainment needs of the army.

Using this multistage supply chain enterprise model for a diagnostic framework, along with basic knowledge about the current state of logistics, reveals initial insight into the potential cause of challenges that have been accumulating over time. For example, unlike the corporate sector

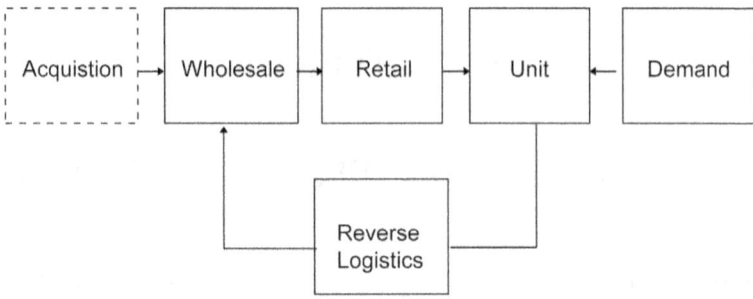

Figure 3. Conceptial approach: Multistage logistics model.

where consumer demand is well defined at the end of the supply chain and product consumption can be measured precisely and forecasted accurately, the "customer" here is "readiness" at the unit needed to meet operational mission requirements.

A well-defined, empirically derived production function, or "readiness equation," especially for army aviation systems, relating capital investment (including spares) and labor (maintenance support) to various aircraft performance standards necessary to meet the "demand" for training and mission requirements does not yet exist. Without it, efforts to forecast logistics requirements have been inaccurate and largely reactive, leading to uncertainty and variability in the supporting logistics system at the point of consumption.

Another example is the reverse logistics or retrograde stage. Rare in the commercial world where products are normally consumed by the market, this stage constitutes the "value recovery" effort to maintain, repair, overhaul, upgrade, and return large subassemblies and replaceable units that are not consumed but used as capital assets. Although these items constitute only about 25% of the number of demand requisitions, they also represent more than 75% of total requisition value.

Nonetheless, an underlying theory for retrograde operations has never been established to guide performance standards for the reverse pipeline, and as a consequence, the organizations responsible for the forward supply chain are also responsible for the reverse. Until recently, ability to measure delay time in the reverse pipeline did not exist, reflecting the lack of importance and priority this aspect of logistics operations historically received within the culture. Yet this multistage conceptual model reveals the importance of viewing the retrograde stage from a systems control theory perspective as a feedback loop with obvious impact on output generated as unit readiness. For every reparable component delayed in an unresponsive reverse pipeline–where delay times average several months—another component must exist elsewhere within the forward supply chain or the retrograde feedback loop will significantly degrade readiness output.

Finally, the multistage model also suggests configuration of the current logistics structure as a series of independently operating organizations, frequently with differing agendas and conflicting goals, struggling to manage the adjacent interfaces between them (Figure 4). Multiple manufacturing, maintenance, logistics, materiel, distribution, and transportation organizations have responsibility for different parts of the supply chain. Not surprisingly, various supply performance metrics have evolved over the years to manage these interfaces. However, these various organizations have not had good visibility of their effect on "readiness" production and could not relate their interface metrics to readiness-oriented outcomes. The sequence of events between initial cause and ultimate effect is so long, obscure, and complex that the connection between what occurs and why it occurs is rarely observed, much less understood. This organizationally induced dynamic complexity essentially precludes readiness-focused management actions.

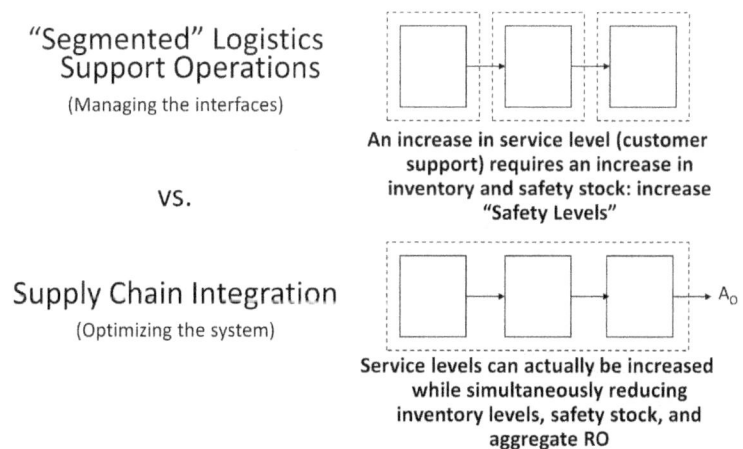

Figure 4. *Improving system effectiveness: Integration and optimization.*

The various organizations have historically been autonomously managed, each with their own missions and objectives. Frequently, these objectives conflict across organizations and have very little to do with the supply chain's overall performance. Even when organizations meet operational goals, these objectives may induce inefficiencies for the overall supply chain.

Consequently, organizations are not able to effectively correlate resource investment levels and coordinate policy decisions—both within the stages and across them—to achieve readiness goals. In effect, the decisions within these organizational stages, which function as structural constraints on the overall supply chain, yield at best locally optimal solutions. Each of these organizations is, by definition, clearly dependent upon others. Yet paradoxically, they have not traditionally cooperated with each other in a closely coordinated manner. In addition to operational inefficiencies, these structural (organizational) constraints also induce counterproductive behavioral effects as a consequence of cognitive limitations on the part of logistics managers who naturally tend to undervalue other elements of the supply chain they cannot see or control.[1] The existing logistics structure, largely a legacy system from an industrial-age environment where "buffers" of stock were created to accommodate uncertainty, variability, and organizational structure, was never designed to adequately address these growing concerns.

The concept of the "extended enterprise," to be differentiated from a single organization in the public sector or a private company in the corporate world, has gained importance. Whereas a "company" has traditionally been defined as a profit-making entity with its own management authority, control over its own actions, and limitations on both ownership and liability, an extended enterprise is a group of institutions that develop linkages, share knowledge and resources, and collaborate to create a product or service. This collaboration ideally maximizes combined capabilities and allows each element within the supply chain to realize its goals by providing integrated solutions to customer needs. This concept of an extended enterprise has special significance for the army's complex supply chains from both managerial and organizational perspectives.

CHAPTER 4

Supply Chain Concepts

Analytical Foundation for Improving Logistics System Effectiveness

> Logistics can no longer be thought about as an annex to our operations plans. . . . It must be inherent in the plan . . . not a "wake-up call."
> —General Paul Kern, commanding general, Army Materiel Command

> Address "root cause" rather than "source." Root cause lies hidden beyond the source.
> —Taiichi Ohno, chief engineer, Toyota Production Systems

The academic development of theory and subsequent practical implementation of supply chain management concepts in the corporate world offer valuable insight into U.S. Army logistics challenges. Two key concepts will be offered here. First, enabled by transportation planning and materiel management, logistics has traditionally been defined as the forward flow of materials from suppliers through a series of production and distribution stages to customers. More recently, supply chain design concepts and management theory expanded to incorporate two other flows through these logistics stages as well: supply demand information and financial transaction flows across organizations comprising the enterprise. Definitions of "supply chain management" (SCM) have recently evolved to capture this more expansive view. For example, the Logistics Management Institute succinctly defines SCM as "the management of *all* processes or functions to satisfy a customer order." In contrast, a more detailed definition is provided in Department of Defense (DoD) Joint Publication 4-09:

> Supply chain management provides an intellectual and organizational approach to managing, integrating, and assuring all the

elements that affect the flow of materiel to the joint force. Military supply chain management is the discipline that integrates acquisition, supply, maintenance, and transportation functions with the physical, financial, information, and communications networks in a results-oriented approach to satisfy joint force materiel requirements.

This view of multiple information and physical flows interacting across these process planes, or "templates" (Figure 5), then led to the second concept, now known as the "bullwhip" effect. When recognized and adequately modeled for understanding and insight, this bullwhip effect illuminates the enormous consequences of these independently operating stages and interacting templates on the system. It is now well known and understood that these independent decisions within decentralized supply chains are inefficient due to the interacting effects of inadequate information and organizational self-interest. Actual consumer demand is magnified at successive stages as a consequence of incomplete and delayed information rippling back through the supply chain, thereby causing amplification, oscillation, and time lags of the original demand signal. Manufacturers must add production capacity and suppliers and distributors more buffer stock to satisfy

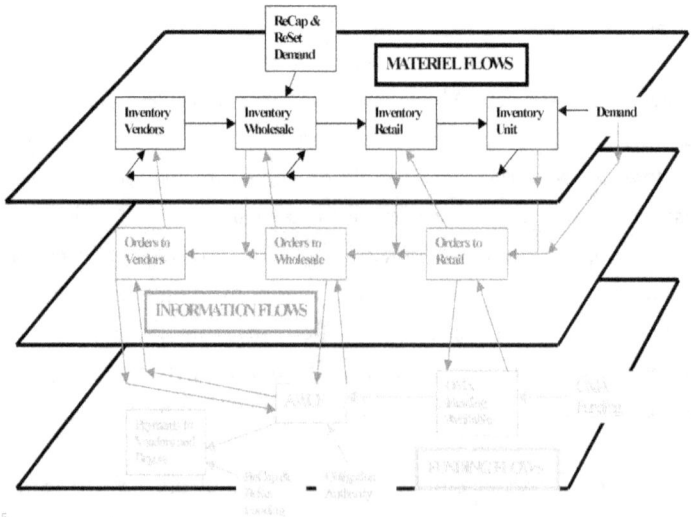

Figure 5. Supply Chain Flows: Materiel, information, and financial.

order streams that are increasingly more volatile the further removed they are within the supply chain from actual demand.

Although operationally recognized for several decades, this induced, cascading variability has only recently been analytically identified, then rigorously quantified and subsequently explained in the academic literature.[1] Enterprise-wide variability grows geometrically as the number of independent stages in the supply chain increases. The value of information sharing, access to centralized databases, and collaboration across the stages, in contrast to independently operating stages, has also been quantified and shown to dramatically reduce system variability and associated requirements for buffer inventory while actually improving performance (e.g., reduced stockouts). In essence, shared information and collaboration have the effect of collapsing several independent stages into only a few "virtual" stages (Figure 6). Growing corporate awareness of this phenomenon has resulted in companies moving away from the traditional view of the enterprise as a collection of separate and independent entities toward a more collaborative model where interconnectivity is increasingly emphasized as a means to mitigate demand variability propagation through the supply chain.

Practical examples of integrating supply chain operations through information and collaboration include electronic data interchange (EDI) to reduce delays and enable a smoother flow of material with smaller, more frequent orders, and vendor-managed inventory (VMI), which requires the supplier to actually manage retail inventory distribution in exchange for receiving customer demand information.

In the commercial sector when a company faces pressures of excessive inventory, degraded customer service, escalating costs and declining profits, or a poor return on assets, its supply chain may be out of control. Similarly, if a company is moving into new markets or new technologies, then its supply chain must be appropriately aligned for new business opportunities, challenges, and uncertainties.

Despite the many new design concepts and management approaches intended to exploit the advantages of the Internet and information technology, successful companies realize that an appropriate supply chain strategy must be tailored to meet the needs of its particular customers and market conditions. For example, a product with stable demand and a reliable source of supply should not be managed the same way as one

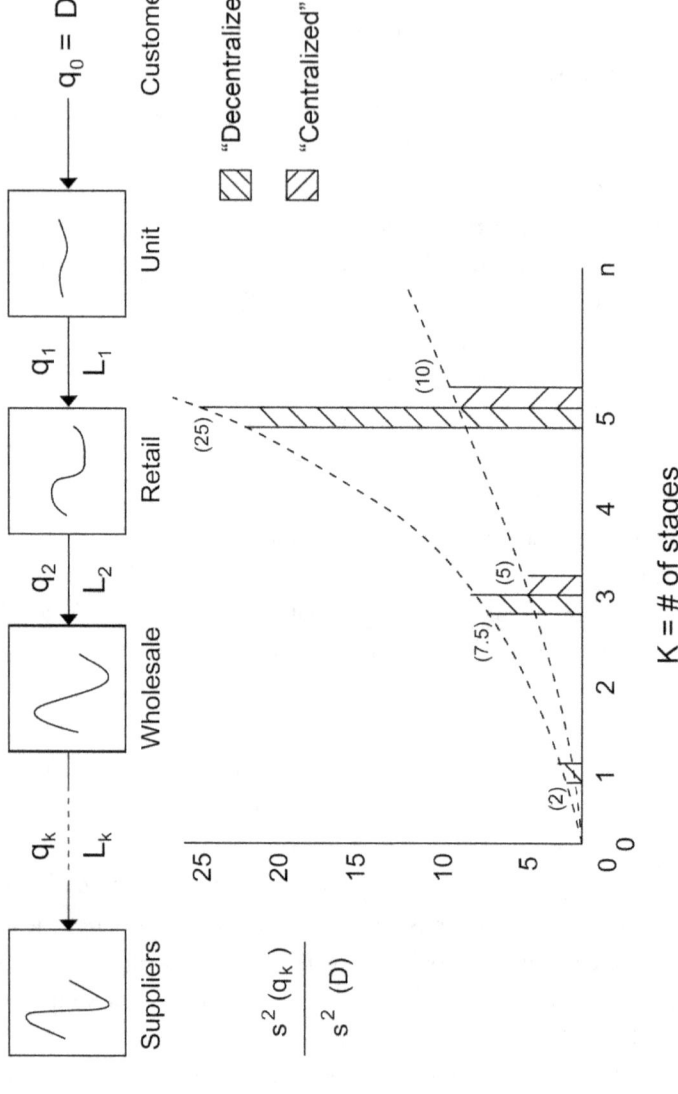

Figure 6. Demand volatility in multistage supply chains: The "Bullwhip" effect.

with highly unpredictable demand and an unreliable source of supply. A model to assist in selecting an appropriate supply chain strategy consistent with demand-side variability characteristics was initially developed by Fisher[2] then later extended by Lee to incorporate supply side variability characteristics as well.

This "uncertainty framework" (Figure 7) illuminates the potential improvement that can be achieved in supply chain performance by adopting both "demand uncertainty reduction strategies" and "supply uncertainty reduction strategies." The goal is to adopt techniques and policies that will reduce aggregate variability in lead time demand as much as possible and then ensure that an appropriate design is chosen to effectively accommodate resulting supply chain characteristics.

In the business world, efforts to reduce the effects of demand uncertainty have focused on information sharing and supply chain collaboration to provide enterprise-wide visibility of actual customer demand, thereby reducing these pernicious bullwhip effects. Supply side uncertainty reduction methods have included collaborative relationships, longer term contracts with suppliers, and the creation of supplier hubs to reduce supply risks in manufacturing lines. Lee[3] has defined four resulting supply chain strategies that should then be "aligned" to these resulting product uncertainties (Figure 8):

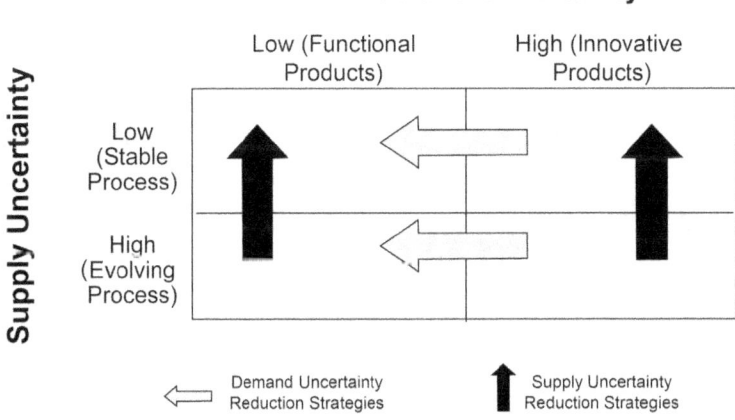

Figure 7. Supressing the "bullwhip."

Demand Uncertainty

	Low (Functional Products)	High (Innovative Products)
Low (Stable Process)	Efficient supply chains	Responsive supply chains
High (Evolving Process)	Risk-hedging supply chains	Agile supply chains

(Supply Uncertainty — vertical axis)

Figure 8. Supply chain strategies.

1. Efficient supply chains: Strategies aimed at creating the highest possible cost efficiencies by eliminating non-value-added activities, pursuing economies of scale, and optimizing capacity utilization in production and distribution
2. Risk-hedging supply chains: Strategies that pool and share resources to reduce risks and that increase safety stock to hedge against supply chain disruption
3. Responsive supply chains: Strategies designed to be responsive to the changing and diverse needs of the customer, including build-to-order and flexible, high-order-accuracy mass customization processes
4. Agile supply chains: Strategies that combine the strengths of responsive and risk-hedging; characterized as "agile," since they are responsive to unpredictable customer demand but also minimize risks of supply disruption

Recent decades have also seen an increasing marketing and sales shift from consumer product consumption to emphasis on the value that customers derive from ownership and use of those products over extended periods. Nationwide, as a percentage of total expenditures, commercial budget growth in purchased goods and services has more than doubled during the past 20 years. For DoD, in FY2002 the total budget was $345 billion; about 44% of this total budget was spent on comparable purchased goods and services (operations and support, or O&S costs).

Supply chain concepts have been extended and adapted to incorporate this trend where after-sales services are increasingly providing a greater proportion of revenue and profit to companies that traditionally focused only on product manufacturing. This new focus on "service supply chains" is having a significant impact for those adopting its use, providing competitive differentiation and improving customer acquisition and retention by offering value propositions for purchase and ownership rather than the traditional approach of simply offering products for sale. However, mechanisms for designing and implementing postsale services and support—delivering "value"—for competitive, cost-effective service supply chains have proven far more complex than those used for the manufacturing and sales of products delivered for market consumption through standard supply chain designs. This after-sales market creates a service management challenge that is much more complex than traditional supply chain planning problems in manufacturing. Technology alone cannot provide the solution. It will require a new mind-set to effectively and efficiently manage service operations toward optimized processes from an integrated perspective to achieve what has been called "strategic service management."

It is the application and adaptation of these service supply chain concepts that appear to align most closely with and offer the greatest insight into military logistics systems providing after-sales services to complex defense and aerospace weapons systems. Until recently, the value proposition for these military logistics service supply chains has been cost-effective delivery of spare parts and maintenance services. However, under DoD's recently mandated performance-based logistics (PBL) concept, this value proposition is transitioning to incorporate availability and other capability measures as readiness output values rather than the selling of repair parts and services per se (i.e., readiness inputs). This PBL approach, discussed in much greater detail in chapter 22, is analogous to "power by the hour" value propositions for service supply chains in the corporate sector.

Using this service supply chain model, we have been able to clearly demonstrate army aviation supply chain vulnerability to the bullwhip. This ability, using system dynamics modeling, provides significant explanatory power regarding these "death spiral" conditions characterizing the current environment mentioned previously.[4] The analytical challenge now is to better understand army logistics system hysteresis by first segmenting the logistics structure into stages and then identifying, understanding, and systematically attacking each of the root causes that contribute to uncertainty, variability, and inefficiency both within each stage and across the system of stages.

The stages can then be linked together using network optimization methods to allocate resource investment decisions to readiness-oriented outcomes with greater confidence. For example, readiness-based sparing (RBS) uses a marginal analysis approach to generate a cost-constrained retail stock policy that optimizes the link between the retail stage and a desired readiness production level at the unit stage. By reducing uncertainty and improving efficiency within each stage, and linking the stages together using multiechelon optimization methods developed for large-scale, complex systems, logistics system performance is moving toward the efficient frontier in a cost-availability trade space (Figure 2).

This project is quantifying efficiency gains from various initiatives using analytical demonstrations, field experiments, and testing. Examples of major initiatives include development of a "readiness equation" for the unit stage; implementing PBL concepts, including availability-based sparing and centralized risk pooling in the retail stage; using empirically derived, operation-based forecasts for the demand stage; and, especially, reducing delay time in the retrograde stage for depot-level reparables (DLRs).

Working backward through the supply chain from the point of readiness production, the stages can be linked together using multi-echelon optimization enabling resources-to-readiness investment decisions to be made with dramatically improved accuracy.[5] Then, return on investment (ROI) estimates can be reliably estimated and credible cost-benefit assessments performed for the wide variety of initiatives that have been proposed. This analytical architecture would guide an ambitious Logistics Transformation endeavor, consistent with a strategic plan for implementation, by pushing the envelope of continuous, measurable, and relevant improvement.

However, the great challenge for the army's unique supply chain strategy, referring to Lee's framework (Figure 8), is that it not only must be both efficient and effective but also must be characterized as agile, responsive, adaptive, flexible, and robust to accommodate both surges in demand and disruptions across the supply chain. What is needed is a logistics network that is efficient, effective, and "resilient." This project endeavors to assist the army achieve such a result using a new, analytically based, performance-focused philosophy and mind-set—a comprehensive decision support system for strategic capability and readiness management to enable and guide Logistics Transformation.

PART II

Multistage Analysis of Systemic Challenges

Unfortunately, current readiness levels reflect an Army in crises . . . Cannibalization of equipment has left the Army without a single combat brigade in the continental United Sates ready for all its wartime missions . . . This problem developed over time due to mismanagement.
—Representative Ike Skelton, chairman, House Armed Services Committee, February 2007

The U.S. military is in a state of strategic peril . . . The U.S. Army is starting to unravel.
—General (Retired) Barry McCaffrey, December 19, 2007

Chapters

5. Readiness Production Stage: Tactical Units
6. Operational Mission and Training Demand Stage
7. Retail Stage: Tactical Level
8. Reverse Logistics Stage: Retrograde
9. Wholesale Stage: National Level
10. Acquisition Stage
11. Summary

As described in chapter 1, the U.S. Army's materiel enterprise is truly enormous in scale and scope. However, it is not merely the size and complexity of the supply chain that causes difficulty, but rather the structure and policies within the system that are the root cause of persistent problems. Because this complex supply chain is a large-scale engineering system, some form of representation is needed to model its essential structure to segment the problem into meaningful components to focus analytical effort, enable root cause analysis, and assist in identifying the various sources of variability and uncertainty that cause the "bullwhip" effect and create persistent inefficiencies across the enterprise. The multistage logistics diagram, introduced in chapter 3 (Figure 3) to simplify and model army materiel enterprise processes, is consistently used throughout the next six chapters to provide this diagnostic framework.

These subsequent chapters sequentially address the organizational components of the multistage model with each chapter devoted to a particular stage of the logistics model. The focus is on analyzing and understanding what actually causes the inventory, rather than the inventory itself. Inventory management theory, supply chain principles, and logistics systems analysis are the key sources of diagnostic power that are used to illuminate the underlying problems in each of the stages as well as identify potential solutions. The final chapter in part II summarizes the problems and challenges identified using the root cause analysis in each of the stages and further explains both their individual and collective consequences for—and opportunities to improve—army supply chain performance and materiel enterprise management.

CHAPTER 5

Readiness Production Stage

Tactical Units

We simply do not know our spare part consumption patterns across DoD. Even in those rare instances where we do, we do not share this information with our suppliers and manufacturers.

—Alan F. Estevez, assistant deputy under secretary of defense for supply chain integration

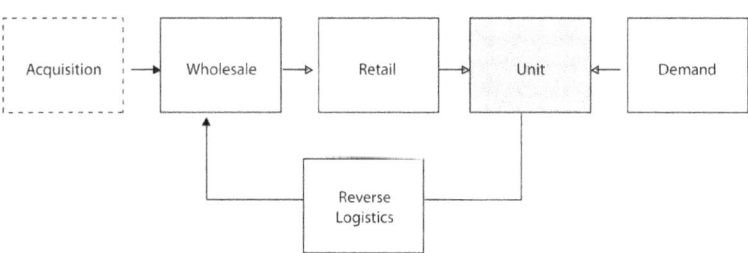

Figure 9. Tactical Unit Stage.

Readiness reporting trends from the field were becoming increasingly worrisome by fall 2002. Overall, short-term aviation readiness seemed to be holding although longer term trends suggested slow yet noticeable decline. This apparently healthy state of tactical aviation units was partly illusion, however, since local work-arounds were masking deeper, more serious readiness problems. For example, aviation commanders were increasingly resorting to controlled substitution as a method to both maintain acceptable readiness rates and also compensate for an inventory system that could not keep up with the growing demands of aging aircraft fleets.[1]

Nonetheless, the dominant cause of non-mission-capable (NMC) aircraft was persistently attributed to repair maintenance downtime

(NMCM) rather than a shortage of spare parts (NMCS). These reported trends were not consistent with an already large and growing backlog of spares (for aviation alone the shortfall was nearly $1 billion at that time), suggesting that the actual NMCS rates were considerably higher than reported. Another indicator for comparison was the fixed-wing aircraft NMC rates for both the U.S. Navy and the U.S. Air Force. Nearly 50% of their NMC rates were due to spares shortages compared to only about 10% reported for army rotorcraft. These inconsistent trends are at least partially the consequence of an inadequately understood "production function" for army aviation readiness.

In most commercial-sector supply chains, products are created in accordance with a well-defined and highly refined production function describing the manufacturing process. Subsequent distribution occurs through international or national wholesale centers, then regional retail distribution centers, and ultimately to customers who "consume" the product. At the end of the supply chain the customer is, ultimately, also the consumer. In military spare parts supply chains, however, the consumption process also involves another production function—the creation of militarily capable and "ready" units available to execute the national military strategy.

The term "supply chain" typically has been applied to commercial organizations and processes that provide raw material into a manufacturing process and then distribute finished goods to retail sales operations for consumer purchase. In addition to manufacturing and distributing repair part "products," military logistics systems also provide maintenance support to "manufacture" readiness for tactical units. Consequently, due to their scope, scale, and complexity, these military "extended enterprises" are far more challenging to coordinate and synchronize than commercial consumer product supply chains.

Unlike demand forecasting for commercial production operations where inputs for manufacturing and retail operations can either be controlled or exhibit high predictability, repair part demand rates needed for military readiness are a function of failure propensities and replacement rates rather than the speed of assembly line operations. The demand-generating processes for these two different production operations—commercial manufacturing and military readiness—exhibit dramatically different characteristics. Although both have stochastic elements associated with demand forecasting, the inherently predictable pattern of raw material requirements for finished goods enables relatively precise and definitive answers for inventory stock quantities. In contrast, consumption and replacement patterns for repair parts are highly volatile, reflecting greater variability in demand due to random failure patterns found in complex aerospace systems such as military aircraft.[2]

For army aviation systems this production function, or "readiness equation," has been well defined from an engineering design perspective where readiness performance levels are typically denoted by aircraft operational availability (Ao) percentages (Figure 10). However, this readiness equation has not been empirically measured in terms of traditional economics relating labor and capital to desired readiness production levels in operational environments. As a consequence, and despite countless initiatives to improve logistics supportability, proposed changes will continue to remain disconnected from the "point of consumption" where readiness is actually generated. Two problems have persisted: first, inadequate knowledge of what is really happening on the ground (or in the air), and second, complexities that are not captured by current management information systems. This failure to observe, measure results, and incorporate feedback has been a critical supply chain design flaw.

Capital in the form of spare parts investments cannot be optimized to an inadequately defined readiness production function. Consequently, numerous work-arounds occur that tend to substitute labor for capital, which is the opposite of what technology advances are intended to yield.

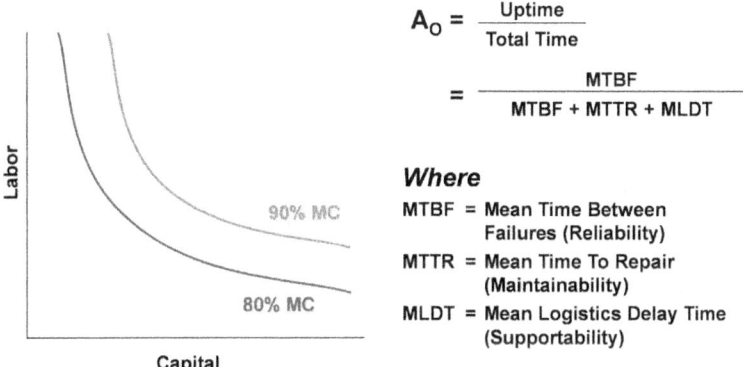

Figure 10. The "Production Function" for readiness.

These work-arounds become necessary alternatives for completing a repair action, since the supply system could not provide needed parts in a timely manner. Typical work-arounds include temporary repair, local fabrication or purchase, cannibalization, and controlled substitution. Increased maintenance man-hours are routinely incurred by resorting to these work-arounds that are needed to compensate for requisition delays or shortages of parts (Figure 11).

Recent project research to develop a readiness equation for army aviation systems indicates these work-arounds are occurring more than 25% of the time for unscheduled maintenance across the army's aviation fleet. We have also been able to estimate the likely reduction in aircraft readiness if these organizational work-arounds were not performed by tactical units. The impact of these work-arounds is significant, suggesting that labor (maintenance man-hours) is indeed substituting for capital (spare part investments): *If work-arounds were eliminated, then estimated readiness would decline by 33%.* We also discovered that army rotorcraft have significantly higher failure rates than ground systems, although repairs tend to be completed in less time.

These labor-intensive work-arounds further exacerbate an already stressed labor supply of existing tactical-level mechanics. Using army regulations (AR 570-4) as a guide, which specify manpower requirements for mechanics based on maintenance standards, recent U.S. Army Forces Command data clearly shows that there are more field-level maintenance requirements than there are mechanics assigned to units and maintenance man-hours available to meet these standards. This manpower shortfall equates to about $300 million of annual unexecutable organic maintenance, of which 20% is accommodated through civilian maintenance contract support agreements. This has been an increasing trend.[3]

In our research effort to empirically measure the "readiness production function," we have been able to operationally link logistics performance to aviation readiness. Four key contributing factors to improved aviation system readiness (or Ao) have emerged. Each factor aligns with unscheduled maintenance events, scheduled ("phase") maintenance activities, or both:

1. Component reliability
2. Spare parts availability for unscheduled maintenance

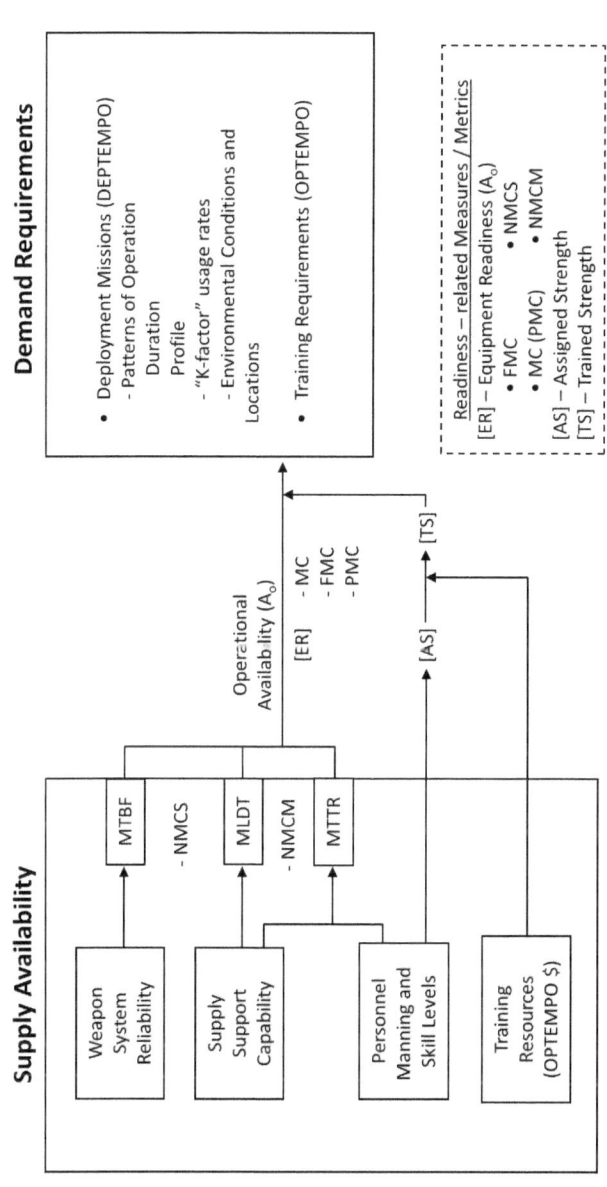

Figure 11. "Production Function": Components of readiness.

3. Intervals between scheduled maintenance inspection and overhaul
4. Customer wait time for parts needed to complete these scheduled maintenance events

Project research has also generated marginal value estimates—the "elasticity"—for each factor's contribution to readiness.[4] We can now associate potential improvements in technology, management, or policy initiatives with each of these readiness factors. Next, implementation costs can be estimated to develop readiness return on investment results and comparative cost-benefit analyses. Three promising initiatives are described here.

First, the U.S. Army Recapitalization Program (RECAP) is intended to extend platform service life through reliability upgrades and technology insertion. We identified and measured differences in failure and replacement rates among various components and subsystems and how these change across aviation platform types. This information will now allow design improvements, better failure detection methods, and condition-based maintenance (CBM) sensor prognostics to be targeted where component reliability improvement and RECAP investments will have the greatest impact.

Second, adopting as army policies both readiness-based sparing (RBS) and mission-based forecasting (MBF), which are described in detail in the next two chapters, will improve spare part availability, reduce back orders, and decrease customer wait times for both scheduled and unscheduled maintenance actions.

Third, the new CBM initiative has the potential to reduce and combine inspections while increasing intervals between, and perhaps eliminating altogether, phase maintenance. As its name implies, CBM takes into consideration the actual condition of equipment when deciding whether maintenance is necessary. CBM enables the transition from costly, highly reactive break-then-fix operations to predictive, proactive maintenance strategies that yield higher asset availabilities, fewer service disruptions (e.g., periodic inspections and phase maintenance), and reduced maintenance costs. No doubt there will be significant interacting and synergistic effects among these initiatives, suggesting tremendous possibilities for improvement. Especially noteworthy is the truly dramatic potential for reducing labor-intensive work-arounds—maintenance man-hours per aircraft—thereby decreasing the enormous burden currently placed on operational units.

A final condition that further clarifies and illuminates the compelling need for a production function—or readiness equation—for army aviation is the universally acknowledged inadequacy of existing tactical-level databases to capture meaningful aviation maintenance and supply data.[5] Obviously, regardless of the sophistication and "fit" of mathematical models used, any sincere effort to align Class IX demand forecasting to readiness targets is critically dependent on maintenance consumption and repair data accuracy.

"Demand information latency," which is the failure to rapidly transmit consumer product use, pattern, and trend information throughout the supply chain enterprise, is one of the greatest contributors to the bullwhip effect. As the army seeks to improve its field data collection systems, especially with the enhanced unit-level logistics system (ULLS) for aviation (ULLS-A(E)), care should be taken to ensure that consumption data is not only captured to enable "readiness production" analysis and trends but also then processed so that re-supplies can automatically be requested similar to point-of-sale collection and inventory reorder triggers in the consumer products industry.

CBM, in conjunction with ULLS-A(E), has the potential to quantify spare parts usage and empirically track the readiness production function for army aviation systems. Consequently, vast amounts of data and information will soon be available at the tactical level. However, if these new tactical-level data collection and warehouse systems are not "connected" to the larger supply chain, then enterprise-wide visibility will not exist to generate the knowledge needed, (e.g., using multiechelon readiness-based sparing) to fully capitalize on their promise.

Conversely, if this "customer" (readiness) demand information is made visible using information technologies and provided to the entire logistics enterprise, then the bullwhip effect can be drastically reduced. This can be accomplished, for the very first time, by providing actual consumption information (in near real time) to all production, provisioning, distributing, and inventory supply elements within the supply chain. By providing such visibility, collaboration among all organizations can be drastically improved and focused directly on supply performance for readiness capability needs that are now apparent to all. Uncertainty is thereby removed and inefficiencies induced by information lag across previously independently operating logistics organizations can be dramatically reduced (Figure 12). The supply chain becomes increasingly more responsive to *real customer demand*, or actual readiness requirements. Capability and readiness performance can be improved and aggregate investment levels reduced *and* tied directly to performance outcomes, thereby linking resources to readiness.

More generally, if uncertainty is viewed as the complement of knowledge, then for a fixed demand the three quantities shown in Figure 13 (inventory, capacity, and knowledge) are substitutes in the following sense: If more of one is available, then less of one or both of the others is necessary for the same level of system performance needed to meet that demand. This trade-off suggests a fundamental truth about inventory management for supply chain operations. If CBM can be "connected" to the supply chain to increase the amount and timeliness of useful data and good information for actionable supply management decisions (i.e., increased knowledge or "what we know"), then with the same capacity ("what we can do") as before, it now becomes possible to improve system performance with lower inventory ("what we have") costs.

READINESS PRODUCTION STAGE 37

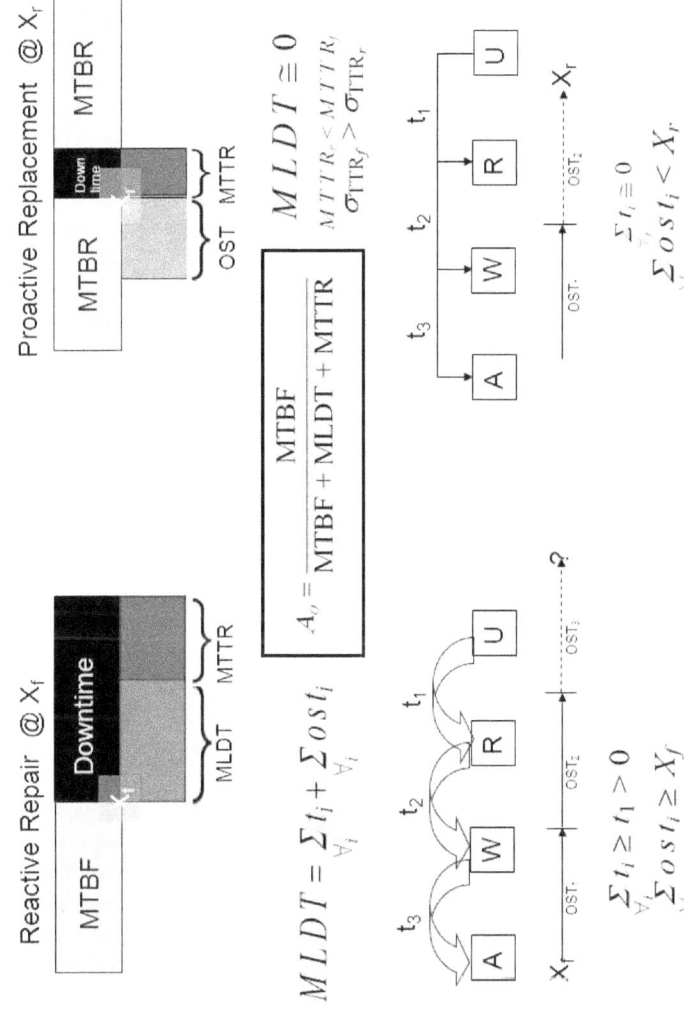

Figure 12. "Connecting" Condition Based Maintenance (CBM) to the Supply Chain.

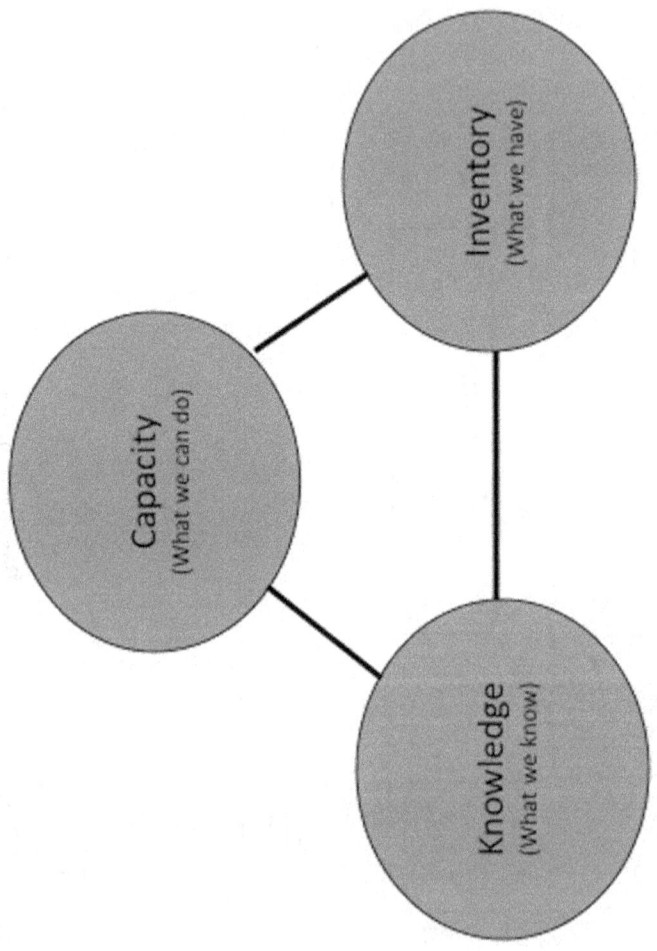

Figure 13. Capacity, inventory, and knowledge.

CHAPTER 6

Operational Mission and Training Demand Stage

We must operationally link logistics support to maneuver in order to produce desired operational outcomes.
—General Peter J. Schoomaker, chief of staff, U.S. Army

Good demand forecasting is the most important thing in controlling the level of inventory.
—Jim Erdman, senior vice president, Penske Logistics

What is surprising is not the magnitude of our forecast errors, but our absence of awareness of it.
—Nassim Nicholas Taleb, from *The Black Swan*

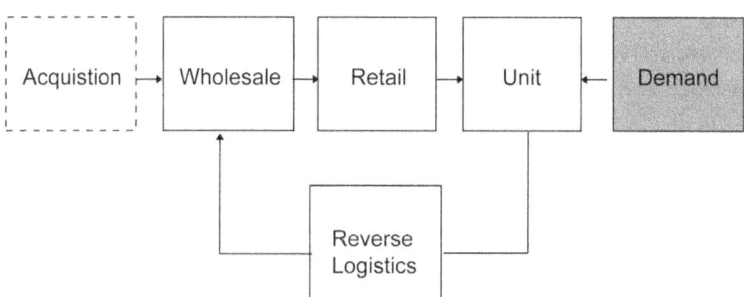

Figure 14. Mission demand stage.

Our military strategy is evolving from the Cold War's "threat-based" force-planning concept, which was characterized by forward deployed, continental U.S. (CONUS) reinforced forces, to an expeditionary "capabilities-based," power projection concept consistent with the changing geopolitical environment. These capabilities are expressed in terms of modular force structure and resources needed to conduct various types of operations, simultaneously and overlapping, across a wide spectrum of anticipated missions. Resources, including sustaining assets such as Class IX repair parts and components, associated combat service support organizations, and doctrine, must be aligned to support these desired capabilities.

Aligning resources with desired capabilities starts with a clear understanding of how resource "usage factors" for various expeditionary operations and locations differ from standard peacetime, home station training requirements. Currently, tactical operations planning typically involves deploying with a logistics support package optimized for peacetime training conditions or, in some cases, multiplying a standard peacetime quantity by a subjectively derived factor. At the strategic level, long-term resource forecasting to support program development usually involves averaging past demands over time (several years), location, and mission types and extrapolating those average results as an estimate for future investment budgets.

Clearly, a great deal of potentially useful information is not being considered in forecasts that generate averages by aggregating data across time, location, and missions in this fashion. This lack of an empirically derived, operation-based forecasting process also contributes to the large "safety levels" that are incorporated into wholesale supply requirement objectives.

"Demand forecasting" refers to the quantitative method used for predicting future demand for spare parts generated by training requirements and operational missions. Reducing both demand uncertainty and variability at the point of consumption where readiness is actually produced and providing both understanding of causes and visibility of effects are crucial to reducing system-wide aggregate variability in lead-time demand. Theoretically, both average demand and variability in demand are confounded with supply-side effects that together interact to magnify system variability, thereby driving up the need for additional safety stock. Even though "demand" may be perceived as an uncontrollable variable, simply ignoring it and concentrating only on supply-side variance reduction efforts throughout the rest of the upstream supply chain will not achieve the dramatic performance improvements that are possible (Figure 15).

Currently, however, we do not know what real demand is, partly due to the lack of a "readiness equation" described earlier. As a recent Government Accountability Office report on defense logistics in Operation Iraqi

OPERATIONAL MISSION AND TRAINING DEMAND STAGE 41

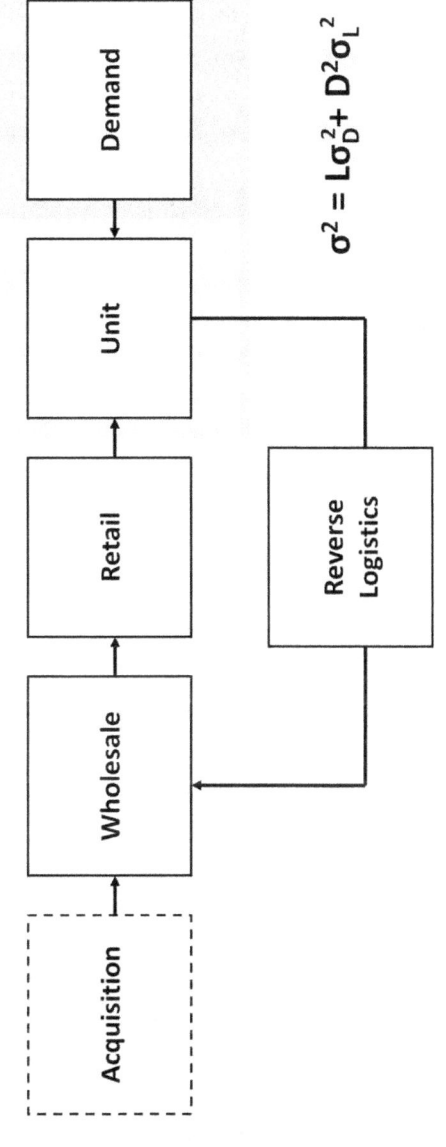

$$\sigma^2 = L\sigma_D^2 + D^2\sigma_L^2$$

- Reduce uncertainty and variability by improving demand forecast accuracy for requirements estimation and operational planning
- Reengineer inventory sparing policies to achieve *cost-effective* readiness goals
- Transition from supply push concept to a readiness-driven demand network

Figure 15. Enhanced class IX planning: Linking operational patterns, demand forecasting, and supply planning.

Freedom notes, "the logistics effort was weakened by long processing times for supply requisitions, which resulted in the loss of confidence and discipline in the supply system, the abuse of the priority designation process, and the submission of multiple requisitions."[1] As recent comments from a former senior defense logistics policy official suggest, this "blindness to true demand" results in a very "high cost of low trust."[2] And as Moshe Rubinstein, distinguished professor of engineering and organizational systems at University of California at Los Angeles, has observed, "There is no survival without trust."[3]

A major project initiative in this "stage" is our effort to significantly improve demand forecasting by borrowing concepts from market segmentation research and population polling statistics. Stratified sampling is a powerful variance reduction technique that enables accurate and precise estimates to be made without the need for larger and more costly sample sizes that are typically required when using random sampling of a large and diverse, heterogeneous population. This straightforward technique achieves these results by capturing and using more of the information in targeted homogeneous subpopulations, or market segments. Not only subpopulation parameters but also overall parameters for the entire, more diverse population can more accurately be predicted with far greater confidence (reduced variation) in the forecast.[4] A key insight from stratified sampling theory that we are applying is recognition that the *method* of sampling, rather than the *size* of the sample, is what matters most for improved forecast accuracy.

In our application we are focusing initially on those intuitively derived factors (explanatory variables) that can or should be expected to affect Class IX consumption. These include weapon system type; training or operational mission category; geographic location and environmental conditions; and system parameters including, for example, aircraft age. We may find, for example, that aggregate flying hours contribute significantly toward predicting spares demand in a stateside training environment. On the other hand, for overseas operational missions it may be that flying hours do not contribute nearly as much explanatory power to the forecast as, for example, mission type or the environment where the mission is conducted. We will also determine whether or not these factors are captured by existing data collection systems and to what extent, if any, they are incorporated into current mission and resource planning factors.

Fundamentally, this is an effort to capture the statistically significant factors influencing future demand using all of the information provided by the empirical evidence of recent experience. It is predicated on the simple notion that practical operational enhancements emerge from the judicious study of discernible reality: *Forecast error is reduced primarily through observed demand.*

Our basis for optimism here is the very successful effort during the past 2 decades to dramatically improve combat medical support by increasing battlefield casualty forecasting accuracy. Previously, for example, medical planning factors were derived from attrition-based, theater-level campaign model casualty projections. However, when compared with actual empirical evidence from recent experiences of modern warfare, including Persian Gulf War results, these projections were overpredicting aggregate casualties by orders of magnitude, thereby creating unnecessary and unaffordable requirements for medical support force structure.

Recent extensive, comprehensive analyses into the nature of modern warfare[5] and the structure and patterns of casualties that result[6] are yielding major improvements in forecasting accuracy and an ability to better design more responsive, effective medical support requirements that, in many cases, result in reduced force structure investments costs. Both of theses seminal analyses, which challenged traditional views and standard practices, have been validated and corroborated by our most recent experiences in both Afghanistan and Iraq and are now being further refined and extended.

Similarly, through a systematic and analytically rigorous evaluation of the empirical evidence contained in past deployment operations, we intend to identify and verify various patterns of use that will have significant predictive power for the future.

We have developed a large experimental design to identify spare part consumption patterns and readiness "drivers" that either dominate, or differ significantly across operational missions and geographic locations and how they may vary from peacetime training. Our major hypothesis states, "If empirically derived Class IX usage patterns, profiles, and/or trends can be associated with various operational mission types, then operational planning, demand forecasting, and budget requirements can be significantly improved to support a capabilities-based force."

The initial research focused on the first portion of the hypothesis to determine whether or not clearly discernable differences could be identified in spare and repair parts maintenance data at the tactical level. Demand patterns distinctive to different operational missions (e.g., training, major combat operations, stability operations) and environments (CONUS, OIF in Iraq) were clearly identified confirming the "if" portion of the hypothesis. Indeed, the differences in these descriptive patterns proved to be even more striking than originally anticipated (Figure 16).

The second phase of research (corresponding to the "then" portion of the hypothesis) has endeavored to determine whether or not relevant data for these descriptive, operations-driven demand patterns could be captured and used to develop a method for improved demand forecast accuracy. For a particular weapon system (e.g., UH-60, AH-64), this new method isolates and captures key explanatory variables, including operational mission type and duration, force size, and environment, using actual part data from unit-level maintenance actions contained in the Army's Sample Data Collection program (*not* supply requisition data from the supply system which current methods rely on), and then estimates future demand for similar operational settings using the information contained in these different, empirically derived parts usage patterns. Since this new method projects parts demand by linking to operational patterns, it has been referred to as "operations-driven demand patterns" (ODDP), or more simply "mission based forecasting" (MBF).

And most recently, to formally prove or disprove our research hypothesis, MBF has been tested against and compared with currently used forecasting methods. Results to date have been truly remarkable: *across platforms and operational settings, MBF has consistently demonstrated nearly an order of magnitude (e.g., 100%) improvement in demand forecast accuracy.* For Blackhawk and Apache aircraft (75% of the Army's rotorcraft fleet), forecast accuracy for both part "breadth" (different parts) and "depth" (actual quantity of each part) is dramatically and consistently improved across operational settings (figures 17 and 18). MBF forecasts are 70–100% more accurate than current methods and, if adopted as policy and implemented, have truly enormous potential for cost savings across major weapon system fleets while sustaining or actually improving readiness.

Another key insight, derived from our ODDP/MBF research, further reinforces an issue previously described and addressed at the end

OPERATIONAL MISSION AND TRAINING DEMAND STAGE 45

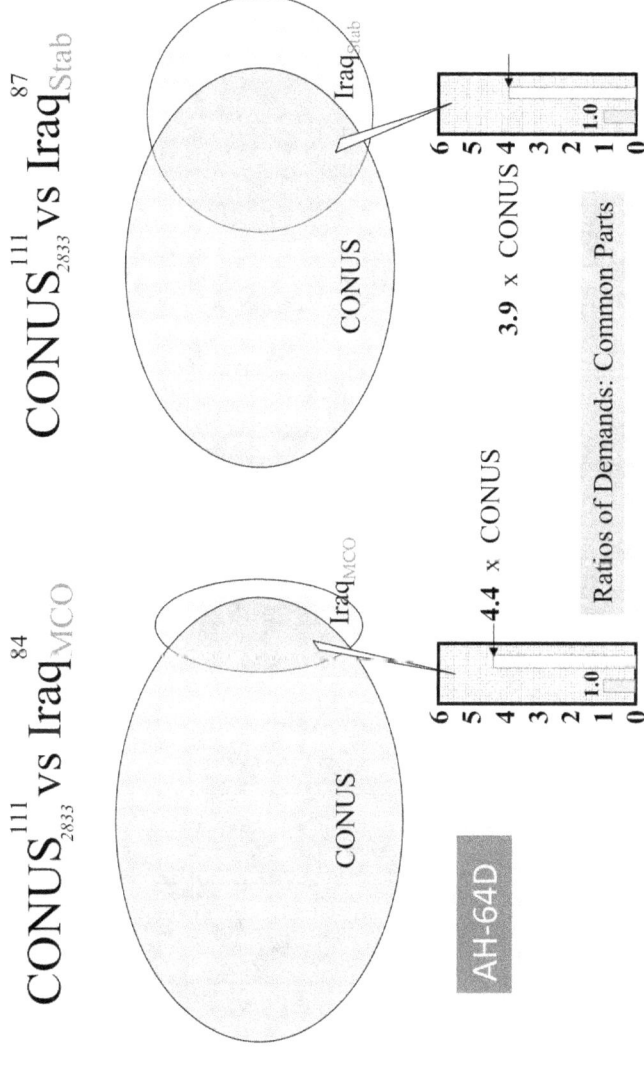

Figure 16. *Part Demand: Relative composition and magnitude.*

46 TRANSFORMING U.S. ARMY SUPPLY CHAINS

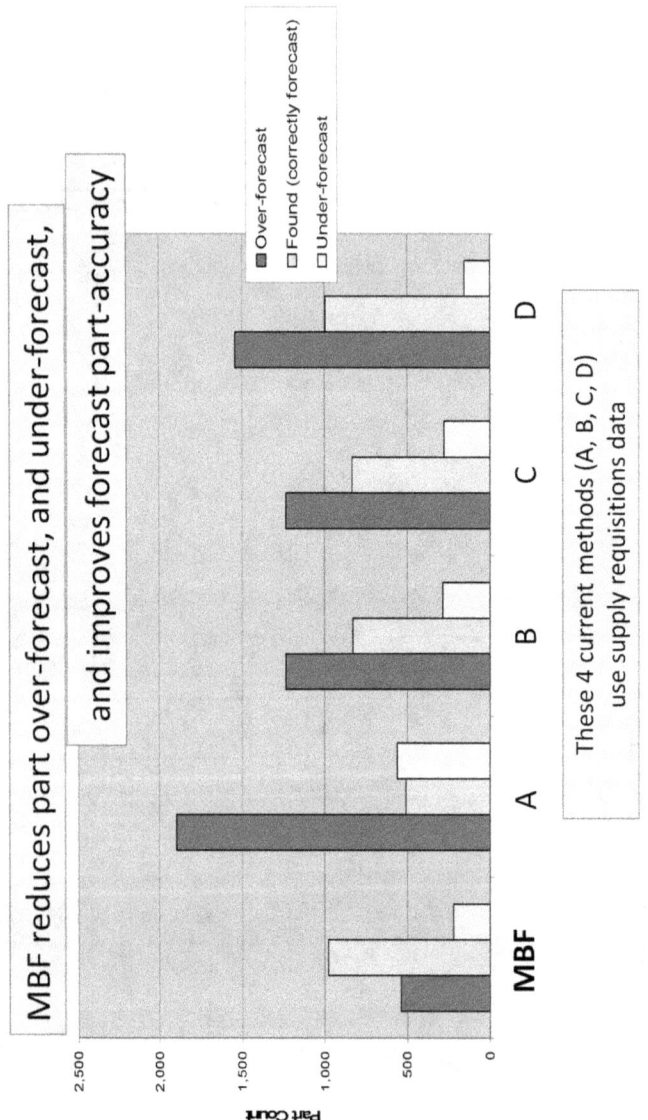

Figure 17. MBF compared to current methods: Part breadth.

OPERATIONAL MISSION AND TRAINING DEMAND STAGE 47

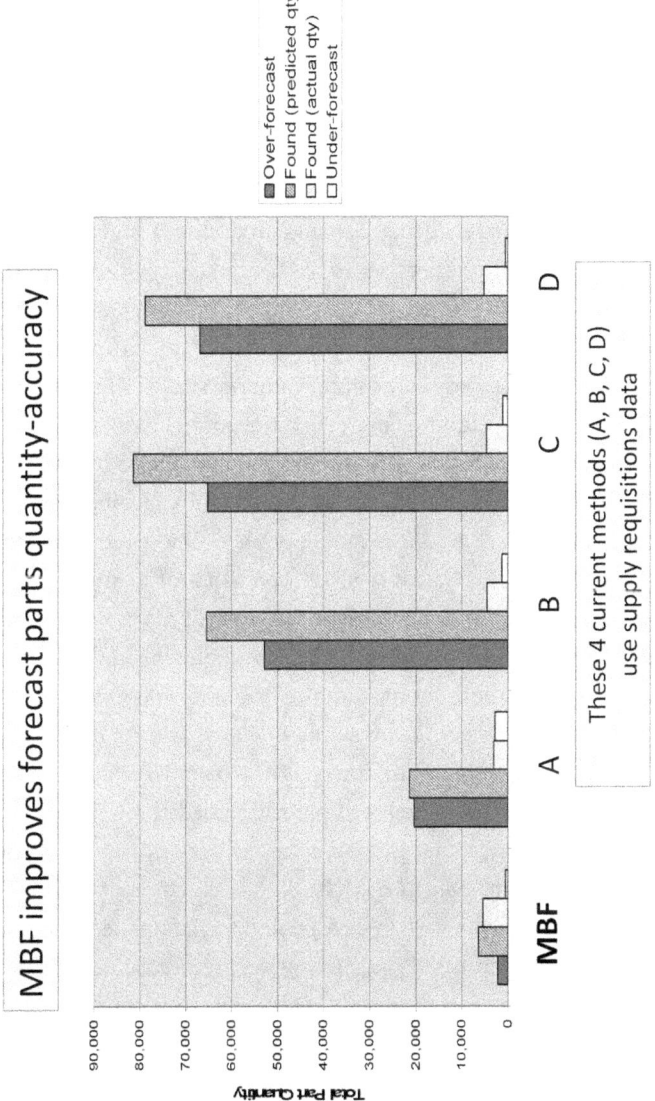

Figure 18. MBF compared to current methods: Part depth.

of chapter 5. Real "customer demand" (spares and repair parts actually used) at the "point-of-sale" (tactical units)—where readiness is actually produced—is not systematically captured by standard, existing data collection systems. Hence, there is no genuine, empirically derived demand history available to compute an accurate, *cost effective* demand forecast to achieve future readiness objectives for the customer. This fatal flaw must be corrected so that demand forecast accuracy can be significantly improved for inventory management across the army's materiel enterprise.

Successfully developing this empirically derived, mission-based forecasting (MBF) capability also has the potential to lead to even more dramatic improvements in reducing demand uncertainty and variability. Conventional *feedback* processes act to reduce the effect of some disturbance on an output. However, they can do so only *after* the effect of the disturbance is seen and subsequently responded to. In contrast, the concept of *feedforward*, defined as anticipatory action oriented on first predicting and then precluding failure, is centered on counteracting disturbances before any change in output actually occurs. These implications are significant even beyond the "sparing to mission" capability outlined previously. For parts that are either failure prone or known to be nearing the end of useful life anyway, this suggests repair and replacement *prior to* executing a particular mission can enhance mission success by preempting failure—"inoculation" in a sense—thereby improving and extending Ao. In fact, this theoretical observation was essentially observed in practice for many years by the 82nd Airborne Division as their initial ready companies (IRCs), division ready force (DRF) battalions, and division ready brigades (DRBs) were prepared for and cycled through their no-notice, global deployment alert process.

Condition-based maintenance (CBM) is the current "reliability-centered maintenance" initiative to develop and use component prognostic sensing and platform-based diagnostics for preemptive, anticipatory part replacement. This contrasts with traditional practices of "replacement upon failure" for unscheduled maintenance, and "flying hour-based replacement" for scheduled, "phase" maintenance. These current maintenance models tend to presume that component condition is exclusively a function of age. Consequently, traditional policies have tended to ignore other important exogenous factors such as environmental conditions, manufacturing variances, preventive maintenance history, and especially the effects of different types of missions flown. Ongoing CBM efforts, however, are now focusing on linking aircraft usage data with various flight conditions to identify potential correlations to component failure.[7]

Nonetheless, this *internal* platform-focused prognostic capability, which is the current focus for CBM, needs to be complemented with an understanding of historical consumption patterns and usage trends associated with operational and environmental demand factors *external* to the platform. These differential effects of operational mission types (e.g., training, combat, stability operations, and humanitarian support) and environmental conditions (e.g., altitude, temperature, humidity and salinity, sand and dust) can be measured by statistically evaluating the empirical consumption patterns associated with recent deployment operations.

This is, of course, the essence of our MBF initiative. Research has shown that "demand lead times behave in a fashion that is exactly the opposite of supply lead times. In effect, an increase in demand lead time improves system performance exactly like a reduction in supply lead time."[8] This insight, coupled with the concept of "feedforward" control from adaptive control theory, suggests that system output (e.g., Ao) can be positively affected a priori.

Adopting Bayesian updating by creatively combining these two new capabilities, CBM and MBF, holds great promise for improved demand forecasting. The basic logic underlying Bayesian methods is the notion of conditional probability and the systematic incorporation of prior knowledge and expectations about probability distributions into statistical analysis. This method consists of a coherent set of axioms that converts prior information (derived empirically from appropriate historical data using MBF) to posterior evidence (i.e., a revised estimate including new information) by conditioning on observed data (current CBM status).[9] Hence, the logic develops an updated forecast in a dynamic environment.

For example, MBF can be used to determine well in advance what will likely be required based on a clear understanding of typical consumption patterns for a platform type (e.g., AH-64) performing specific missions (e.g., major combat operations, stability operations, noncombat evacuation operations, etc.) under environmental conditions associated with, or similar to, the geographic location where the deployment operation will occur. Much of the uncertainty associated with *external* factors in operational demand forecasting will be significantly reduced by using

MBF in this way. Then when the operation is actually conducted with a designated unit and its particular complement of AH-64s, each with its own *internal* set of depot-level reparable life-cycle reliability profiles (for remaining useful life), CBM can be used to "revise" the original (albeit much improved) a priori estimates provided by MBF.

As CBM matures, and both data collection and analytical methods improve, this Bayesian approach is likely to dramatically improve demand forecast accuracy for spares and repair parts (Class IX). The promise now exists that these empirically derived conceptual advances will serve as a foundation and methodological guide for similar progress for improved demand forecast accuracy for other planning domains and classes of supply as well.

CHAPTER 7

Retail Stage

Tactical Level

As we create, define, and redefine future warfighting doctrine, we must develop options—not mandates—for creating flexible logistics for quick response to a changing operational environment. We have a tendency to come up with a rule—five days of supply, 14 days of supply, whatever the number of days of supply—frequently with little bearing on the facts, just to set parameters that fill carts. . . . We cannot afford to plan for future logistics by segmenting the logistics planning from the overall operations planning. . . . Customized packaging based on actual and operational needs enables responsiveness to future challenges.

—General Paul Kern, commanding general, Army Materiel Command

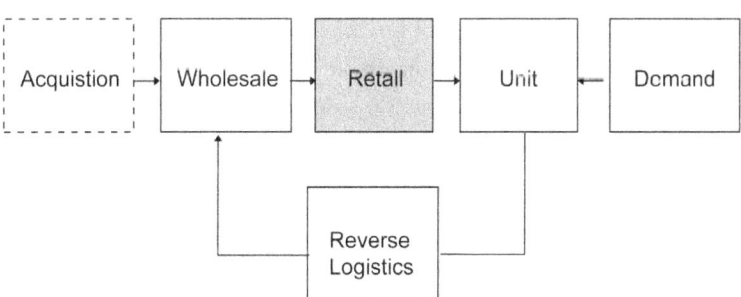

Figure 19. Retail Stage.

The retail stage in this multistage logistics network model consists of globally dispersed supply support activities (SSAs) containing hundreds of authorized stock lists (ASLs) that are typically located near their supported battalion and brigade tactical units. Historically, the U.S. Army has managed supply parts in ASLs based on an item-level, "demand-based" stock policy (AR 710-2): During a given period of time, if a minimum quantity of a particular part was ordered that meets an "add/retain" threshold, then the part could be stocked at some prescribed level; in general, all parts were stocked according to the same rules, and no special considerations were given to either part cost or part impact on readiness.

During recent years the army has transitioned to a modified policy that does consider part costs, although the cost categories used in this dollar cost banding (DCB) policy are arbitrarily designated. Steady improvement has been measured where this new, improved stock policy has been implemented. Nevertheless, metrics used to assess effectiveness are still "supply performance" focused, including satisfaction rates, accommodation rates, and fill rates, rather than "readiness metrics," including operational availability (Ao). Although both the Department of Defense and the army's current logistics policy documents require Class IX inventory levels to be established to maximize weapon system materiel readiness performance, this has yet to happen for the army in actual implementation and execution.[1] Consequently, it has been and continues to be difficult—essentially impossible—to develop consistent cause-effect relationships between retail investment levels and readiness-oriented outcomes, since there is no specific objective function to optimize using currently mandated army stock policy methods.

The fundamental purpose of any military inventory system is to sustain the supported force, in this case aviation end items. The true measure of inventory system performance should be the ability of that system to achieve required mission-capable system objectives. Nonetheless, traditional supply performance standards have focused on "interface metrics" (Figure 4 in chapter 3), especially "fill rate," to gauge inventory system performance. This can yield very misleading indications, however. Fill rate is not an adequate diagnostic of operational performance because it does not measure the degree of order lateness—the duration of backorders.

Fill rate measures only what happens when demand occurs, whereas backorders also measure the duration of the shortage. Since backorder durations are not considered, fill rate is insensitive to the trade-off between a few of short duration relative to rare but very lengthy ones. For example, two supply chains with the same 90% fill rate may differ dramatically on how responsively they fill the remaining 10%. Fill rate does not consider aircraft complexity, yet more complex aircraft require a higher fill rate to achieve a given Ao than simpler aircraft.[2] While a high fill rate may suggest healthy supply support, it is not directly related to inventory system impact on end item readiness, or Ao.

Conversely, a more relevant and insightful indication of inventory *system* performance relative to a readiness-oriented outcome is the relationship between backorders (supply shortfall) and non-mission-capable supply (NMCS, or Ao degradation due to supply shortfalls): As inventory *system* responsiveness improves over time, backorder rates should decline and both customer wait time (CWT) and NMCS should decrease accordingly with a positive effect on readiness. Historically, however, these data scatter plots associating NMCS ratings with backorder rates are indeed "scattered," showing essentially no relationship between the two, although fill rate metrics are, at the same time, within acceptable limits. Consequently, it has been difficult to establish correlation between backorder rates and readiness. Critical parts that incur long delivery delay times or must be back ordered by higher supply echelons, thereby impacting readiness, tend to be resolved at the tactical level through various work-arounds that increase maintenance labor workload.

Recent evidence also shows that as CWT increases for unscheduled repair at unit level, work-arounds likewise increase. This effect, in turn, masks what otherwise would have been declining readiness. This compensating action at unit level is isolating readiness results from wholesale supply system performance rather than illuminating supply system ability to affect Ao. Consequently, managing the supply system to "fill rate" interface metrics actually precludes identifying and implementing meaningful cost-effectiveness choices within an investment-performance (readiness) trade space. This *must* be corrected.

Therefore, to both illuminate this managerial shortcoming and identify a better, outcome-oriented approach, the most important initiative in this stage has been the analytical demonstration, and subsequent field testing, of a retail stock policy focused on weapon system readiness for aviation performance (Ao) rather than supply performance. For each repair part, this policy considers cost, frequency of use, and contribution to readiness and then uses a marginal analysis approach to determine a minimum-cost ASL to achieve a desired system readiness goal. This method has been variously referred to as a multiechelon technique for recoverable item control (METRIC), sparing to availability (STA), and readiness-based sparing (RBS).

The key difference between this method and others, which typically focus on managing individual items, is the ability to adopt inventory policies focused on the weapon system itself, such as aviation rotorcraft, and readiness goals needed for those combat platforms. This enables a systems approach to be applied that incorporates the differing contributions of all components across the entire supply chain rather than focusing on individual item supply performance interface metrics such as fill rate and stock availability that, as described previously, can be very misleading.

The item-level approach may be easier to implement during ASL quarterly reviews and wholesale-level supply control studies, but it is impossible to know whether individual item decisions will achieve an acceptable level of combat system availability within budget constraints. Additionally, the item approach historically tended to use the same "protection level" (safety stock) regardless of costs, yet dramatic improvements in system performance have been demonstrated when these other factors are included.[3] RBS enables efficient solutions to be developed and relationships between ASL costs and weapon system availability to be established. Relationships between resource investments and readiness outcomes can then be determined. If the initial link between the retail and unit stages has not been optimized to achieve tactical aviation readiness production goals (Ao), then the potential benefits of improving many other, more costly and inefficient upstream logistics network stages will not be fully realized. In terms of the "resources to readiness" challenge, implementing RBS is therefore a crucial first step in integrating the supply chain.

Although the army has experimented with RBS, initially over 2 decades ago, it has never officially implemented the policy for routine use beyond initial spares packages for newly fielded systems. Additionally, the testing and experimentation previously conducted was limited to ground-based systems. Our recent RBS analytical demonstration using UH-60 aircraft in the 101st Airborne Division (Figure 20), followed by implementation of an ongoing, large-scale field test at Fort Rucker (where nearly a third of the army's flying hours are executed at the Army Aviation School using several different aircraft types), is now clearly demonstrating the significant advantages of implementing RBS in the retail stage of the aviation supply chain.

Extrapolating these results across all army division-level retail ASLs, over 10 years ago the Army Materiel Systems Analysis Activity (AMSAA) estimated that the requirement objective (RO) could then be reduced by several hundred million dollars, yielding potential savings that could have

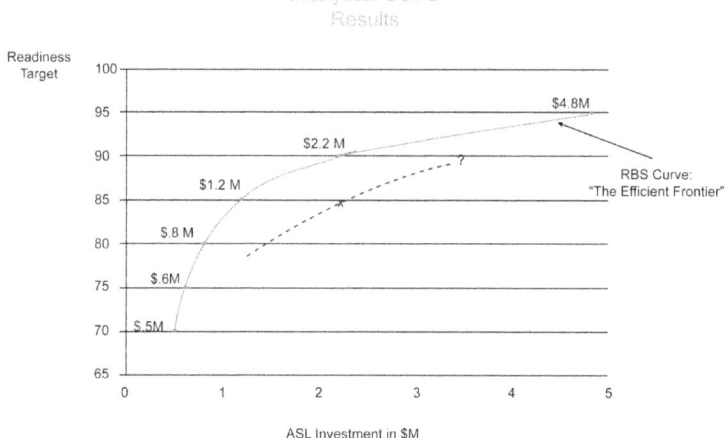

Figure 20. Readiness-based sparing at 101st Airborne - Blackhawk parts.

been applied, for example, against the growing backlog of backorders. An additional benefit obtained from RBS is a significant reduction in "footprint," or the weight and volume of ASLs that must be deployed to provide Class IX sustainment for supported units. This has several positive effects including reducing both deployment lift needs for supporting units and theater closure times for the deploying force during the initial phase of an operation, as well as requirements for sustainment during follow-on phases.

Over the past decade, the original military-focused, theoretical inventory management models developed and refined in academia (e.g., Wharton, Stanford) and the federally funded research and development centers (FFRDCs; e.g., RAND Corporation and Logistics Management Institute) have since spun off into commercial firms. Several commercial off-the-shelf applications now fully capitalize on the use of sparing to availability (STA) and RBS algorithms and are applying them increasingly to support the proliferation of performance-based logistics (PBL) contracts in the military, other government agencies, and corporate arenas including the commercial airlines and global service support providers (e.g., Caterpillar Logistics).

These commercial applications have been successfully applied to very complex supply chains, some in conjunction with enterprise resource planning implementations, and are now competing in a growing market. The current focus is on accelerating computer processing times through heuristics and so-called greedy algorithms to achieve approximate solutions. For example, the U.S. Navy conducted an FFRDC-hosted "RBS Olympics," inviting several commercial firms to demonstrate their respective capabilities to adapt and apply their software and algorithms to navy-unique supply chains.

A second major effort is the incorporation of "inventory pooling" to realize the benefits of reduced costs and improved supply performance through centralized stocking, especially for high-value but relatively low-demand depot-level reparables (DLRs). Also referred to as "risk pooling," this approach dampens variability and reduces backorders by consolidating safety inventory through either physical (central location) or virtual (IT-enabled) means. In general, safety stock required to achieve a desired performance level will increase with the square root of the number of supported locations exhibiting independent demand. Hence, as the number of these supported units increase, the benefit of risk pooling improves at an increasing rate.

This potential was demonstrated with M1 Abrams tank engines across several major installations supporting III Corps armor and mechanized units dispersed across five states near Fort Hood, Texas. Several risk-pooling alternatives were evaluated by AMSAA. Each of the alternatives achieved significant tactical-level improvements across all 17 division-level ASLs for both RO reduction (ASL investment levels) and footprint, measured by both aggregate ASL weight and volume: RO decreased 55–75%; ASL weight was reduced 65–75%; and ASL volume declined 60–70%.[4]

Additionally, by transitioning from a hierarchical "arborescence" logistics design (treelike branching structure with serial, vertical supply channels) to a supply network incorporating responsive lateral supply links, risk pooling coupled with improved asset visibility will enable the eventual attainment of a much more efficient, responsive, and resilient, readiness-driven supply network (RDSN). Analysis suggests backorder reductions of 30–50% for DLRs are likely, especially for the many forward-positioned locations within the retail stage.[5]

RBS should be expeditiously adopted and implementing as retail stock policy. Then, further enabled by (a) risk pooling (for low demand but expensive spares), (b) responsive lateral supply between ASLs and SSAs, and (c) mission-oriented demand forecasting described in the previous chapter, army inventory management policy can then transition from an archaic rule and mandate-based (e.g., "days of supply") support concept, which is neither mission nor readiness based, to a more flexible RDSN to be discussed in greater detail in the section on adaptive network design (chapter 13).

Major benefits from such a policy include an ability to better anticipate what mission-specific spare part demand is likely to be and then to react and adjust more responsively according to the changing operational environment. Within the retail (forward-located) theater distribution system, the key enablers to achieve RDSN for a capabilities-based force are (a) mission-based forecasting (MBF) and (b) RBS.

CHAPTER 8

Reverse Logistics Stage

Retrograde

During OIF [Operation Iraqi Freedom], retrograde either was not specifically planned or became forgotten in the "fog of war".... From a logistics planning point of view, retrograde should be an integral part of the logistics process.

—Joint Staff report, "Objective Assessment of Logistics in Iraq"

In spite of over a decade of investments in asset visibility technology, the DoD still struggles with asset visibility at the tactical level and the overall retrograde process.

—Lou Kratz, assistant deputy under secretary for logistics plans and programs, DoD

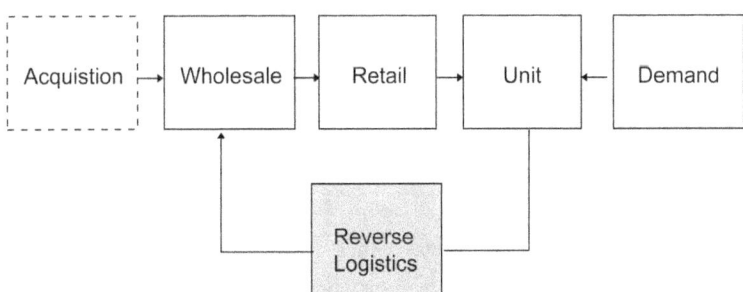

Figure 21. Reverse Logistics Stage.

The reverse logistics stage, or retrograde supply pipeline, constitutes the U.S. Army's value recovery process for reparable spares and includes nearly 80% of the value requisitioned at the unit stage. From theoretical perspectives, both system dynamics and control theory suggest the responsiveness of this retrograde stage should have considerable impact upon readiness or the "output" of the system; it is clearly a feedback loop in the supply chain (Figure 21).[1] For these reparable items, the cycle created by the combination of unit→reverse logistics pipeline→wholesale (depot)→retail→then back to the unit readiness stage again forms a closed-loop supply chain to return, rebuild, redistribute, then reuse (repeatedly) capital assets (e.g., depot-level reparables [DLRs]) to continuously produce readiness. Operating within the larger logistics structure, this closed-loop chain creates internal dynamic system behaviors that can potentially be changed through feedback to regulate the output variable of interest, readiness (operational availability, or Ao). However, opportunities for more cost-effective supply chain operations by implementing a synchronized, closed-loop DLR processing cycle have not yet been realized.[2]

From a practical logistics network perspective, the more DLRs that are delayed in the reverse pipeline awaiting evacuation for repair, the more inefficient and unresponsive the reverse pipeline becomes, thereby increasing the overall requirement objective (RO) for those DLRs. For every DLR in retrograde, another similar serviceable DLR is needed somewhere in the forward supply pipeline, thereby increasing system-wide RO for that DLR. Or, if the DLR is not available, then customer wait time for a backorder increases thereby impacting readiness at the unit.[3] Although not well recognized yet, this is characteristic of a very tightly coupled system that can have potentially disastrous results without warning.

An operational environment inducing greater stress on weapon systems may for some parts cause higher failure rates than "normal." In the case of obsolescent DLRs that can no longer be quickly procured or repaired through commercial supply sources (if at all), they must be retrograded to Army Materiel Command (AMC)-level depots for repair and then returned for serviceable issue again through the forward supply chain. The responsiveness of the reverse pipeline then becomes crucial to support sustained operations when higher failure rates occur, resulting in temporary spikes or sustained surges in demand. This situation occurred during Operation Iraqi Freedom (OIF), for example, in the case of wave guides for deployed Patriot Missile Systems. Near-heroic intervention, necessary to compensate for lack of visibility into an unresponsive retrograde process, was required to avert an extremely dangerous situation that could have otherwise resulted in disaster.[4]

Despite these theoretical and practical implications, army logistics regulations, processes, and culture have not fully recognized the importance of this portion of the logistics network. Reflecting a lack of strategic focus and awareness of retrograde operations as an indispensable value recovery effort, the traditional army supply system has placed very little emphasis upon expediting, prioritizing, managing, or even monitoring DLR returns. For example, there was no ability to differentiate between types of return transportation used, surface or air, or the priority of a returning item. So broken musical instruments, M1 Abrams tank engines, and Patriot Missile System wave guides all have, by default, the same lack of visibility and priority in retrograde even though their respective contributions to battlefield outcomes are dramatically different.

And since retrograde in-transit visibility did not previously exist, unserviceable DLR returns could not be anticipated for repair depots to accurately forecast workload. A final challenge, which significantly impacts the financial system, has been a disparity in DLR returns compared to issues for tactical units. Prior to OIF, the trend had been more issues than returns for several years, but that has now reversed with more returns coming from OIF than issues. Recent data analysis indicates that the ratio of issues to returns across deployed units is highly variable, ranging between 40% and nearly 100%. Furthermore, less than 20% of unserviceable DLR returns from deployed units currently could be traced to a final disposition.[5] Until recently, the army has been forced to request an annual waiver to Office of the Secretary of Defense policy mandating exchange pricing for DLR returns. This was necessary because the army has been unable to track unit returns through the reverse pipeline.[6]

During the initial phase of our retrograde research, the U.S. Army Logistics Support Activity (LOGSA) focused on identifying, measuring, and quantifying delay times for DLRs awaiting retrograde in the reverse pipeline. These total retrograde time (TRT) average values vary considerably across the various overseas commands but are generally measured in several months, not days or weeks. Additionally, there has been extreme variability in these return times to various sources of repair (e.g., original equipment manufacturers [OEMs] and depots), ranging from a few hundred to several thousand per month.[7]

LOGSA efforts then oriented on ways to capture reverse logistics (RL) information, measure TRTs for the various theaters, and estimate the value of reparables delayed in the RL pipeline. However, until recently there has been no focus on defining and quantifying both the potential reduction in aggregate DLR inventory requirements (RO) *and* the effects of reduced DLR customer wait time on improved readiness (Ao) that can potentially be achieved by synchronizing RL flow and depot operations with the forward supply chain. For example, U.S. Transportation Command (TRANSCOM-US), the new Department of Defense (DoD) "distribution process owner," recently announced "improved" retrograde operations. But the metric used was exclusively oriented on transportation cost reduction by shipping greater retrograde quantities by surface means (98% now) rather than more expensive air transport.[8]

Moreover, the "value" of the RL stage is not to be found by minimizing reverse pipeline transportation costs but rather by estimating the contribution to readiness, through cost-effective and responsive value recovery, that those DLRs provide (Figure 22).[9] Enormous improvements are possible if we begin to view retrograde logistics as dynamic "feedback loops" with multiple effects–closed-loop supply chains–rather than as independently operating, disconnected operations with linear, additive effects.

As mentioned earlier, our initial research efforts focused on empirically capturing and analyzing actual retrograde delay times and understanding their theoretical consequences from system dynamics and control theory perspectives. Our latest efforts have quantified key relationships between aggregate inventory size (and investment costs),

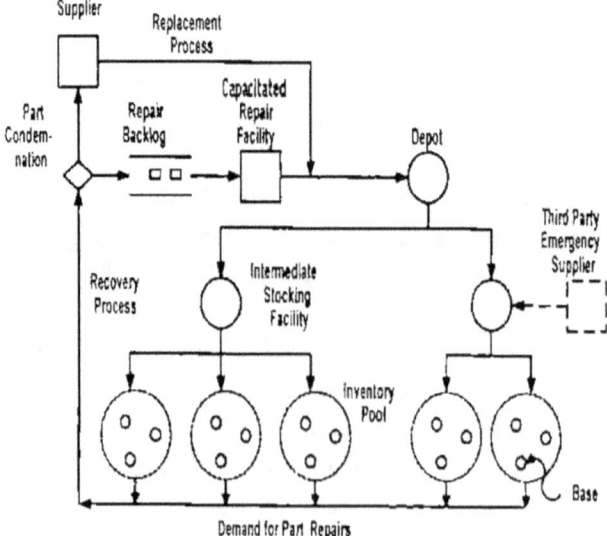

Figure 22. Reverse logistics structure.

retrograde "velocity" (the speed of DLR returns from tactical units to depot facilities for repair and overhaul), and associated transportation costs and their impact on tactical readiness for aviation units. Using actual data for specific DLRs, we established retrograde process relationships and tradeoff curves between inventory cost, retrograde speed, transportation cost, and readiness.

The prevailing wisdom has been that "there is no retrograde problem" simply because reported readiness ratings for deployed combat units have remained relatively high in recent years. This argument, however, fails to incorporate a cost-effective readiness view for closed-loop supply chain operations. Consequently, reducing reverse logistics pipeline delay times has little effect on readiness since very high inventory levels ("mountains of iron") are masking feedback loop dynamics. However, we have identified threshold inventory levels where the feedback dynamics do become apparent and balancing retrograde speed, inventory, and transportation costs with desired readiness objectives can clearly be achieved at significantly reduced inventory levels and lower total costs.

The army should recognize this readiness-producing perspective and urgently adopt a new paradigm for this crucial closed-loop supply chain within the larger logistics enterprise. Readiness Responsive Retrograde—R3—has enormous potential to both improve readiness and reduce total life-cycle costs.

As the criticality of responsive retrograde operations becomes evident and the potential for improvement acknowledged, materiel managers will need supporting metrics that capture and provide greater visibility into this enormous hidden cost inventory. Consideration should be given to adapting Hewlett Packard's (HP's) inventory-driven cost (IDC) approach that links system-wide inventory costs to financial performance. HP discovered that it was particularly important to include product return costs that previously were neglected. Such an approach, return on net assets (RONA), enabled HP to overcome its standard management accounting metrics that had failed to keep pace with the evolution of the company's global supply chain network (Figure 23):

> HP now oversaw a complex, multitiered manufacturing network made up of many disparate entities . . . making it impossible for them to assess the overall dollar impact of their local decisions. . . .

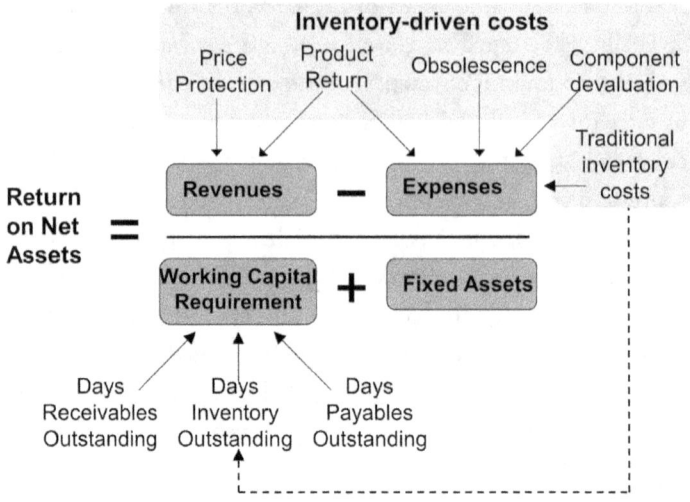

Figure 23. Evaluating retrograde efficiency: Readiness return on net assets.

Apart from incurring operational costs, returns lengthened the time a product spent in the supply chain before reaching an end user, increasing . . . inventory finance costs. . . . Existing cost metrics did not track all of HP's inventory-driven costs (IDC), pieces of which were often mixed in with other cost items, scattered over different functions and geographic locations, and recorded with different accounting conventions.[10]

Implementing RONA made it easier to link operational decisions to corporate goals by better aligning company interests and management decisions across the entire supply chain. HP concluded that its competitive advantage derived less from market share than from its ability to efficiently manage assets throughout its entire supply chain.

Of course the army, unlike HP, is not "profit motivated" to increase revenues and reduce expenses but instead attempts to balance them over time using the Army Working Capital Fund (AWCF) unit cost goal (UCG) formula. Nonetheless, the appeal of such an approach can be visualized with a modified application of HP's numerator in the RONA formula by replacing the "profit" measure (revenues minus expenses) with a "readiness" measure (e.g., Ao or perhaps more specifically 1 − [DLR non-mission-capable supply]). Then, using this new metric to gauge performance, intense management attention should be focused on improving retrograde efficiency, thereby reducing both backorders and AWCF RO expenditures for DLRs. This will result in increased "*readiness* return on net assets," which, in sharp contrast to the current focus on minimizing retrograde transportation costs, is a performance metric aligned with the goal of an R3 process.

According to a recent estimate by AeroStrategy Consulting, efforts in the commercial aircraft industry have resulted in a reduction of inventory throughout supply chains, from $3.6 million worth of inventory to $2.6 million per active aircraft. Total inventory value in the aggregate supply chain is still estimated to be $44 billion, however, so ongoing efforts to further reduce inventory and improve service will require higher levels of coordinated management across all elements of the industry including suppliers, aircraft OEMs, maintenance providers, and customers (the commercial airlines). A simple management metric such as this (DLR inventory value per aircraft) for army aviation supply chains, especially applied to DLRs, would illuminate the tremendous potential for improved performance, in terms of both increased readiness and reduced costs, that could be achieved.

From a closed-loop supply chain performance perspective, the retrograde process contribution to tactical readiness and supply chain efficiency could also be measured using the following two metrics: DLR turnover ratio and materiel availability. The first, DLR turnover ratio, is the simple ratio of DLR "sales" to inventory where the denominator represents the sum of DLRs in retrograde, those in repair depots, and those in the forward supply chain. This metric would be analogous to "inventory turns" in private sector supply chains for consumer products. The second, fleet-wide "materiel availability" (or "Am"), defined as the ratio of DLR tactical unit quantity divided by system-wide totals throughout the closed-loop supply chain, would provide an indicator of retrograde responsiveness and efficiency (reverse logistics "readiness") comparable to Ao (operational availability) as an indicator of tactical level readiness.

Given extremely long retrograde times and the enormous value of recoverable capital assets delayed within the reverse logistics pipeline, the potential for improvement seems considerable. These various DLR network links and flows, including reverse pipeline flow, depot production and scheduling operations, and forward supply chain flow, must be connected and made visible through in-transit visibility. Then the army's extensive investment in DLR assets can be reduced *and*, through better management within a synchronized, closed-loop supply chain, both current readiness (Ao) and future capability improved.

Those assets that are no longer required due to reductions in overall RO could be released and used to create a variety of "mission support packages" comparable to Cold War–era army prepositioned stocks (APS)(Figure 24). These mission support packages would augment the readiness-driven supply network and better support a capabilities-based force as described in the final paragraphs of chapter 7. This would be especially valuable for aviation DLRs that currently have limited war reserve stock but instead rely upon enhanced depot repair capacity from the Army National Guard Aviation Depot Maintenance Roundout Unit/Aviation Classification Repair Activity Depot to meet higher repair and replacement demand rates.

REVERSE LOGISTICS STAGE   67

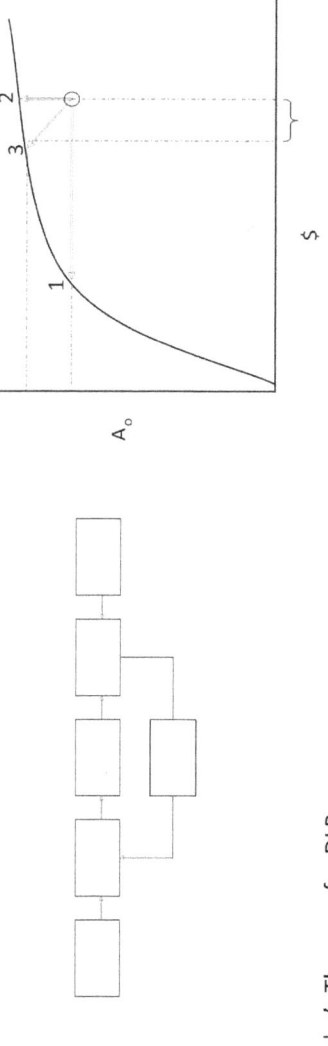

- Palm's Theorem for DLRs:
  - Average demand is m
  - Average repair time is t
  -Then, Avg number in repair pipeline is mt
- Reduce t, then mt decreases
- As mt decreases, DLR RO is reduced
- As CWT decreases, A_o improves

1) Significantly reduced RO for same A_o
2) Improved A_o at current RO
3) Improved A_o & reduced RO with savings allocated to Army Prepositioned Stocks

Figure 24. Effects of improved retrograde operations.

CHAPTER 9

Wholesale Stage

National Level

Without a significant effort to increase resources devoted to recapitalization of weapon systems, the force structure will not only continue to age but, perhaps more significantly, become operationally and technologically obsolete.

—*Quadrennial Defense Review Report*, Office of the Secretary of Defense, 2001

Our defense industrial supply chain is broken.

—Dr. Richard Amos, deputy to the commanding general,
U.S. Army Aviation and Missile Command

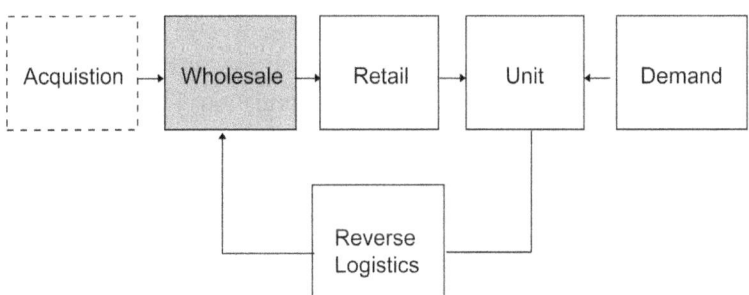

Figure 25. Wholesale Stage.

For U.S. Army Class IX spares, the wholesale stage incorporates two major functions. First, maintenance depots repair, overhaul, and rebuild "end items"—major weapon system platforms—and their major assemblies or subassemblies (engines, transmissions, blades, etc.). These components and end items, arriving through the reverse (retrograde) pipeline at the depot for rebuild or modification upgrades, are considered reusable capital assets rather than consumable parts or items, hence the term "depot-level reparable," or DLR. These commodity-oriented repair depots (e.g., Corpus Christi Army Depot for aviation systems; Letterkenny Army Depot for missile systems) belong to Army Materiel Command's (AMC) subordinate life-cycle management commands (LCMC). Second, defense supply and acquisition centers procure and distribute consumables, including repair parts. Most of the items and parts common to multiple armed services are managed by the Defense Logistics Agency's (DLA) three supply centers.

This wholesale system includes theater and strategic maintenance, supply, and transportation systems that receive, account for and report, store, manage, repackage for shipment, distribute, and transport Class IX materiel to operational units. This system also delivers unserviceable capital stock to appropriate maintenance depots for repair and overhaul, then back to the forward supply chain for redistribution as serviceable assets. However, this very large, functionally differentiated, and complex system must rely on organizations in the retail stage, described in chapter 7, to provide demand information on unit and equipment status, requisition and maintenance actions, and materiel received and returned.

From a supply chain enterprise perspective, this "demand information latency" introduces inefficiencies and uncertainties caused by the wholesale stage belatedly reacting to retail stage information. These information delays discourage or prohibit short production planning cycles, leading to large forecast errors and both inventory and backorder accumulation. Longer planning cycles increase forecast errors and reduce manufacturing's ability to respond to updated order information. Consequently, manufacturing ends up building products at the wrong time, which then leads to high inventory levels *and* high backorder rates.

Furthermore, this delayed "demand" information that is provided by the retail stage does not reflect actual readiness requirements measured empirically at the "point of consumption." As described previously in the unit stage section (chapter 5), this is partly due to the lack of a recognized, well-defined "production function for readiness"—a readiness equation. Information is not only delayed, thereby affecting responsive and efficient supply chain materiel distribution, but also inaccurate. Since a readiness production function has not been empirically defined, the army has historically used retail stage supply system "demand" information as a surrogate for "consumption" information generated by tactical units where readiness is actually produced.

As mentioned in the reverse logistics stage discussion in chapter 8, in-transit visibility for DLRs in the reverse pipeline has not existed until just recently. Consequently, depots could not accurately anticipate the quantity, quality, or timing of returns for repair to manage depot workload and synchronize returns of serviceable DLRs to the forward supply chain. This lack of visibility and useful information further magnifies uncertainty and variability—the bullwhip effect—for DLRs, which are also the most expensive spares, further driving up the aggregate system-wide requirement objective. Long turnaround times (TAT) for repairs are further affected by obsolescence issues, diminishing manufacturing sources and material shortages (DMSMS), and especially depot parts stock for repairs, which historically has been managed to a standard army-wide 85% wholesale supply availability target.

Recently, AMC incorporated Lean and Six Sigma manufacturing concepts into depot management practices with measurable success in reducing process variances and rebuild times. One clear example at the Corpus Christi Army Depot (CCAD) has been the success of T700 engine remanufacturing that achieved a requirement objective (RO) reduction estimated at nearly $70 million as a result of reduced depot repair cycle time. The focus of Lean, a manufacturing concept originally pioneered, developed, and refined by Toyota in Japan, is on better synchronizing process flow, thereby reducing work in progress (stagnant inventory) and "waste" leading to a "just-in-time" approach to meet the pull of customer demand. In contrast, Six Sigma's complementary focus is on reducing defects to improve product quality by reducing variation, the proximate cause of product defects within the manufacturing process.

However, significant additional improvements can now be obtained by adopting synchronized manufacturing (also known as "optimized production technology" from the theory of constraints, or TOC) for depot repair management. In essence a business-process redesign approach, TOC enables realization of significant "effectiveness" gains, in contrast to "efficiency" gains, that become possible within a truly synchronized closed-loop supply chain for DLRs (Figure 26). This becomes possible because, unlike Six Sigma with its use of statistical methods to uncover flaws in the execution of an existing process without actually challenging

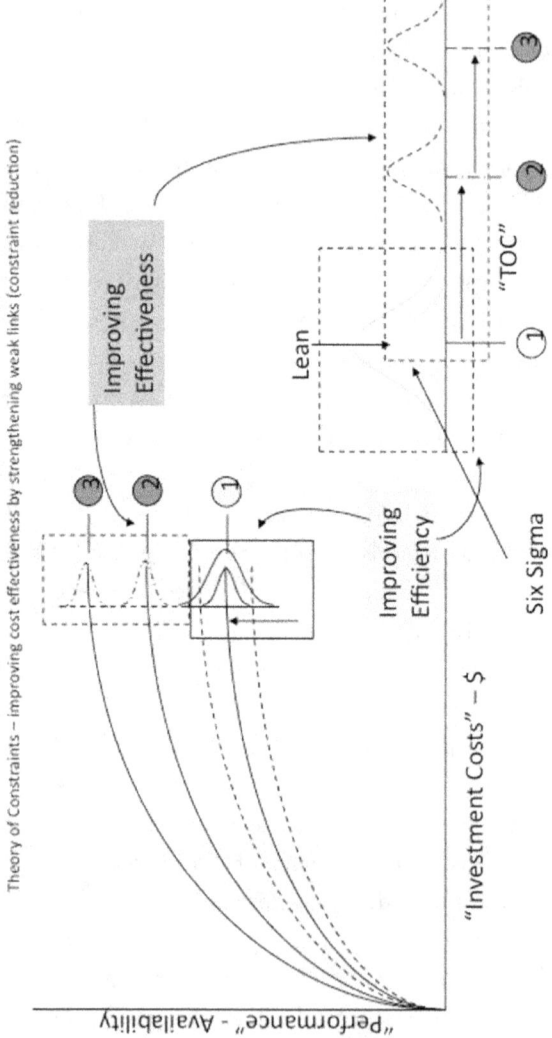

Figure 26. *Six Sigma, lean, and theory of constraints: Contributions in the cost-performance trade space.*

the business-design process itself, TOC views the process itself as potentially flawed, an approach generally referred to as identifying "weak links in the chain." Increasingly, those companies following their Lean and Six Sigma efforts with this process redesign approach are finding "more success redesigning whole processes (e.g., Caterpillar, Merck, Johnson & Johnson, IBM)," improving weak links, and reducing or eliminating constraints to improve cost-effectiveness and productivity.[1]

The key perspective TOC emphasizes is that systems-wide performance (throughput) is limited by the capacity of specific "bottlenecks" within the manufacturing or supply chain network. As the optimization theory for capacitated network flow models suggests, output can be improved by focusing exclusively on these bottleneck operations, since they control the productivity of the entire enterprise. These efforts to synchronize operations dampen the demand volatility effects of the bullwhip in commercial supply chains, improving predictability, cost-effectiveness, and profitability. The ideal state is achieved when the entire supply chain is managed and synchronized to actual customer demand.[2]

An example of the dramatic improvement that can be obtained using TOC within the military depot system is the U.S. Marine Corps maintenance facility in Albany, Georgia, where costs, work in progress, and repair cycle times have been reduced resulting in increased throughput and improved scheduling. The specific results for MK-48 engines have been especially dramatic: Averages and variances for both repair cycle time and labor-hours per engine have been cut in half, with MK-48 engine output per month more than quadrupling.[3]

Depot maintenance activities have historically experienced delays in obtaining consumable parts for repair and overhaul. This is partly due to the 85% target used by the wholesale system for supply availability but is also increasingly attributed to obsolescence issues, especially wiring, avionics, corrosion, and dynamic component degradation caused by aging aircraft systems and subassemblies. As retrograde efficiency and responsiveness improve, however, the combination of in-transit visibility and emerging weapon system "health monitoring systems" (on-board diagnostics and prognostics), including condition-based maintenance, can provide anticipatory, feedforward information for depot repair before the component actually arrives through the reverse pipeline. Hence, particular or unusual parts can be ordered before, rather than after, components and end items arrive for repair induction, further reducing depot repair TAT and aggregate system-wide RO.

The Intelligent Collaborative Aging Aircraft Spare Parts Support (ICAAPS) project, a Logistics Management Institute (LMI) initiative for the navy, explored the value of such an anticipatory ability, illuminating the potential for reducing these forecasting lag effects, especially on consumable parts needed in the maintenance repair process. Since current projections for depot-level consumable part requirements are based on historical depot repair maintenance data, there is considerable delay between actual need, particularly for aging aircraft that are experiencing increases in consumable parts requirements and when these same parts are incorporated into future requirement projections.

The ICAAPS project successfully established correlations and relationships between both depot-level discrepancies and consumable parts usage and also operating environments and field maintenance activities that could be expected to affect future depot-level maintenance requirements. This predictive power to more accurately anticipate parts usage requirements, and ensure the necessary parts were available for repair upon induction, rather than some later time, cut the growing gaps between predicted usage rates and actual usage by over 50% for many consumable parts. Consequently, by expanding the maintenance planning horizon to include all relevant information gathered during the entire operating cycle *before the aircraft arrived at the depot for repair*, ICAAPS was able to significantly reduce forecasting lag, improve part requirement forecasting accuracy, and reduce depot repair cycle time (Figure 27).[4]

One of the great challenges in better synchronizing depot repair operations is overcoming the inability to "see" all of the potentially useful information that could contribute to better forecasting. No integrated "knowledge base" currently exists to combine aircraft onboard data with potentially relevant unit-level operational information and program depot maintenance (PDM) data since each information source is typically maintained by different organizations in multiple, geographically dispersed locations.

Recognition of this limitation recently led to a joint initiative between the U.S. Air Force Oklahoma City Air Logistics Center, which overhauls KC-135 tankers, and the Department of Energy's Pacific Northwest National Laboratory (PNNL). Using visualization techniques originally developed by PNNL for the U.S. intelligence community, several

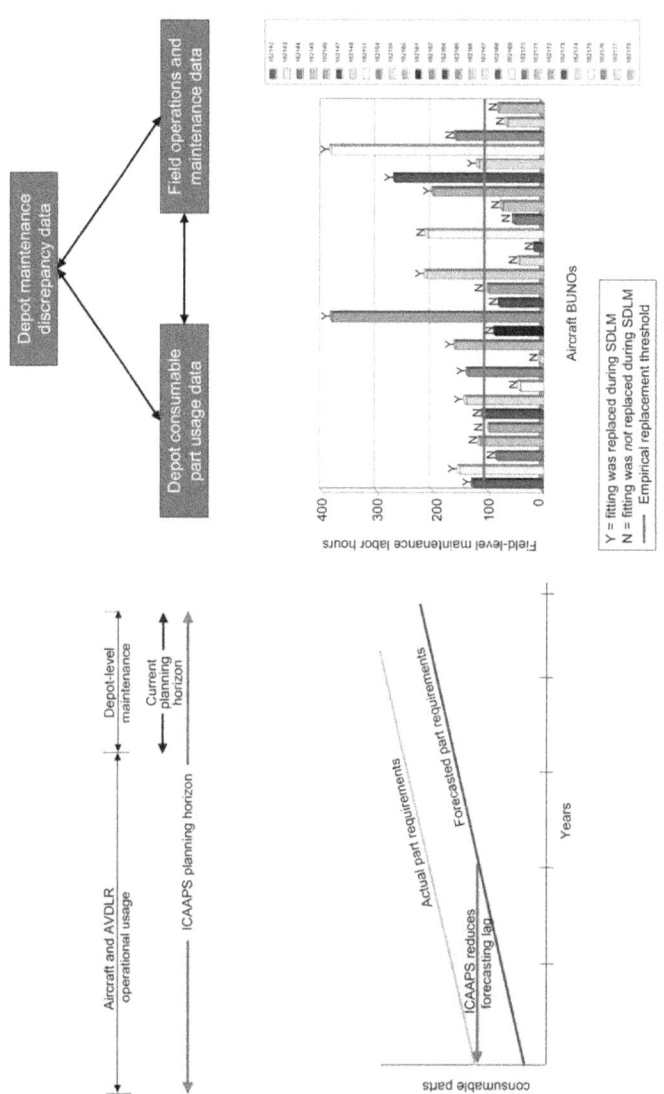

Figure 27. ICAAPS: Intelligent Collaborative Aging Aircraft Parts Support.

disparate data types and sources are linked, transformed, and then presented on large computer graphic displays. These multidimensional spatial mappings portray information using complex visual patterns that humans can much more easily recognize compared to interpreting standard graphics, data tables, or text.

Known as the Visualization of Logistics Data (VLD) project, the analysis of trends, patterns, and relationships in a large maintenance data warehouse enables logistics managers to capitalize on and exploit the ability of the human brain's visual processing capabilities to rapidly perceive and absorb visual representations of large amounts of data in a manner not possible through listening or reading. This capability provides for a consistent and integrated picture of the health of the aircraft fleet, better parts forecasting, and reduced depot repair time and enables more informed decisions for PDM workflow, scheduling, and resource forecasting.[5] Consideration should be given to combining the capabilities offered by both ICAAPS and VLD. The potential for improvement appears enormous and, when used in conjunction with an improved reverse logistics stage, could pave the way toward a truly synchronized retrograde process, enabling a responsive closed-loop supply chain with both reduced RO *and* improved readiness.

To adequately support initial force deployment requirements for warfighting scenarios, the army established overseas prepositioned stock to accommodate in-theater demand for ammunition and other classes of supplies, including medical supplies, end items, and spare parts. These stocks are intended to provide sustainment until the industrial base can ramp up production levels to meet higher demand rates.

In the case of additional demand for aviation DLRs, however, there are no prepositioned stocks. Instead, the additional depot repair capacity needed to support higher repair and return rates is provided through four continental U.S. (CONUS)-based Aviation Classification Repair Activity Depots (AVCRADs) operating under the Army National Guard's Aviation Depot Maintenance Roundout Unit (ADMRU). In peacetime, these units are regionally located within CONUS and manned by reserve component soldiers to support National Guard aviation units located in states within their respective regions. When activated to support an operational theater, an AVCRAD is then mobilized for deployment and attached to Aviation and Missile Command (AMCOM) to increase capacity needed for initial surge and sustained aviation repair requirements. By design, when deployed and operational in theater, the AVCRAD reduces retrograde requirements by conducting repair in theater for DLRs, thereby improving deployed aviation readiness.

In practice, however, several organizational challenges emerged in support of Operation Enduring Freedom (OEF) and, subsequently, Operation Iraqi Freedom (OIF). The AVCRADs were already operating at or near capacity in their peacetime roles supporting their regional state National Guard aviation units and providing some overload relief to AMCOM's CCAD. When requirements for weapon systems needing overhaul exceed depot repair capacity, which had been occurring, this backlog is deferred to future years as "unexecutable deferred maintenance." By the end of FY2002, over 50% of army aviation-related depot-level maintenance requirements had been deferred and therefore not funded. Additionally, in 2002 AMCOM was short $1.4 billion for DLR repair that was already approved for *current*-year PDM. As a result, there was no additional DLR surge capacity available either at CCAD or in the AVCRADs by late 2002.[6]

Consequently, despite the mobilization and ongoing rotations of the regional AVCRADs to Kuwait needed to support higher in-theater repair demand in Iraq, there may still be a growing gap in overall capacity relative to higher repair demand requirements. This is, of course, the opposite result of what the AVCRADs were designed and intended to achieve but nevertheless the consequence of insufficient "slack" capacity to accommodate surge requirements in the current organizational design.

Resolving this challenge, reversing this trend, and developing additional maintenance capacity are crucial. Three converging demand trends are combining and interacting to dramatically increase aviation maintenance requirements and associated repair and spare part aggregate demand rates. These include (a) increasing stateside demand, especially for National Guard units; (b) the continuing demand to support overseas global operations, including OEF and OIF; and (c) the sustainment demands of rotorcraft fleets that are near or within their original design "wear-out regions." These "aging aircraft" issues, largely due to the cancellation or postponement of several modernization programs, are causing average fleet ages to increase at a ratio of 1 year per calendar year.

Chapter 20 addresses possible organizational solutions to these persisting maintenance challenges.

In addition to ongoing challenges to wholesale repair capacity described previously, there are two major programs that will also stress wholesale supply availability. The U.S. Army Recapitalization Program (RECAP) affects several weapon systems across the army, both ground and air, and is intended to compensate for extending life durations—the "useful" life—caused by the absence or cancellation of major acquisition programs to replace these aging systems. This is a service life extension program using selected upgrades and component replacement or rebuild to, in effect, delay the system's entry into the "wear-out" region of the failure rate curve where growing sustainment and repair costs become prohibitively expensive.

Without modernization, time (and age) will eventually degrade operational readiness and increase demand on repair resources as aircraft inevitably progress from useful life to the wear-out region (Figure 28). In the absence, or delay, of modernization programs, which is the situation now for army manned rotorcraft systems, various service life extension programs have frequently been used to further extend useful life, particularly for major components (DLRs). More recently, with entire

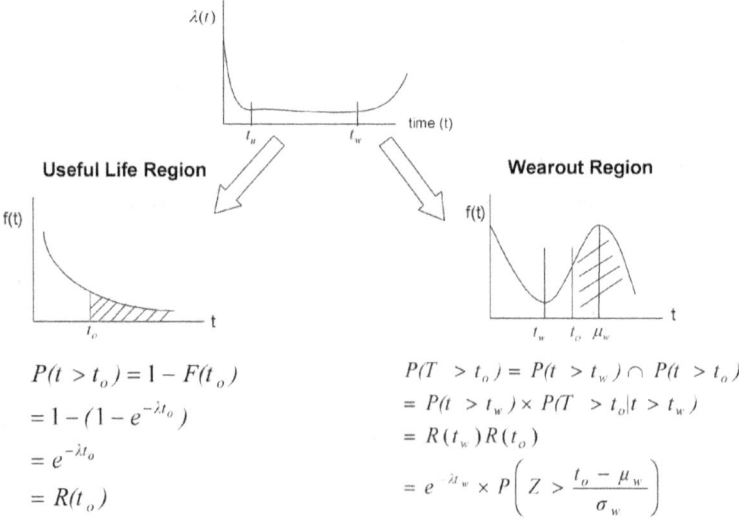

Figure 28. *System life-cycle failure rate pattern: The "Bathtub" curve.*

fleets beginning to enter the wear-out region, it has become necessary to develop extensive, comprehensive "recapitalization" programs—hence simply RECAP—for 17 major army weapon systems, including UH-60s, AH-64s, and CH-47s.

The previously existing need to mitigate the effects of aging fleets has now been further compounded by sustained, higher usage rates with greater wear and tear on these same systems due to ongoing Global War on Terror operations. The recapitalization need is now chronic and, consequently, the army RECAP program is extensive. Knowledge of rebuild and procurement costs, and especially differential failure rate and remaining useful life patterns for various DLRs and subsystems, should help RECAP program managers to optimize their RECAP programs.[7]

The army should incorporate lessons learned from the two issues highlighted previously. The goal should be to select for replacement or upgrade those DLRs and subsystems that minimize total program costs (including future operations and maintenance, or O&M) subject to extending and achieving system availability goals. Or, similarly, if faced with a fixed RECAP budget, DLRs should be selected and prioritized to maximize their contributions to overall system availability. RECAP is, in essence, a "reliability design to readiness" program where additional reliability is "built into" a platform within the useful life (or even wearout phase, e.g., M1 tanks) instead of the traditional design phase of the system life cycle.

The Center for Systems Reliability at Sandia National Laboratories (SNL) recently demonstrated an impressive "optimization" methodology using the AH-64 RECAP program as a demonstration. Using genetic algorithms and artificial neural networks, the center's modeling and simulation methodology identified several specific DLRs and other cost availability drivers. Then, using current mean time between replacement data and marginal analysis (similar to the readiness-based sparing [RBS] methodology), optimal solutions were developed that identified a range of RECAP investment costs with associated O&M savings. Analysis identified where additional RECAP effort yielded diminishing marginal O&S savings. This powerful and insightful methodology demonstrated an ability to significantly reduce RECAP costs by evaluating a wider range of potential DLRs to prioritize while also nearly tripling the availability improvement that had been projected for the baseline case (Figure 29).

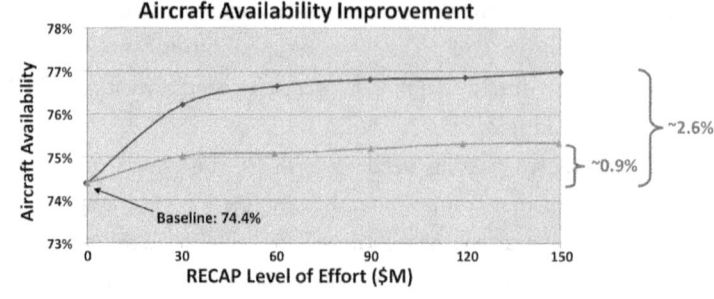

Figure 29. *Availability improvement analysis.*

An additional benefit of this approach was realization of a threshold beyond which operational availability (Ao) could not be increased regardless of the RECAP investment level. This result highlighted the importance of reviewing other potential sources of readiness improvement, including phase maintenance requirements and especially inventory management policies focused on reducing mean logistics delay times.[8] SNL's capability is portable, transparent, fast running, and adaptable to other RECAP programs, and it exhibits potential to evaluate future alternative "prognostic and health monitoring" concepts as well. The various army RECAP programs should expeditiously adopt and implement its use. Savings generated can be used to further improve selected system Ao and also to support the growing demand for RESET programs as well.

The second more recent program, initiated as a consequence of the extreme wear and tear and higher consumption rates experienced after more than 4 years of war, is referred to as the RESET program. RESET, unlike RECAP, is instead intended to restore existing equipment and systems to "10/20 standards," which represent normally accepted conditions of maintenance and repair to achieve intended equipment operational readiness capability. RESET also procures new replacement systems for those that have been destroyed through battle damage or that can no longer be economically repaired. In most cases now, RESET is needed to rapidly return equipment to a ready-to-fight condition for the next unit rotation back to operational theaters. Although overall PDM funding increased by over $50 million from FY2005 to FY2006, the army continued to fund this program at less than 75% of actual requirements.[9] Estimates for RESET, RECAP, in-theater sustainment, depot maintenance, and battle loss and damage replacement were $9.2 billion in the FY2005 supplemental budget. There was, however, an additional requirement of $7.5 billion that was considered "unexecutable," since repair capacity did not exist to expend these funds within the FY2005 supplemental time frame. In 2007, the army RESET budget alone had grown to $17.1 billion and by 2008 was projected to cost more than $40 billion according to the AMC commanding general.[10]

The consequence of all these additional wholesale spare demands has been a dramatic increase in the aggregate overall RO for Class IX within the army's supply planning system. In the case of aviation Class IX, this funding requirement had already been growing substantially even before OEF and, subsequently, OIF (refer to Figure 1). The AMC RO in 2002 was estimated just under $11 billion but had grown to exceed $20 billion by 2006. (The army budget, for comparison, was about $100 billion.) The various elements that contribute to this aggregate RO, and their differential growth rates, can be identified, measured, and associated with each of the various stages in the army's multistage logistics model. Additionally, safety stock must also be included in this aggregate RO computation. This accommodates (buffers against) various sources of demand uncertainty within the "demand" and "unit" stages and lead time variability across the "supply" stages—the bullwhip effect—which historically have not been isolated, measured, and quantified.

However, wholesale safety stock investment levels cannot currently be related in any meaningful way to readiness-oriented outcomes. This is a consequence of both the existing lack of integration across the logistics stages and also, as emphasized in chapter 7 in the retail stage, a persistent inability to relate downstream retail investment levels to readiness outcomes, since RBS has not yet been adopted. Moreover, this inability is reflected in the "interface metric" the army has traditionally used to measure or gauge this protective buffer safety level. This term—"safety level"—actually confounds two distinctly different inventory management metrics: (a) "safety stock," which represents the inventory investment (budget) in protection, and (b) "service level," which measures the degree of customer satisfaction in terms of a meaningful output metric (Figure 4).

By confounding both safety stock and service level into "safety level," the only means to improve customer satisfaction (Ao) is to increase wholesale safety level (spend more) although the actual effect on Ao is unknown. However, buying more safety level—the standard managerial response—merely perpetuates masking long-term structural problems in procurement practices, supply management processes, and logistics doctrine.

Consequently, both safety stock *and a readiness-focused performance metric (e.g., backorders)* should be adopted by AMC as management objectives for wholesale operations, rather than safety level. Measuring safety level and supply availability as wholesale management objectives (interface metrics), which are the standard measures, do not permit assessments of improved logistics network efficiency. As with the case of "fill rate," discussed in chapter 7, managing the supply system to these interface metrics actually precludes identifying meaningful and cost-effective initiatives, programs, and policies within an investment-performance (cost-availability) trade space. Other actions, especially work-arounds at the unit level, have persistently compensated for poor wholesale supply performance and, in effect, masked potential wholesale stage contributions to readiness from the larger supply chain perspective.

Regarding the second major function performed by the wholesale stage, national supply inventory management, recent Logistics Management Institute (LMI) research sponsored by DLA's Aging Aircraft Program has focused on stock policy for consumable inventory characterized by highly irregular demand patterns. These encouraging results appear to have significant carryover implications for the army's wholesale system as well, especially for aviation fleets. Across all armed services, specific repair parts in this category are infrequently demanded yet must be stocked because they are essential to sustaining aerospace weapon system readiness and safety standards.

Traditional DLA practice has been to classify parts demand into two basic categories: (a) demand patterns for parts that meet minimum requisition quantity and frequency thresholds (specifically, at least four requisitions with a total quantity of 12 during the previous year) are stocked under "replenishment" policy requisition objectives governed by standard inventory management models; and (b) low, infrequent, "sporadic" demand for parts that do not meet this requisition threshold are ordered under a numeric stock objective (NSO) policy.

Because of their sporadic demand, it has proven difficult to decide when to buy these items and in what quantities. Typically, "heuristic" policies have been used with arbitrary levels for reorder points and RO. These approaches are unable to relate investment levels to supply performance, much less readiness, and generally have not worked well. This existing NSO policy has failed to produce good results at reasonable cost for over 30 years. Furthermore, DLA's new business modernization enterprise resource planning does not provide an improved policy either. Nonetheless, as systems become more reliable and infrequent demand patterns increase due to reduced failure rates, these sporadic demand parts are expected to grow.

LMI studies for both DLA and the Federal Aviation Administration—large organizations that manage huge inventories for repairing complex systems across vast distances—have shown that this new "peak ordering policy" reduces both delivery delay times and backorders for these particular consumable parts.[11] Additionally, experimental results for a range of aircraft (C-5, E-3, E-2C, F/A-18, and AH-64) are proving that this new policy can substantially reduce both inventory levels and procurement workload within a short period of time after implementation.

These results are significant, since DLA's sporadic demand inventory is currently valued at over $1.6 billion with annual sales to the armed services of over $400 million. This "peak" ordering policy, which now enables DLA (and the army if adopted) to make three-way trade-offs between service levels, inventory investment, and frequency of procurement actions, is estimated to reduce overall delay times by 50%, the number of procurement actions by 35%, and the value of the sporadic demand inventory by 15%.

By simulating the distribution of backorders for aviation units operating under this peak policy, LMI has also been able to estimate Ao improvement by reducing non-mission-capable supply due to better supply performance for these sporadically demand parts. In the specific case of the army's AH-64, experimental results show the peak policy, relative to the current baseline during the period 2001–2003, reduced delay times by 25% and DLA procurement actions by 40%, while improving both on-hand inventory and fill rates by nearly 10% for these sporadic demand items.

After 5 years of development, experimentation, and review, this new methodology is now considered mature enough to implement as DLA policy for aircraft parts. Current LMI work is now focused on assessing "peak" policy effects for both sea- and ground-based systems and also examining the policy's application for sporadic demanded DLRs. The army, following DLA lead, should consider adopting this policy and also supporting LMI's current investigation into peak policy implications for DLRs as well.

In addition to adopting readiness-oriented metrics (including Ao and backorder rate) inventory should also be assessed for quality as well as contribution to readiness. The latter, contribution to readiness, can be achieved by implementing multiechelon RBS stock computations as discussed at length in chapter 7. The former, quality, is typically captured in commercial supply chains with product "inventory turns" needed to meet customer demand. However, within the structure of military inventory systems, "products" are more complex. For example, multiechelon supply chains must be designed to support DLRs such as transmissions and engines that consist of multi-item and multi-indenture assemblies and subassemblies. They are also prone to both aging and obsolescence challenges associated with long life cycles, or "clockspeeds." Hence, a simple metric that could be considered to capture inventory quality is 100% − (excess inventory% + obsolete inventory%). These initiatives and supporting metrics will ultimately enable the necessary transition from a focus on internal traditional, but arbitrary, interface metrics between stages to an ability to manage the entire inventory system toward equipment readiness performance objectives required by the customer.

CHAPTER 10

Acquisition Stage

Up to 80% of total costs and lead times are with suppliers.
—James Womack and Daniel Jones, *Lean Thinking*

In DoD we continue to compete externally against commercial industry, and internally within our own Services, for key strategic materials and specialty metals.
—Alan F. Estevez, assistant deputy under secretary of defense for supply chain integration

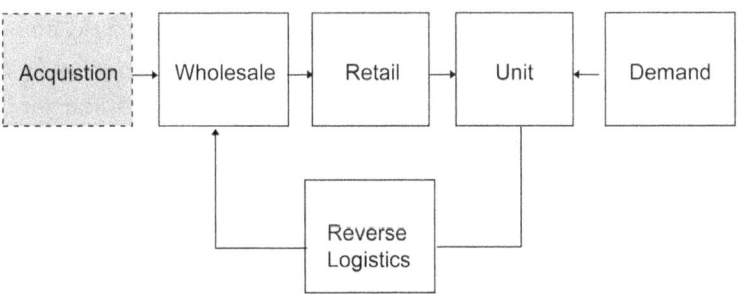

Figure 30. Acquisition Stage.

The acquisition stage in our graphical, multistage supply chain model (Figure 30) represents procurement and purchases from original equipment manufacturers (OEMs) supporting the Department of Defense (DoD) and their multitiered labyrinth of more than 100,000 suppliers. Collectively, they constitute the manufacturing capacity resident within the larger defense industrial base that responds to the procurement and sustainment needs of the U.S. Army. Though furthest removed from the readiness production stage, this procurement function impacts supply chain responsiveness in two major ways: (a) relatively short-term operational availability of spare parts, components (line replaceable units, or LRUs), and end items that can have a direct, even immediate, impact on readiness (operational availability, or Ao) at the unit stage; and

(b) longer-term operations and maintenance (O&M) support costs contributing to life-cycle costs (LCC) over the extended duration of system use, typically several decades after research, development, test, and evaluation; procurement; and initial fielding.

Furthest removed organizationally from actual readiness production (consumer demand), this acquisition stage is at the "whip" end of the supply chain bullwhip. All of the volatility and inefficiencies in down-range stages impact this stage (refer to Figure 6). Moreover, additional inefficiencies induced here further magnify those that have already accumulated through the cascading ripple effects in previous stages. From a theoretical supply chain system perspective, both average demand and variability in demand interact with supply-side effects to magnify system-wide variability, further compounding the need for additional safety stock (refer to Figure 15).

The basic challenge of inventory management is ensuring the proper amount of items is on hand when actually needed. If inventory levels are too low, then supply shortages develop, customer demand cannot be satisfied resulting in backorders, and readiness consequently suffers. This condition causes costly reactions and wasteful recovery efforts. On the other hand, if inventory levels are too high, then resources are invested in a series of unnecessary expenditures for warehousing and transportation while storage and distribution facilities become more crowded. These inventory excesses might never be used, ultimately resulting in disposal at significant financial losses.

Inventory levels are also influenced by the amount of time between the initiation of a procurement action and the receipt of the item into the supply system. This period is known as "acquisition lead time," and consists of two parts: administrative and production lead times. Administrative lead time is the time interval from the initiation of a procurement action to the contract award, while production lead time is the interval from contract award to delivery of the items. Since acquisition lead time estimates are predictions of when items will arrive, variation from these predicted delivery dates results in all the undesirable consequences described previously when items arrive significantly late or early.

Because of persistent weaknesses in DoD supply chain management and the resulting effects of these acquisition lead times on both readiness and procurement levels, the Government Accountability Office (GAO) has conducted several congressionally mandated studies since 1990. In its March 2007 update report, it noted that limited progress has been made in estimating and reducing these procurement lead time forecasts. When comparing actual to expected lead times, GAO found that the Defense Logistics Agency had *overestimated* 40% of its procurement lead times by more than 90 days yet, in contrast, the Army Materiel Command (AMC) *underestimated* nearly 60% of its lead times during the same period. Within AMC, the U.S. Army Aviation and Missile Command (AMCOM) accounted for the overwhelming proportion of this figure with $10.3 billion (of the $10.6 billion AMC total) worth of inventory arriving more than 90 days later than expected. *For AMCOM, nearly two-thirds of the value of all procurement action in FY2005 arrived more than 90 days late.* The GAO report stated,

> Army officials acknowledged that AMCOM has experienced a problem in meeting supply demands for several years, especially after Operation Iraqi Freedom began, because of the surge in demand for their items, depleted on-hand supplies, long lead times for aviation-related items, industrial capacity limitations, and lack of sufficient funds.[1]

However, this persistent underestimation of procurement lead times was caused by a systemic failure to routinely update lead time forecasts with actual, observed delivery results. Instead, lead time "standards of performance" or even system default values were being used rather than the actual results that were repeatedly occurring over extended periods of time. The GAO report acknowledged that continued failure to maintain, update, review, and validate actual lead time data in automated supply systems will result in perpetuating delivery delays and parts shortages. By failing to correct and update these estimates, inventory errors accumulate, further impeding the organization's ability to manage inventory and control backorders. This is another example where Bayesian updating should be incorporated by updating delivery estimates with the actual empirical data of observed reality to yield improved supply chain performance.

Economic aspects of globalization are proving dominant in structuring the new global economy, especially in defense industries where the distinction between domestic and foreign ownership is blurring. Since the late 1990s major defense contractors have pursued three strategies: (a) buying related small defense units from U.S. conglomerates (e.g., GM and TRW); (b) acquiring defense-related businesses outside of aerospace and electronics (such as IT or shipbuilding); and (c) expanding abroad by purchasing foreign defense firms. In this new environment of domestic mergers and buyouts coupled with international partnerships and subsidiaries, it is increasingly challenging to maximize U.S. competitiveness without compromising national security. Through restructuring and consolidation, globalization in many ways has strengthened defense companies at the expense of national governments.[2]

The post–Cold War slowdown and cancellation of weapon system programs left critical U.S. technology areas at risk due to years of uncertainty and low defense budgets that caused capital and companies to merge or leave the defense business altogether. Procurement funding levels were also jeopardizing the viability of the industrial base. All of this necessarily meant fewer domestic competitors pursuing more sole source contracts, and conducting less research, and therefore higher costs. Even compensating efforts to adopt new "efficiency" management principles seem to have backfired in many cases. For example, Boeing Airplane Company's commercial manufacturing experience is instructive: Without suppliers adapting to Lean manufacturing as well, the entire supply chain grinds to a halt.

As a result, the aviation supply chain's acquisition stage is increasingly fragile and vulnerable to price and lead time escalation. It also includes an increasingly higher proportion of sole source suppliers that, in many cases, are sole sources to several different military and commercial OEMs. Until recently, the army had little visibility into its second-, third-, and fourth-tier vendor base. At the same time these vendors had no visibility into actual demand patterns and were incapable of anticipating future army needs. So while procurement managers routinely modify their inventory polices in an effort to reduce backorders during manufacturing, little has been done to actually improve supplier delivery performance, one of the root causes of the problem. As a result of this lack of visibility, and with lead times of well over a year for many critical components, the only solution has been even higher "safety levels," again contributing further to the bullwhip effect.

Additionally, many of the high-strength alloys, metals, and aerospace steels used in helicopter turbine engines and transmissions are in tight supply and subject to dramatic price increases. Price and supply are very cyclical and highly volatile, varying more than other industrial sectors. This volatility is partly due to the combination of limited original sources for strategic materials used in these alloys and steels and also the fact that the aerospace industry, which itself is vulnerable to cyclical market dynamics, represents about 70% of global demand for these materials.[3]

However, these aerospace supply chain dynamics are not new. They have been studied extensively by the commercial airplane manufacturers that account for about 40% of this demand. Boeing, for example, now monitors these strategic material price fluctuations and cyclical market patterns and their impact on manufacturing capacity for the commercial airplane industry. Using system dynamics and discrete-event simulation to better understand cause-effect relationships, Boeing has modeled its supply chain to quantify the impact of better positioned inventory, improved collaboration and coordination, and reduced inherent delays within its supplier base. These "dampening" effects provide a more stable, cost-effective source of acquisition supply.[4]

It is not surprising, then, that a recent study for the army's cargo helicopter (Boeing CH-47) program management office (PMO encountered these same cyclical effects within the army's aviation acquisition stage. Production lead times for transmission gears are ranging from 8 to 13 months and for bearings 8 to 12 months—all from sole source suppliers—many of whom are also sole source to other army helicopter program offices as well as the commercial sector. Market prices for many of the materials needed to create the special alloys and steels used for these components have skyrocketed, literally growing exponentially in recent years.[5]

These conditions were occurring at a time when the acquisition and wholesale stages were already overwhelmed with growing demand to support recapitalization program (RECAP) and RESET requirements as described in the previous section. This is another example similar to the Patriot Missile System wave guide retrograde issue described in chapter 8, where the interactions between an unresponsive retrograde stage, a disconnected wholesale depot repair stage, and an inefficient and unaware acquisition stage can directly and immediately affect readiness (Ao) at the unit stage, potentially constraining the production of readiness needed to achieve demand-stage requirements for operational missions. At the time, this increasingly dangerous situation confronting army aviation readiness appeared to be widespread.

Again, however, this was not the first time the U.S. military had confronted these particular "supply chain" challenges.[6] One of the strategic materials used in aerospace steel that was afflicted by rapidly growing market price is cobalt, which has a very limited source of supply and is mined in central Africa. In the late 1970 to early 1980 time frame, during a similar, earlier phase of this aerospace supply chain dynamic, F16 turbine engine blades were in high demand for production by the OEM. At the same time, cobalt prices were not just increasing but supply access was actually completely disrupted by rebels who controlled a crucial railroad in Zaire. The solution then, since the situation could not be tolerated given Cold War tensions and U.S. Air Force readiness needs at the time, was to literally fly C-141s into central Africa, bypassing the "disruption," in an effort to reconnect the supply chain at a crucial time by hauling cobalt in military aircraft cargo bays back to U.S. OEMs.

The current perception of professionals who have actually experienced and understand the consequences of these dynamics is that, especially for the military, these cyclical trends are worsening. This is partially a consequence of the contraction and consolidation of the defense industrial base in this early post–Cold War era. Fewer suppliers are facing greater demands from multiple customers. Potential solutions to mitigate such effects, in addition to first clearly understanding the implications of these worrisome trends, include the use of long-term, performance-based logistics (PBL) type contracts, which have built-in product surge capacity provisions as part of the contract award criteria.[7] Such contracts provide incentives for OEMs and their suppliers to incorporate and adopt supply chain management concepts, such as defining push-pull boundaries for the optimal placement of critical high-value, strategic materials inventory thereby providing for more stable and cost-effective operations.

The logic here is comparable, though of course the specific details are different, to using PBL or contract logistics support (CLS) where the contract logistics provider now has an incentive to adopt supply chain management concepts to achieve readiness requirements (e.g., Ao) specified by the contract but also must do so profitably. This is surely one reason why the commercial sparing to availability- or readiness-based sparing providers, especially those with responsive multiechelon, multi-item, multi-indenture software capabilities, are beginning to flourish now in partnerships with OEMs and armed service program managers, especially for complex commercial and military aircraft.[8]

The second, longer-term impact of the acquisition stage is on lifecycle costs, primarily those associated with growing O&M support costs as a consequence of aging aircraft fleets coupled with the current lack of modernization programs that historically have constituted weapon system recapitalization. So far, the primary focus of this text has been on improving logistics performance using supply chain and inventory management concepts to derive efficiencies and improve readiness (e.g., Ao). This emphasis then, using Figure 31 and Figure 32 as guides, has been on reducing mean logistics delay time, or "supportability," a measure of supporting supply chain adequacy and responsiveness to reduce and mitigate effects that adversely impact readiness including, for example, decreasing backorder rates and work-arounds.

Obviously, other weapon system "design factors" also affect the operational readiness "production function" as well, notably maintainability (mean time to repair, or MTTR) and reliability (mean time between failure, or MTBF). Maintainability and reliability are complementary aspects of aircraft availability and mission generation capacity: "Reliability" keeps an aircraft operational while "maintainability" enables an aircraft to undergo rapid repair and return to operational status when a failure occurs.

The implications of both MTTR and MTBF on O&M sustainment costs, although recognized from a theoretical design perspective, are

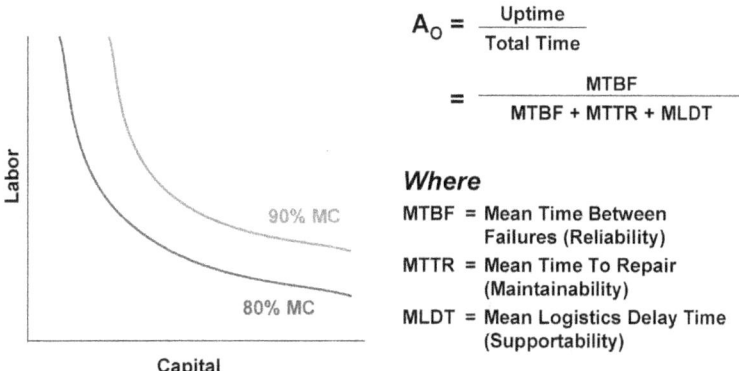

Figure 31. The "Production Function" for readiness.

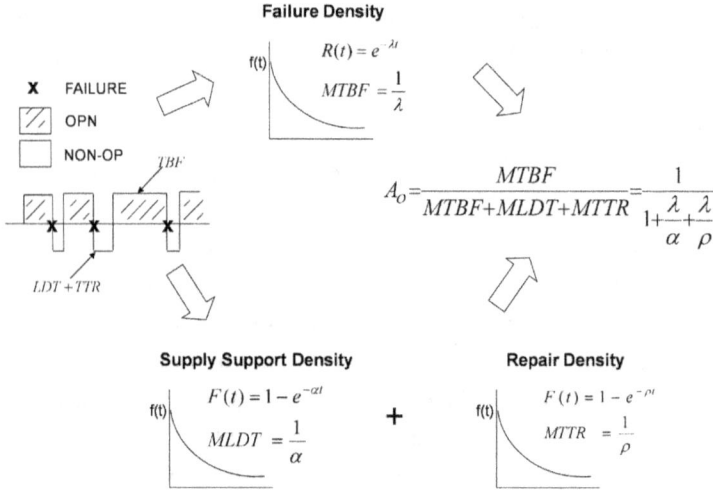

Figure 32. Components of operational availability.

becoming operationally significant and more costly due to the unprecedented length of service for aging fleets. Previously this has not been a major concern due to the normal 20- to 25-year replacement cycle for modernization programs. Two issues are briefly highlighted here: (a) the previous failure to credibly incorporate reliability and maintainability design considerations into total system life-cycle costs that are now severely impacting today's downstream O&M costs, and (b) the failure to recognize and correct for deviations between original design MTBF parameters and subsequent actual MTBF (or mean time between replacement [MTBR]) empirical evidence derived from operational experience and the resulting consequences of this gap on supply system performance.

Regarding the first issue, reliability design to readiness, significant work previously undertaken by the Institute for Defense Analyses (IDA), which focused on U.S. Air Force and U.S. Navy/U.S. Marine Corps fixed-wing aircraft, suggests it is indeed possible to quantify relationships between these design factors (MTBF and MTTR), operational availability goals, and life-cycle costs. Furthermore, despite the lack of standardized cost-estimating relationships for reliability improvement, analysis and modeling using actual aircraft data revealed significant improvement to availability, and also to reducing life-cycle costs, that can be obtained by increased investment in reliability and maintainability.

Traditional maintainability concepts that improve availability have included use of line-replaceable units, accurate fault isolation and detection, and commonality. Another emerging concept is condition-based maintenance, described previously (chapters 5 and 6), which capitalizes on prognostics and health monitoring systems to detect potential failure modes, thereby ideally anticipating and precluding failure from occurring in the first place.

Three major potential benefits accrue from this increase in aircraft availability. Life-cycle costs are reduced as a result of O&M savings. Also, procurement quantities can be decreased without sacrificing the number of effective aircraft. And third, for ground systems, land combat modeling and simulation results suggest that higher reliability and availability lead to improved loss exchange ratios across a range of scenarios according to a recent study for the army by RAND Corporation's Arroyo Center. IDA's work also reveals a strong correlation between increasing aircraft complexity with their associated greater costs and this cost-savings effect: The more complex the aircraft, the greater the potential savings from this "reliability design to readiness" approach.[9]

Regarding the second issue—failing to correct and adjust for actual MTBF operational experience—analysis at the Naval Postgraduate School, focusing on naval aviation using the F/A-18 as an example, emphasizes that "reliability is the single most dominant life cycle cost driver and is the key enabler of acceptable cost effective operational availability."[10] When new systems or components are fielded, engineering reliability estimates for failure rates are usually the only information available to predict parts usage rates and to forecast inventory requirements.

However, these initial engineering design estimates are likely to prove inaccurate as operational experience is gained. Revising and then periodically updating these estimates with empirically based replacement rates from operational experience is necessary to ensure inventory levels appropriate for tactical readiness goals are maintained. In statistical terms, this is yet another, albeit simple, example of applying Bayes' Theorem in risk assessment: taking an initial estimate for likelihood of occurrence of an event and then periodically updating that "prior" estimate as new information is obtained to derive a more accurate, updated ("posterior") estimate as time unfolds and events actually occur.

This particular case study, examining one of the aircraft's actuators, reveals the impact of failing to periodically review recent patterns and trends and then recompute spare support requirements in light of actual operational experience. Patterns of failure were found that exceeded provisioning stock levels by more than an order of magnitude. Although experience clearly had shown that reliability declined over time, inventory support computations had not been updated (using Bayesian statistics or any other method) and requirements adjusted to accommodate those changes. This resulted in "under-budgeting logistic support, cannibalization and its costs, increased workload on maintenance personnel, potential safety risks and most significantly an operational readiness potential that was unrealized."[11]

CHAPTER 11

Summary

DoD's materiel distribution structure has changed little since it was first put in place during the World War II era.
—"Beyond Goldwater-Nichols: U.S. Government and Defense Reform for a New Strategic Era, Phase 2 Report," Center for Strategic and International Studies, July 2005

There are chinks in the aviation repair parts supply chain.
—Major General James H. Pillsbury, Commanding General, U.S. Army Aviation and Missile Command, remarks at Army Aviation Association of America Conference, April 11, 2006

The U.S. Army's materiel enterprise is truly enormous in scale and scope. However, it is not merely the size and complexity of the supply chain that causes difficulty but rather the structure and policies within the system that are the root cause of persistent problems. Army aviation logistics has especially suffered from several disorders that are both systemic and chronic. These problems have been illuminated throughout these chapters using inventory management theory, supply chain principles, and logistics systems analysis as key sources of diagnostic power. To summarize generally, these causal disorders and their respective effects include the following:

1. Lack of an aviation readiness production function that induces both uncertainty and variability at the point of consumption in the supply chain, resulting in inappropriate planning, improper budgeting, and inadequate management to achieve readiness objectives
2. Limited understanding of mission-based, operational demands and associated spares consumption patterns that contribute to poor operational and tactical support planning and cost-*in*effective retail stock policy
3. Failure to optimize retail stock policy to achieve cost-efficient readiness (customer) objectives, which results in inefficient procurement and reduced readiness

4. Failure to proactively synchronize and manage reverse logistics, which contributes significantly to increased depot-level reparable (DLR) requirement objectives (RO), excess inventory, and increased delay times (order fulfillment) with reduced readiness
5. Inadequately organized depot repair operations that may be creating a growing gap in essential repair capacity while simultaneously precluding the enormous potential benefits of a synchronized, closed-loop supply chain for DLRs
6. Limited visibility into and management control over disjointed and disconnected original equipment manufacturer and key supplier procurement programs that are vulnerable to boom and bust cycles with extremely long lead times, high price volatility for aerospace steels and alloys, and increasing business risk to crucial, unique vendors in the industrial base, resulting in diminishing manufacturing sources of materiel supplies and growing obsolescence challenges for aging aircraft fleets
7. Independently operating, uncoordinated, and unsynchronized stages within the supply chain creating pernicious "bullwhip" effects, including large RO, long lead times, and declining readiness
8. Fragmented data processes and inappropriate supply chain measures of effectiveness focusing on interface metrics that mask the effects of efficient and effective alternatives and further preclude an ability to determine "readiness return on net assets" or to relate resource investment levels to readiness outcomes
9. Lack of central supply chain management and supporting analytical capacity results in multiagency, consensus-driven, bureaucratic work-arounds hindered by lack of an army supply chain management science and an enabling "analytical architecture" to guide Logistics Transformation
10. Lack of an "engine for innovation" to accelerate and then sustain continual improvement for a learning organization

The existing aviation logistics structure is indeed vulnerable to the bullwhip. While endless remedies have been adopted over the years to address visibly apparent symptoms, the fundamental underlying disease has not been adequately diagnosed or treated, much less cured. Now, better understanding these underlying causes of failure, a new approach to logistics management is required for the U.S. Army.

The analytical challenge is to conquer unpredictability and to better understand and then attack the root causes of variability and uncertainty within each stage and their collective contributions to volatility across the system of stages—the bullwhip effect. Analysis clearly reveals that inventory investment levels can be significantly reduced while maintaining or improving performance (e.g., readiness) simply by linking stock policies to the sources of uncertainty and inefficiency that require inventory in the first place. However, to reduce the impact of this variability, some of which is unpredictable but much is predictable, supply chain managers must understand their sources and the magnitude of their impact.

In general, these various contributions to aggregate system-wide RO—induced by the bullwhip effect—can be identified, measured, and then systematically reduced by understanding and attacking root causes. The first step, then, in suppressing the bullwhip effect is to isolate, detect, and quantify these inefficiencies within each stage and their respective contributions to Army Materiel Command system-wide aggregate inventory RO. The next step is to use this knowledge to drive inventory policy. Since army inventories are managed to these computed ROs, reducing the value of the RO is critical to eliminating unnecessary inventory. Demand uncertainty can be reduced by adopting empirically derived, mission-based demand forecasting. Variability can be reduced on supply-side lead times for all components that contribute to higher RO, including administrative, procurement, retrograde, and repair cycle times. And order fulfillment can be improved while reducing backorders and requisition wait times by implementing readiness-based sparing, inventory pooling, and ultimately, tactical-level readiness-driven supply networks.

As prescriptions for improved performance recommended throughout this chapter are implemented in each of the stages, their respective contributions to reducing RO—while sustaining or actually improving readiness performance—can be measured, compared, and assessed within a rational cost-performance framework (Figure 33). An especially compelling and urgent need, and also one with lucrative potential benefits (so-called low-hanging fruit), is the reverse pipeline: As retrograde operations become more responsive and contribute to a synchronized closed-loop supply chain, it becomes possible to reduce RO and safety stock for

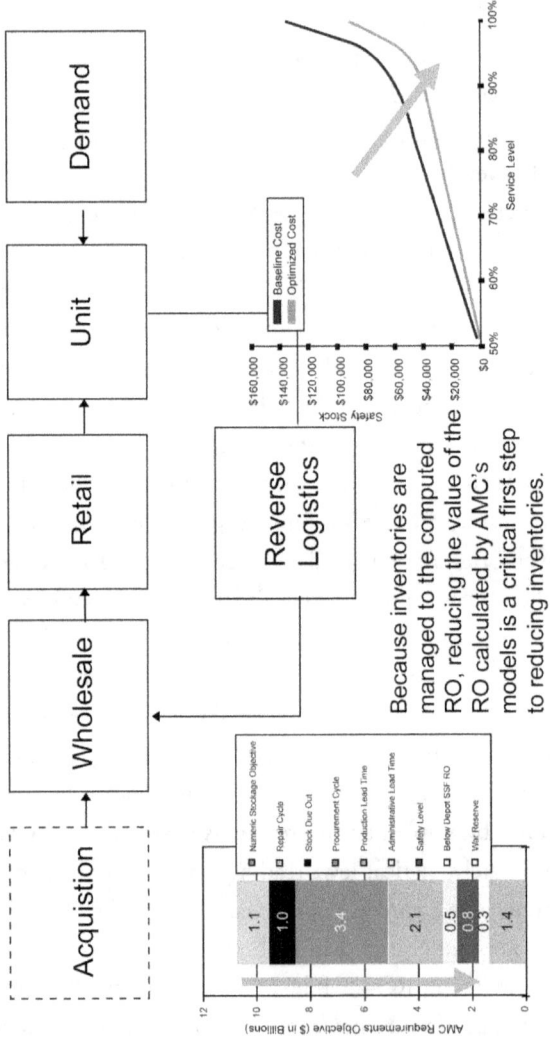

Figure 33. *Improving system efficiency: Across the system of stages and within each stage.*

specific DLRs while simultaneously reducing backorders and *increasing readiness* (operational availability, or Ao).

By improving demand forecasting and reducing supply-side variability and inefficiencies within each of the stages, logistics system performance is moving toward an efficient frontier in the cost-availability trade space. As these efforts are systematically pursued, the logistics system becomes more efficient: RO (safety stock, etc.) is reduced while performance (backorders and Ao) is increased, thereby moving toward the "efficient frontier" in the spares investment-readiness performance trade space (Figure 2). So far, however, the collective organizational pathologies described in these chapters have impeded analytically based management. This project is a first effort to link a comprehensive analytical approach to army supply chain performance as a whole.

PART III

Multistage Integration for Efficiency, Resilience, and Effectiveness

Despite spending billions on logistics systems improvements in recent decades, the results have always been less than expected and often years later than promised . . . [A] dramatic coordinated effort to improve the military's strategic supply chain planning and execution capability is badly needed.

—Roger Kallock, deputy under secretary of defense for logistics and materiel readiness

Chapters

12. Achieving Efficiency: An Integrated Multiechelon Inventory Solution
13. Designing for Resilience: Adaptive Logistics Network Concepts
14. Improving Effectiveness: Pushing the Logistics Performance Envelope

Although its recognition provides important insight into U.S. Army logistics, merely acknowledging that the aviation supply chain is vulnerable to the "bullwhip" does not, of course, automatically solve the problem. Simply recognizing that these conditions exist does not guarantee that needed changes will actually be made. However, these persistent effects can be avoided if dysfunctional management processes contributing to them are both acknowledged and addressed. And as distinguished systems management Professor Russell Ackoff reminds us, the historical record also cautions that many of the "panaceas, fads, and quick fixes" that operate under the guise of new management approaches are likely to fail because they are fundamentally "antisystemic."

In addition to reducing demand uncertainty, identifying the causes of inefficiencies, and reducing the effects of supply and demand variability within each of the logistics stages, the stages must also be integrated, or linked together in meaningful ways. This integration, or synthesis in analytical terms, is needed to identify and quantify credible cause-and-effect relationships among new initiatives, Department of the Army resource allocation investment levels, and the contribution of both to readiness-oriented tactical outcomes.

Complex challenges typically require an analytical approach where the problem is systematically broken down into smaller, more manageable elements based on process, function, and organization. As we have seen in part II, component-based analysis provides great insight into sources of uncertainty and variability. However, we must guard against treating the entire materiel enterprise merely as an aggregation of its component parts that can be improved independent of one another.

This component-based modeling approach, in which the pieces of a complex problem are modeled as segments, must then be complemented with an integrating perspective, or synthesis, where the segments are then incorporated into a larger representation encompassing the broader scope of the original challenge. How do you actually achieve integration and interoperability for complex systems where challenges of both vertical and horizontal integration persist?

A compelling need now exists for prescriptive, integrating concepts that focus these interdependent efforts among the stages toward army supply chain system-wide objectives and goals. The next three chapters recommend and explain three integrating army supply chain goals for Logistics Transformation and how modeling and analysis can be used to pursue them: efficiency, resilience, and effectiveness.

CHAPTER 12

Achieving Efficiency

An Integrated Multiechelon Inventory Solution

Synchronized and integrated leadership of logistics is a must. . . . Fragmentation and fiefdoms result in a mess. The solution is not to take separate existing stove pipes and merely add a larger organization on top and announce, "Well, we are now joint and integrated."
—General Paul Kern, commanding general, Army Materiel Command, 2003

We have got to become more efficient . . . we are not doing forecasts well. Our stats are terrible.
—Major General James E. Rogers, commanding general,
Aviation and Missile Command, December 9, 2010

One of Army Material Command's (AMC) most challenging functions is the requirement to position and effectively manage a large, globally distributed inventory with millions of parts in hundreds of locations. The challenge is further magnified because these geographic locations are situated in different tiers, or echelons, of the supply chain. One of the major difficulties in managing this enormous multiechelon network is achieving an enterprise-wide inventory optimization solution. Multi-echelon inventory optimization is difficult for at least two reasons: First, replenishment policies are applied to a particular echelon without regard to the impact of that policy on other echelons ("suboptimizing" within independent stages of the supply chain); and second, higher echelon (in this case, wholesale stage) replenishment decisions tend to be based on specious, uncertain, or unreliable demand forecasts.

Visualizing a set of hierarchies helps to understand this complexity. A geographic hierarchy addresses the question of *where* spares and repair parts should be deployed across multiechelon, global supply chains. A product hierarchy exploits the multi-indentured nature of major assemblies and subassemblies, such as aircraft turbine engines, addressing *which* specific parts should be placed within the various echelons of the geographic hierarchy. And a planning horizon hierarchy addresses the question of *when* parts will be needed, since demand is triggered by events that are highly uncertain, yielding demand patterns that are both probabilistic and dynamic, and hence stochastic processes.

This demand uncertainty cannot be completely eliminated through forecasting, yet increasing inventory to buffer this uncertainty is costly. This phenomenon results in a classic risk management challenge.

Failure to achieve an integrated solution results in several inefficiencies and degraded performance:

- The supply network carries excess inventory as redundant safety stock.
- Customers face shortages even when inventory exists elsewhere in the network.
- Shortfalls and backorders occur, yet interface metrics between echelons (e.g., fill rates and safety level) appear to be acceptable.
- Upstream suppliers receive distorted and delayed demand projections and cannot deliver reliable performance.
- Short-sided internal allocation decisions are made for parts with limited availability.

Commercial enterprises characterized as "multiechelon" have typically used one of two approaches to address this inventory positioning challenge: a sequential application of the single echelon approach; or, more recently, distribution requirements planning (DRP), an extension of materials requirements planning used in manufacturing. Both approaches (Figure 34), however, result in excessive inventory without necessarily improving performance levels. This occurs because an optimal solution for the entire network has not been achieved; total inventory has not been minimized subject to an outcome-oriented result such as customer service performance objectives. Inefficiencies occur due to lack of visibility both up and down the supply chain; the retail stage has no visibility of the wholesale-stage inventory balance, and wholesale lacks visibility into retail demand.

Independent demand forecasts among the stages result in greater demand variation between them—the bullwhip effect—leading to bloated but undifferentiated inventory levels, especially at wholesale.

ACHIEVING EFFICIENCY 105

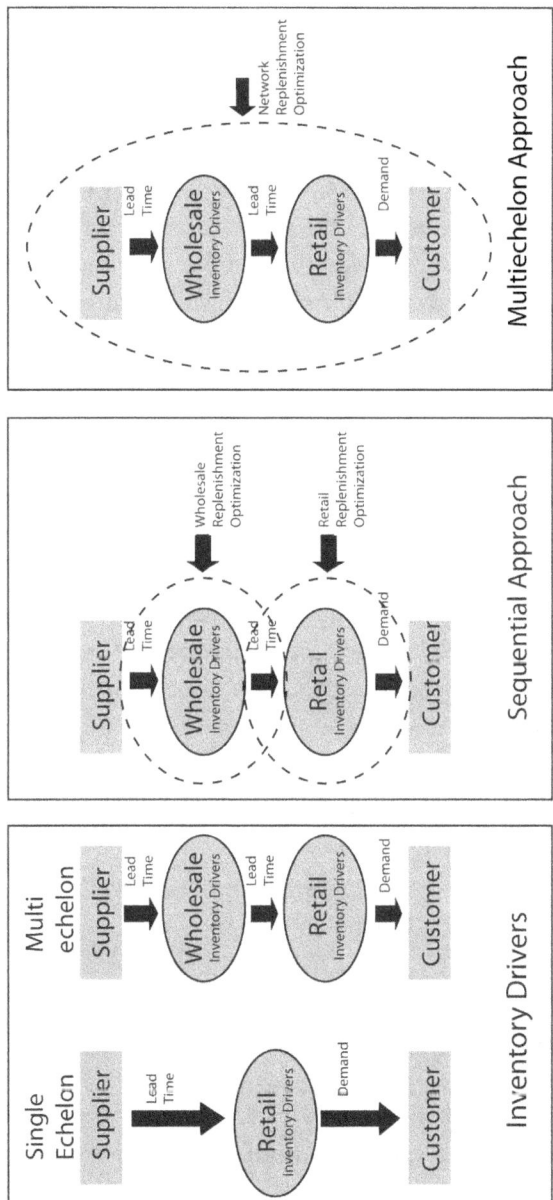

Figure 34. Multiechelon integration.

Furthermore, total network costs are difficult to assess, and the enterprise-wide implications of new initiatives or strategies cannot be accurately evaluated, since this sequential approach can only focus on their impact one stage at a time. Similarly, DRP, which uses a deterministic approach, cannot rigorously compute safety stock for the wholesale stage, since retail stage demand variability has not been incorporated. As with the sequential approach, there is no linkage between safety stocks in the two stages.

In complex supply chains, a recurring management challenge is determining where, and in what quantities, to hold safety stock in a network to protect against variability and to ensure that target customer service levels are met. To improve supply chain efficiency, an appreciation for the interdependencies of the various stages is required to fully understand how inventory management decisions in one particular stage or location impact other stages throughout the supply chain.

For military and aerospace logistics systems, optimizing these decisions requires a decision support system that captures multiechelon, multi-item, multi-indenture interactions and also the dynamics of the reverse flows for reparable components. Such a decision support system must also be linked to the various supply information transaction, depot repair and overhaul, and long-term planning systems that affect the overall responsiveness, support adequacy, and capacity of the fleet supply chain enterprise—the "readiness" of the entire globally dispersed logistics support system. These supporting management systems include maintenance, repair and overhaul scheduling, procurement and order fulfillment, asset visibility, and transportation support.

An integrated, multiechelon network, if achievable, offers several opportunities for supply chain efficiency:

- Multiple, independent forecasts in each of the stages are avoided; variability in both demand and lead time (supply) can be accounted for.
- The bullwhip effect can be observed, monitored, and managed
- Its various root causes can be identified and their effects measured, corrected, and tracked.
- Common visibility across the supply chain stages reduces uncertainty, improving demand forecasting and inventory requirements planning.

- Order cycles can be synchronized (this has special significance for DLRs in the retrograde and depot repair stages).
- Differentiated service levels (e.g., operational availability [Ao] targets for different units) can be accommodated.
- Action can be taken to reduce unnecessary inventory and operational costs while simultaneously improving readiness-oriented performance.[1]

Although the calculations are not trivial to incorporate key variables, their relationships, and associated costs, they *can* be performed using advanced analytic methods, including readiness-based sparing (RBS) optimization methods mentioned previously and described in greater detail shortly. Multiechelon optimization methods generate ideal inventory targets across an entire network of sites and stages. Improved results are then possible and the organization can have far greater confidence that it is operating on the efficient frontier on the investment-performance trade space. (See Figure 35 for a comparison of these approaches.)

Within the Department of Defense (DoD) and its supporting federally funded research and development centers, the mathematical theory

Key areas	Sequential approach	DRP approach	True multiechelon approach
Optimization objective	Meet immediate customer's service goals at minimum inventory; suboptimal for network	Not optimization; objective is to provide net requirements upstream to determine replenishment needs	Meet end-customer service goals at minimum inventory
Demand forecasting	Independent forecasts in each echelon based on immediate customer's demands	Pass-up demands or projected orders with no measures of their variabilities	Forecasts based on lowest echelon's primary demand signals and other information; demand variations also are forecasted

Figure 35. Multistage optimization advantages.

Key areas	Sequential approach	DRP approach	True multiechelon approach
Lead times	Uses immediate suppliers' lead times and lead time variabilities	Uses immediate suppliers' lead times; ignores variabilities	Uses all lead times and lead time variations of upstream suppliers
Bullwhip effects	Ignored	Ignored	Effects measured and accounted for in overall replenishment strategy
Network visibility	*Immediate* downstream customers' demands and *immediate* upstream suppliers' lead times; *myopic* view of the network	Some downstream visibility; no upstream visibility	All echelons have complete visibility into other echelons; this visibility is exploited in the replenishment logic
Order synchronization between echelons	Ignored	Maybe, probably not	Fully modeled to reduce unnecessary lags in network
Differentiated customer service	Not possible	Not possible	Achievable, as orders out of a higher echelon location to a lower echelon are fully controllable; allocation schemes using set-aside inventories can be used
Cost implications between echelons	Not possible	Not possible	Fully modeled so true network optimization can be achieved

Figure 35. Multistage optimization advantages (continued).

for multiechelon, multi-indenture, multi-item optimization supporting military inventory systems has been developed and refined over recent decades. Much of this pioneering theoretical work, primarily focusing on ground-based land combat systems, was accomplished by scientists and mathematicians at the U.S. Army Inventory Research Office (IRO) in Philadelphia. However, IRO was abolished in the early 1990s as part of the post–Cold War drawdown and much of the original talent at IRO has retired or been reassigned to other organizations.

For military aircraft it has also been demonstrated that DLRs most directly relate to aircraft performance, and in general, minimizing the sum of DLR back orders is equivalent to maximizing aircraft availability.[2] Significant effort has also been placed on determining optimal stock levels and locations for reparable components in a multiechelon system. While the subsequent extension of this theory has been widespread,[3] the focus of practical implementation within DoD has been on fixed-wing aircraft in the navy and the air force rather than rotary wing aircraft in the army.

Another structural constraint that previously precluded an integrated multiechelon approach for army supply systems was the existence of separate stock funds used by the army financial management system for retail and wholesale operations. In recent years, however, these separate funds have been combined into one "revolving fund," the Single Stock Fund (SSF) within the Army Working Capital Fund. In theory, this should both facilitate and encourage adoption of an integrated multiechelon approach. For example, in the Aviation and Missile Command's case, the wholesale stage now has both visibility into the retail stage and more control over stock policy in the wholesale *and* retail stages, which it previously did not have for aviation and missile Class IX. Upon achieving milestone III for the SSF program, it becomes possible for AMC to incorporate a multiechelon optimization model and enable wholesale stock levels, *in addition to retail RBS solutions*, to be directly related to readiness (Ao; Figure 36).

However, although AMC now "owns" these retail stocks under this new SSF policy, in practice authorized stock list and supply support activity stocks are still being "managed" by retail organizations as in the past. Consequently, if the SSF policy implementation is not complemented with business process reengineering, including multiechelon, multi-item, multi-indenture optimization methods, then the full potential of SSF will not be realized.

It is not possible to truly optimize performance output from large-scale, complex systems if their component parts—in this case, the stages in our multistage enterprise model—have not first been integrated. Adopting

110 TRANSFORMING U.S. ARMY SUPPLY CHAINS

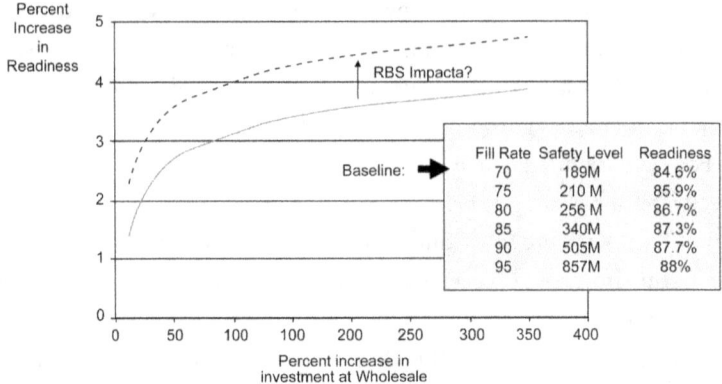

Figure 36. Impact of increased investment at wholesale on Blackhawk equipment readiness at 101st Airborne.

multiechelon RBS is a key integrating enabler for improved efficiency in army weapon system supply chains—and the more complex the system, the more crucial the enabler. Indeed, this is a *precondition* for Army Logistics Transformation.

CHAPTER 13

Designing for Resilience

Adaptive Logistics Network Concepts

Our wars have not been one size fits all, and neither have our logistics. We need to remain flexible in planning for future logistics . . . We need to sense, anticipate, respond, and do logistics better.

—General Paul Kern, commanding general, Army Materiel Command

Lean operations create brittleness in supply chains. With no redundancy to fall back on, operations can shut down quickly once a disruption takes place. Hence, a tight supply chain, by itself, may be an indication of danger…

—Yossi Sheffi, professor of engineering systems, MIT, from *The Resilient Enterprise*

resilient (definition) adj. 1. Springing back to a former shape or position; elastic. 2. Capable of rebounding or recoiling from pressure or shock unchanged or undamaged; buoyant. 3. The ability to recover from or adjust to misfortune or change.

—*Funk & Wagnalls Standard Encyclopedic Dictionary*

The intent is certainly not to blindly *adopt* the latest management "fad" inundating the corporate world. Instead we must consider *adapting* proven concepts to the unique needs and challenges the U.S. Army now faces. For example, the idea of "integration," when achieved by reducing slack or "waste" in the system, does not necessarily enable greater flexibility. The opposite result could occur with "just-in-time" methods. Lean manufacturing concepts have certainly helped firms to become more competitive through the application of just-in-time principles that exchange "industrial age" mass for "information age" velocity. And many of the original Lean manufacturing concepts, especially the focus on reducing "stagnant" work-in-progress inventory, have been successfully adapted for supply chain management across the entire enterprise.

Just-in-time manufacturing concepts, although a powerful inventory reduction method, need stable, predictable supply chains for maximum efficiency. Even when enabled by information technology (IT), Lean supply chains can be fragile, vulnerable to disruption, and unable to meet surge requirements to accommodate an immediate increase in demand. Official documents describe exactly such a condition for army logistics in recent years. Under greater duress and the compounding stress of ongoing wars, the military logistics system has indeed resulted in "a lean supply chain without the benefit of either an improved distribution system or an enhanced information system."[1]

Rather than a fragile and easily disrupted serial "chain" or hierarchical arborescence (Figure 37), a more appropriate analogy for army logistics structure is a flexible, agile, robust network or web, as in spiderweb. This more adaptive structure can be enabled by a strong analytical foundation with supporting IT to achieve an integrated, flexible, responsive, efficient, and effective logistics capability.

These adaptive network concepts are driven by an overarching Department of Defense "transformation" program coordinated by the Office of the Secretary of Defense Office of Force Transformation (OFT). For logistics, which is one of six major battle-space functional area groupings (others are fire; maneuver; protection; Command, Control, and Communications; and intelligence, surveillance, and reconnaissance [ISR]), this visionary adaptive enterprise capability is referred to as sense and respond

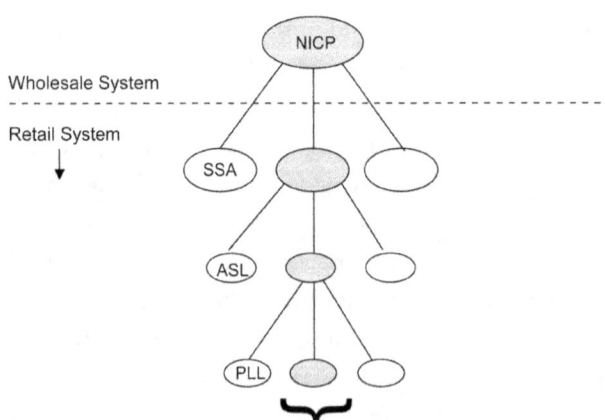

- Vertical "serial chains" create vulnerable supply channels
- Increased buffer stock is required to reduce risk
- Results in increased inventory investment costs

Figure 37. Current structure: Arborescence.

logistics (S&RL).² The basic foundational theory for S&RL is derived from the autonomous nervous system in biological systems that, in conjunction with the sensory perceptions of sight, smell, taste, hearing, and feeling, enable reactive and anticipatory protective responses to be taken.

This S&RL concept builds upon IBM's "autonomic computing initiative" in which machines use onboard diagnostic sensors to assess and monitor system "health," forecast and predict system- and component-level failure using prognostics, and then employ automatic identification technologies to alert maintenance and logistics managers and engineers to developing problems even before they become visible. S&RL further extends this "autonomic logistics" platform-level concept to the larger logistics support network, thereby providing the capacity to predict, anticipate, and coordinate logistics support wherever and whenever it is needed across the battle space. Conceptual documents currently describe S&RL as a "network-centric, knowledge-driven, highly adaptive, self-synchronizing, dynamic and physical functional process [which] achieves 'effects-based' operations and provides a precise, highly agile, end-to-end, point-of-effect to source-of-support network of logistics resources and capabilities."³

Adaptive network concepts have evolved from pioneering work performed at the Santa Fe Institute.⁴ The institute's research has focused on understanding how immensely complicated networks, made up of large numbers of interacting "agents" that cooperate and compete, regularly arrange themselves into complex organizations that are efficient, adaptive, and resilient even though the various agents are pursuing their own respective self-interests. According to this "complexity theory," efficient, self-organizing systems like this emerge only at the edge of "chaos," somewhere between a prescribed rigid order that is unresponsive to new information (including threats) resulting in paralysis and a system so overloaded with new information that it dissolves into chaos.

The research and subsequent understanding of behavior in self-organizing systems has been rapidly advancing in recent decades, extending originally from cybernetics to incorporate growing knowledge in cognitive science, evolutionary biology, dynamical systems, stochastic processes, and computational theory and culminating now in "complex adaptive systems."

Complex adaptive systems become self-organizing by responding to external conditions while maintaining an internal integrity that keeps them together and cohesive. System-level behavior "emerges" from the complex interactions involved, resulting in a higher level of order that enables the system to adapt in ways that continually benefit its member "agents." One consequence of this "emergent behavior" is that it is not possible to precisely predict future evolutionary patterns for such a complex adaptive system. Therefore a unique, "optimal" solution cannot be engineered in advance. Research is showing that some of the greatest improvements occur when these self-organizing systems are forced to respond to random or unexpected events, and creative solutions are thereby discovered.

This ambitious vision endeavors to replicate and highly accelerate these evolutionary, nonlinear biological concepts characterized by terms such as "versatile," "adaptive," "elastic," "agile," "robust," and "resilient." This approach differs from linear, mechanical engineering system concepts that have been the traditional province of large-scale systems design. For military operations, this network-centric future force will be linked and synchronized in time and purpose, allowing dispersed forces to communicate and maneuver independently while sharing a common operating picture. Conceptually, the traditional mandate for overwhelming physical "mass," in the form of a linear array of land combat forces converging at the decisive place and time, is replaced by attaining comparable "effects" derived from dispersed and disparate forces operating throughout a nonlinear battle space.

Our ability to logistically support at least some of these concepts, especially the notion of an agile supply network at the theater and tactical levels for army and joint logistics distribution, may be much closer at hand now than previously recognized. At the tactical level, for example, the readiness-driven supply network (RDSN), which includes mission-based forecasting on the demand side and readiness-based sparing (RBS), lateral supply, and risk pooling (especially for depot-level reparables, or DLRs) on the supply side, provides the foundational basis for a more agile and resilient network "web" (Figure 38).

Through theoretical development corroborated by recent field tests, this RDSN concept has also been shown to attain *both* improved effectiveness (Ao) and, as total asset visibility and in-transit visibility IT-based technologies are incorporated, increasingly better efficiency.[5] Such a tactical-level RDSN is not only effective and efficient but also both resilient

DESIGNING FOR RESILIENCE 115

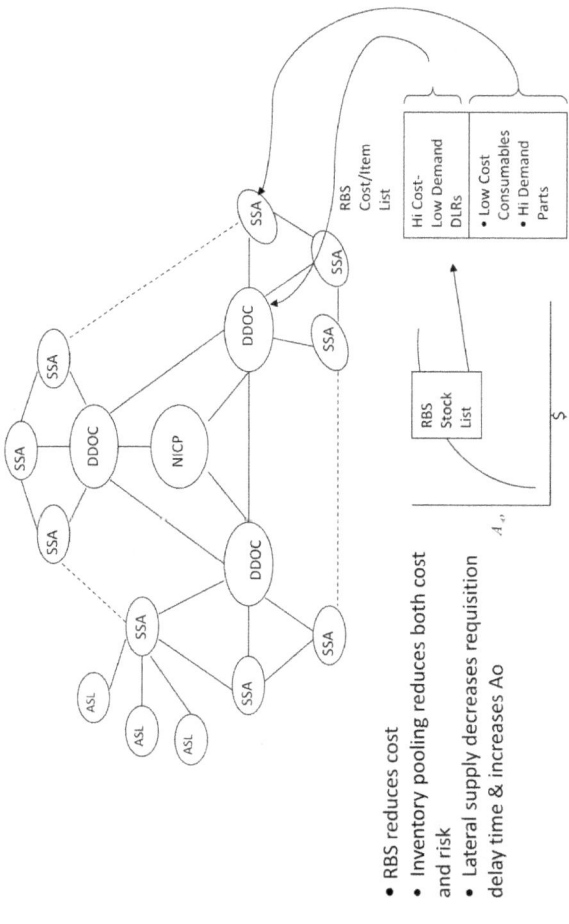

Figure 38. Readiness-driven supply network (RDSN).

and adaptive. This concept offers an opportunity to rapidly transition from the traditional hierarchical arborescence structure, which required "mountains of iron" necessary to buffer uncertainty, inefficiencies, and rigidity, toward an adaptive network design consistent with S&RL.

An example at the theater level pertains to the discussion in chapter 9 on additional aviation repair capacity, currently provided by the Aviation Depot Maintenance Roundout Unit/Aviation Classification Repair Activity Depots (AVCRADs) concept, needed to sustain overseas operations. Although the conventional view, from an "efficient" supply chain perspective, would be that surplus capacity (repair capacity in this case) and inventory (DLR safety level) are undesirable, the operational disposition of such additional capacity and inventory is clearly beneficial as a means for creating "agility" and "adaptability" for supply chains that must react quickly to sudden demand shifts due to operational mission requirements or to disruptions of various components within the supply chain.

By applying design principles for supply chain resilience,[6] a supply chain operating a large-scale (global), demand-driven ("pull") system under stable and predictable demand can quickly adapt to support localized (e.g., theater scenario), forecast-driven requirements that may involve considerable uncertainty, but must be "pushed" to the customer (combat units) to achieve maximum effectiveness (mission Ao in this case). Resilient design concepts include the identification of "push-pull" boundaries separating "base" from "surge" demand. This is achieved using decoupling points for the placement and use of strategic capacity and inventory. This concept enables "readiness pull" for peacetime training resource efficiency in relatively stable environments where risk is low. "Capabilities push" then complements "readiness pull" to achieve effective results for higher risk operational missions and deployed operations that involve considerable uncertainty in time, location, and mission type.

These concepts suggest, first, creating prepositioned mission-tailored support packages (e.g., authorized stock lists) designed using RBS in conjunction with mission-based forecasting. Or, if not prepositioned, the same effect could be achieved by "setting aside" small, similarly constructed packages that could be rapidly deployed along with the army aviation unit similar to the U.S. Marine Corps "flyaway element" or the U.S. Air Force "war reserve spares kit." These tailored mission support packages can then accommodate Class IX replacement needs at deployed locations where existing (e.g., host nation) sustainment is not immediately or readily available. This is an example of defining a "decoupling" point in the existing supply chain and creating additional slack inventory to accommodate a short-term surge that the existing logistics supply network infrastructure cannot support.

Second, to accommodate sustained, rather than temporary, higher demand for extended operations, resilient supply chain design principles would suggest creating additional capacity or relocating existing capacity closer to the demand source. This strategic supply chain concept shifts decoupling points and push-pull boundaries by dynamically changing the supply chain configuration. Hence, the logistics network responds quickly to initially accommodate a short-term need with built-in slack inventory and then adapts, if and when necessary, by actually changing its configuration to sustain increased longer term requirements by relocating production (repair) capacity closer to the source of demand. During OIF, U.S. Army Aviation and Missile Command acted belatedly to achieve the latter by activating, deploying, and now rotating AVCRADs for in-theater repair. However, the former (prepositioned stock) could not be accomplished, since army aviation assets currently are neither included in prepositioned stocks nor set aside as mission-tailored deployable support packages.

In summary, effort for attaining resilience must focus on strategically designing and structuring supply chains to respond to the changing dynamics of globally positioned and engaged forces constantly conducting different operational missions under a wide range of environmental conditions. Ultimately, this necessitates innovation in supply chain design, implementation, and especially management.

CHAPTER 14

Improving Effectiveness

Pushing the Logistics Performance Envelope

> When conditions finally permitted maintenance operations, repair parts were not to be had.... Shortages of predictably high-demand repair parts and vehicular fluids had the most lasting effect on fleet readiness.... A valuable lesson learned during OIF was that "just-in-time" logistics does not work during continuous offensive operations.
>
> —Third Infantry Division Operation Iraqi Freedom (OIF) After Action Report

So far, using supply chain concepts and the graphical army multistage logistics model (Figure 3 in chapter 3), several challenges and opportunities have been isolated and identified both within these stages (chapters 5–10) and across them (chapters 12–13). However, "efficient" and "effective" solutions should be explicitly differentiated within the investment-performance, or cost-availability, trade space. This chapter clarifies and illuminates these distinctions using the graphical trade space construct that has been consistently used throughout the book. Then, using additional analytical methods and concepts, part IV (chapters 15–19) develops and explains an "analytical architecture" to guide materiel enterprise transformation for the U.S. Army.

Economists commonly make a distinction between efficiency and productivity: Efficiency refers to the output achieved from inputs using a given technology, while productivity also encompasses the results of changes in technology. By "efficient" we refer to those methods (whether policies, techniques, procedures, or technologies) that, if adopted, reduce uncertainty and variability both within any particular stage as well as across the system of stages that compose the multistage logistics enterprise. The results of these methods would have the effect of moving toward the "efficient frontier" in the cost-availability trade space (Figure 39).

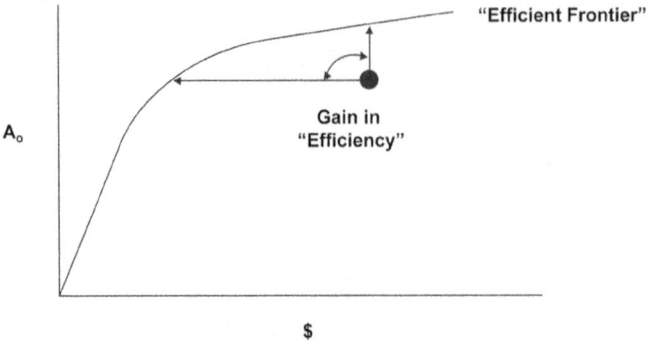

Figure 39. Achieving "Efficiency" in the cost-availability trade space.

Achieving an efficient solution results in operating on the existing efficient frontier and implies the best possible use of existing resources *within the constraints of the current system design and business practices* using existing technology.

In contrast, a more "effective" (productive) method is one that actually shifts the existing efficient frontier representing an improved "operating curve." This reflects the changed reality where previous business practices have been modified and new or different technologies are now being exploited. Cost-benefit analyses can be performed on various initiatives that yield improved but different results (Figure 40). The relative magnitude of each of these cost-benefit alternatives, however, is dependent on knowing the location on the current efficient frontier and, to some extent, the expansion trace of the new and improved frontier that results when taking an existing "efficient" operation and, through organizational redesign, business process reengineering, or technology insertion, creates a more "effective" operation characterized by an improved operating curve. In summary, efficiency is about doing existing things better to reduce costs; effectiveness is about doing things differently to achieve improved performance.

Finally, then, the obvious (graphical) goal to is sustain continual improvement and progress over time through "innovation" in all of its various forms—the notion of "pushing the envelope" (Figure 41). This is the essence of productivity gain and differentiates, in competitive markets, those commercial firms that successfully compete, survive, and flourish over extended periods from those that do not.

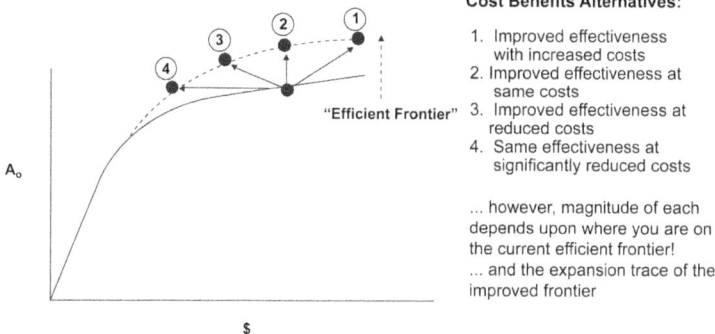

Figure 40. Increasing "Effectiveness" in the cost-availability trade space.

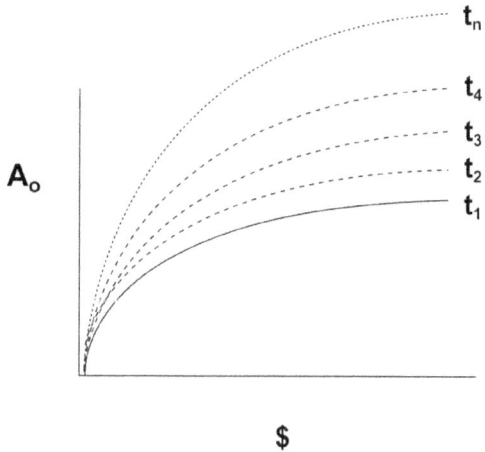

Figure 41. Pushing the envelope: Innovation to sustain continual improvement.

For a noncompetitive governmental activity an "engine for innovation" is needed to compensate for the lack of competitive marketplace pressures typically driven by consumer demand and customer loyalty. The most obvious such engine for a military organization is imminent or evident failure on the battlefield. Failure in battle, especially if sufficient to cause the loss of a major war, clearly constitutes an "unmet military challenge," which is one of several key historical prerequisites for a revolution in military affairs.[1]

However, the U.S. military, especially the army, has been extraordinarily successful in recent battle, despite several acknowledged logistics shortcomings and inadequacies. The current issue then is whether or not these very real, persistent, and serious logistics inadequacies are sufficiently compelling to warrant the attention, resources, sustained intellectual support, and extended commitment required for necessary change.

Indeed, a fundamental question is, Will, or even *can*, a so-called Logistics Transformation actually occur, especially with the nation at war?

> Every Army Chief of Staff, Chairman of the Joint Chiefs of Staff, and Secretary of Defense in the last 15 years has stated unequivocally that a true transformation of the U.S. Army cannot occur without significantly changing the way we conduct logistics. The premise is that logistics is clearly the one area that absolutely must be transformed if the Army's vision of the future force is to be realized.[2]

So far, however, the actual experience of over 2 decades of both Logistics Transformation and the Revolution in Military Logistics that preceded it offers a resounding "no" to this fundamental question. As with many large commercial firms, the army appears to be paralyzed by an "innovation trap." The consistent pattern has been one of internal cognitive capacity denying the need for change and thus causing an inability within these organizations to commit to large-scale transformation efforts before it becomes too late.[3]

In the absence of imminent or evident failure resulting in wartime losses that threaten the nation's interests or values, an alternative "engine for innovation" is an extensive experimentation capacity providing an ability to "see" the impact of alternative concepts, policies and procedures, doctrine, tactics, and organizational design—a virtual or synthetic environment that can realistically illuminate a better way and thereby possibly preempting future failure.

This experimentation capacity must also have a receptive organizational climate including strong, sustained leadership support; mechanisms that actually enable discovery and "learning" to be derived from these experiments; and the institutional means to incorporate positive results into new or existing policies, doctrine, and resource programs—in short, an organizational capacity to both encourage and accommodate change. There are certainly illustrative examples of very successful engines for innovation within the army that have had extremely influential and positive results, some with long-term effects and others of short-term impact.

One example with relatively long-term, sustained effects is the transition toward simulation-based training to capitalize on the emerging power of live, virtual, and constructive simulation technologies. This "opportunity" was initially forced on the army by both increasingly prohibitive training costs and decreasing availability of adequate real estate for live maneuver training areas, largely a consequence of the environmental movement. The resulting revolution in training and training technology has been ongoing for well over 2 decades and has yielded a remarkable ability to provide a quasi-realistic, surrogate environment for the crucible of actual combat at nearly every organizational level. Training simulation is now ubiquitous, spanning individual soldier combat skill training, weapon system team training in crew simulators, highly stressful command and battle staff exercises up to and including multinational corps exercises, simulation-driven theater and global war games, and especially our combined training centers in the continental United States and Europe. This transformation has produced the best-trained and arguably most dominant conventional army in history.

A less conspicuous example within a much shorter time frame, yet one with far more immediate consequences, is provided by the dramatic challenges to the army's recruiting mission in the late 1990s. After nearly a decade of decline during the post–Cold War drawdown, the need to stabilize army end strength led to increased recruiting requirements at a time when youth market conditions had become the most difficult and demanding in the history of the modern All-Volunteer Force (AVF). The interaction of these and several other trends was not well understood at the time. As a consequence of several years of failed recruiting missions and retention challenges, army combat organizations were struggling to meet personnel readiness objectives. Two of the army's 10 active component divisions reported the lowest possible readiness rating then. Indeed, recruiting forecasts at the time portended "imminent catastrophic failure" and, although not well known, the AVF was indeed in jeopardy as the military manpower system of choice for the U.S. Army.

As a consequence of imminent failure, both Department of the Army and U.S. Army Recruiting Command (USAREC) senior leadership focused attention on the creation and successful implementation of an engine for innovation. Creative solutions that directly addressed the fundamental nature of the challenge were found and quickly implemented. This transformation was achieved through nationwide testing, experimentation, modeling, market and recruiter surveys, extensive simulation, and rigorous analysis, all conducted by newly formed but very cohesive multidisciplinary teams of experienced recruiters, demographers, labor economists, statisticians, advertising experts, military psychologists and sociologists, market research and operations research analysts, and systems engineers. USAREC suffered its worst recruiting year, completely reengineered itself while transforming its approach to the youth market, then enjoyed its best year yet in its 30-year history, all within a span of less than 3 years from 1999 to 2001.[4]

These examples, though very different in form, duration, and content, suggest the power, value, and enormous contribution provided by a strong, comprehensive, analytically based engine for innovation to motivate needed organizational transformation. The simulation revolution in training has now spawned an entire growth industry in Orlando, Florida, an area that has truly become a global training simulation center of excellence.

However, consensus-driven "demonstrations," which have been adopted in recent years replacing analytically sound, empirically based experiments and field testing for war-fighting concept development, do not provide—and are not a substitute for—an adequate engine for innovation. The bad news is that such an approach clearly has not yet been adopted to support, much less accelerate, Army materiel enterprise transformation. However, as these two examples illustrate, the good news is that the army clearly has the experience and the potential capacity for doing so, if its leadership so chooses.

PART IV

Design and Evaluation

An "Analytical Architecture" to Guide Logistics Transformation

> Despite decades of attempted modernization, the DoD still largely relies on its 1960s requisitioning process and 1970s inventory management system.
> —Lou Kratz, assistant deputy under secretary of defense (logistics plans and programs)

> Transformation is a journey—there is no end.
> —Jim McCullough, Dean, Defense Acquisition University, South

Chapters

15. Multistage Supply Chain Optimization
16. Systems Dynamic Modeling and Dynamic Strategic Planning
17. Operational and Organizational Risk Evaluation
18. Logistics Systems Readiness and Program Development
19. Accelerating Transformation: An "Engine for Innovation"

The analysis presented in part II was largely "descriptive" in nature. An assessment of the current logistics structure was conducted using supply chain concepts to diagnose and better understand root causes of persistent challenges, their consequences, and effects. Part III presented three "prescriptive" supply chain objectives—efficiency, resilience, and effectiveness—to focus various technology initiatives, policy reforms, and management actions on performance-oriented outcomes to improve supply chain operations for the U.S. Army's materiel enterprise.

A viable strategy is now needed to transition from the existing state of affairs, described in part II, toward a desired outcome defined by the characteristics presented in part III. Inherent in developing such a strategy are needs to (a) understand and anticipate in advance the consequences, likely outcomes, and risks associated with an unlimited array of tasks that must be identified, selected, sequenced, and synchronized for implementation; and (b) optimize the allocation of limited resources accordingly.

These two analytical approaches—optimization modeling to efficiently allocate constrained resources toward desired objectives; and predictive modeling, including testing, experimentation, and simulation, to anticipate likely outcomes and effects within a complex system—must be used together in a complementary manner to illuminate a viable plan for implementation. They provide an analytically based strategy to link means (resources) with ways (concepts and plans) to achieve desired ends (objectives), or in other words, an "analytical architecture" to guide Logistics Transformation.

Furthermore, changing operational conditions, emerging test results, or outcomes from previously enacted policy changes may illuminate a clear and compelling need for adjusting the materiel enterprise transformation plan at a point in time (most likely doing so several times). These conditions may reveal certain project tasks that should be resequenced; possibly accelerated or conducted in parallel; or implemented in a more comprehensive, widespread, and rapid manner. Further testing and evaluation may be needed to resolve key anomalies or concerns thus causing delays or completely eliminating those initiatives that are not sufficiently mature for implementation or have been precluded by better methods. These options and resulting decisions should be grounded in thorough cost-benefit analyses conducted in a large-scale systems modeling environment representing the army's logistics structure and processes. Today, however, our analytical capacity to evaluate new ideas and concepts is inadequate.

The modeling, simulation, and analytical methodologies outlined in these next chapters would provide this much-needed decision support capacity and could constitute a "dynamic strategic planning" capability for Logistics Transformation. The intent is to avoid the typical project management "master plan" approach that prescribes a predefined, although detailed, set of tasks with tightly specified milestone schedules. Dogmatically following such rigid master plans admittedly may be mandated by various Department of Defense regulations and federal contract laws. Yet these constraints discourage the possibilities of adjusting program initiatives and tasks when either necessity requires such adjustments or opportunities are presented through adaptation and experimentation. A more responsive, adaptive planning approach is needed to accommodate doctrinal changes driven by evolving mission needs and operational concepts and to capitalize on emerging results from experimentation, field testing, and unanticipated breakthroughs yielded by a supporting engine for innovation.

This logistics analysis test bed could be patterned after any one, or a combination, of several organizational constructs, including the U.S. Army Training and Doctrine Command "battle lab," U.S. government "reinvention center" provided for by the National Performance Review and Reinventing Government Act, or a think tank–based "center for innovation" design described further in chapter 19. The purpose of this engine for innovation, regardless of the form it ultimately takes, is to provide large-scale systems simulation, analysis, and experimentation capacity and expertise needed to serve as a credible test bed. This capability will generate the compelling analytical arguments needed to induce, organize, sequence, and synchronize the many changes needed to gain momentum and then accelerate transformation for army logistics, including those identified and described previously.

Furthermore, it would offer potential for quantum improvement—real substance—over the PowerPoint "analysis" that has become pervasive. Indeed, PowerPoint presentations have been elevated to an art form, yet they are as insidious as they are pervasive. Managers devote increasing time to packaging their ideas in media-friendly ways rather than to the rigor and resulting implications of their analyses. In contrast, rigorous analysis offers insight and alternative solutions to complex, seemingly intractable challenges that have persistently yielded to emotionalism and myth.

Finally, overall "system efficiency" across all components of the multistage logistics structure should be visualized as the multiplicative *product*, rather than the additive *sum*, contributed by all parts of the supply chain process. In linear systems, changes in output are generally proportional to input; the sum of the inputs equals the output in a relatively predictable pattern. However, complex supply chains are inherently nonlinear, and outcomes cannot be predicted or understood by the simple act of adding up the parts and component relationships.

The purpose, function, and relationships of key components of this enabling "analytical architecture" are described in the following chapters.

CHAPTER 15

Multistage Supply Chain Optimization

The most difficult part of transformation is the complex task of managing the change itself.
—Antulio Echevarria II, director of research, Strategic Studies Institute, Army War College, from *Challenging Transformation's Cliches*

Evolutionary progress for an Army Logistics Transformation trajectory can be conceptualized along a spectrum transitioning from "legacy-reactive" to "future-anticipatory" concepts:

- reactive, cumbersome, World War II–era mass-based, order-and-ship concept where "days of supply" is the primary metric
- modern supply chain management incorporating velocity-based, sense-and-respond concept where "flow time" is the metric
- adaptive and dynamic, inference-based, autonomic logistics network concept to anticipate and preempt, where the metrics are "speed and quality of effects"

However, a clearly defined implementation scheme for "transformation" is certainly not self-evident. Analytical methodologies are needed to properly sequence the vast array of new initiatives, modern technologies, process changes, and innovative management policies in cost-effective ways: Which ones are dependent on others as "enablers" for their success? How many can be done in parallel? For those that can be, will it be possible to identify and quantify the different effects of their respective contributions? Will the synergistic consequences of interactions among complementary initiatives be measurable? Which ones may be precluded by combinations of other, more cost-effective options? And how can we be assured that these various initiatives are not inadvertently discarded because their potentially positive effects on readiness are "lost" in the existing "noise" of such a complex, massive supply chain? In short, how can cause and effect be "disentangled" as transformation proceeds?

The earlier use of a multistage conceptual model to analyze the army's logistic structure throughout part II of this book naturally lends itself to the use of dynamic programming (DP) or a comparable problem-solving technique. DP is designed for complex, nonlinear, mixed discrete/continuous problems that can be decomposed into smaller, more manageable parts for analysis and then recombined in such a manner as to yield an overall system-wide optimal solution while avoiding the normal pitfalls and inadequacies of so many other methods that lead to suboptimal results. The basic concept that makes DP relatively unique in the field of mathematical programming optimization theory is referred to as the "principle of optimality." DP works "backward" through the several stages of the problem to ultimately enable an optimal solution to be derived using a solution procedure, rather than a mathematical algorithm that is typically used for most other optimization methods.[1]

Using Figure 42 for reference, four of the six logistics model stages are aligned for illustrative purposes. Working backward from the point of consumption where readiness output occurs at the unit stage, the DP solution procedure moves from stage to stage—each time finding an optimal policy for each state (impacting operational availability, or Ao, in this case) at that stage—until the optimal policy for the last stage (N) is found. A recursive relationship is used to relate the optimal policy at each successive stage (n) to the n – 1 stages that follow. Once the final N-stage optimal policy has been determined, the N-component decision vector can be recovered by tracing back through all the stages. In this graphical example, the challenge is to determine the optimal allocation of a defined budget across a range of initiatives associated with these several logistics stages. Consideration must be given to various constraints that may be imposed within each of the stages as well. The overall goal is to maximize output from the "system of stages"—readiness (i.e., Ao).

From a practical perspective, this illustrative example especially reinforces the crucial importance of developing a clearly defined aviation readiness production function and adopting sparing to availability- and readiness-based sparing (RBS) stock policies as enabling prerequisites to realize further cost-effective improvements to the system. For example, if the link between the unit stage (where readiness is produced for specific

MULTISTAGE SUPPLY CHAIN OPTIMIZATION   131

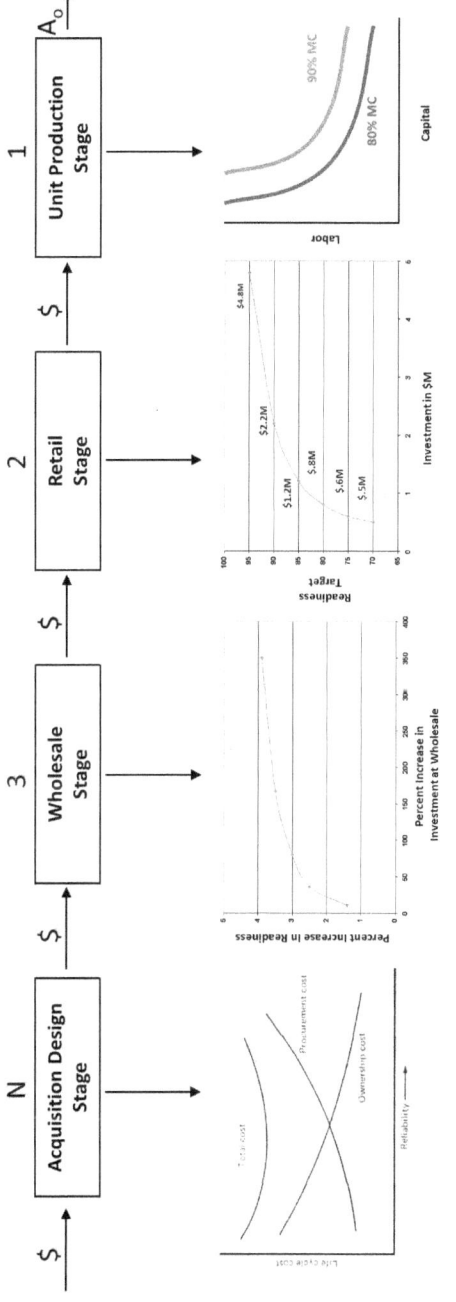

The dynamic programming problem is therefore given by the following expression at the nth stage:

$$f_n^*(S_n) = \max_{0 \le d_n \le S_n/r_n+1} \{r_n(S_n, d_n) + f_{n-1}^*(S_{n-1})\}$$

where: $S_{n-1} = S_n - d_n L_n$
and $f_0^*(S_0) \equiv 0$
         $f_n(S_n, d_n) = r_n d_n$
         $n = 1, 2, 3, 4$

DEVELOPING AN OPTIMAL DECISION POLICY

If our multistage system actually looks like the one just illustrated, then we can notice some interesting characteristics; namely.

1. There are exactly N points at which a decision must be made.
2. If we start at stage 1, then nothing affects an optimal decision except the knowledge of the *state of the system at stage 1* and the choice of our *decision variable*.
3. Stage 2 only affects the decision at stage 1; the choice we make at stage 2 is governed only by the state of the system at stage 2 and the restrictions on our decision variable.
4. And so on to stage N.

Figure 42. "Optimizing" the system: Applying a dynamic (multistage) programming model.

capabilities) and the retail stage (inventory management policy) has not been optimized to desired readiness objectives (Ao) by adopting RBS, then the potential positive effects of a wide range of other improvements throughout the supply chain will not be clearly visible and fully realized. Additionally, initiatives should not be chosen independently but rather on how they interact with and contribute to others. If such interdependencies within a system-wide context are not considered, then their real and potentially very positive performance impacts will simply be lost in the downstream "noise" of a very volatile, disconnected, and inefficient supply chain.

CHAPTER 16

System Dynamics Modeling and Dynamic Strategic Planning

> An act, a habit, an institution, a law produces not only one effect, but a series of effects. Of these effects, the first alone is immediate; it appears simultaneously with its cause; it is seen. The other effects emerge only subsequently; they are not seen; we are fortunate if we foresee them.
> —Frederic Bastiat (1801–1850), French economist

> It's hard to make predictions, especially about the future.
> —Yogi Berra

Use of a *multiperiod* model must be incorporated into Logistics Transformation to accommodate both the extensive and extended nature of this enormous undertaking. As events occur and a transformation trajectory evolves, a mechanism is needed to routinely update the "optimal" solution that, inevitably, will change over time due to (a) the inability to perfectly forecast future conditions, (b) consequences of past decisions that do not always reveal the results expected, and (c) the opportunities provided by adaptation and innovation as they materialize and offer improved solutions requiring new decisions.

This dynamic strategic planning (DSP) approach is, in essence, a multiperiod decision analysis challenge that also encourages and assists in identifying, clarifying, and quantifying risk to the transformation effort. Risk "assessment," a precursor to risk "management," is needed to reduce and mitigate the inevitably disruptive consequences of any major transformative effort with all the uncertainties surrounding significant change.

Most planning methods generate a precise, "optimized" design based on a set of very specific conditions, assumptions, and forecasts. Optimization techniques that provided the foundation on which DSP would subsequently evolve are primarily mathematical programming methods such as linear programming and its many derivatives, including integer programming, goal programming, and geometric programming. Although powerful and essential, a practical limitation of these techniques is that they require a specific set of conditions and explicit assumptions. While these conditions and assumptions may be appropriate in the short term for tactical operations, they are almost certainly never valid over longer planning horizons as strategic designs for technological systems.[1]

In contrast, DSP instead presumes forecasts to be inherently inaccurate ("the forecast is always wrong") and therefore "builds in" flexibility as part of the design process. This engineering systems approach incorporates and extends earlier best practices including systems optimization and decision analysis. It has recently evolved by adapting "options analysis" now commonly associated with financial investment planning. DSP allows for the optimal solution—more precisely, optimal "policy"—which cannot be preordained at the beginning of the undertaking, to reveal itself over time while incorporating risk management: a set of "if-then-else" decision options that evolve as various conditions unfold that, even when anticipated, cannot be predicted with certainty.

This planning method yields more robust and resilient system designs that can accommodate a wider range of scenarios and future outcomes than those more narrowly optimized to a set of specific conditions. Though perhaps easier to engineer and manage, traditional "optimal" designs can quickly degenerate toward instability when such conditions no longer exist.[2]

The human mind also exhibits difficulty inferring accurately the behavior of "complex, dynamic systems" characterized by feedback loops and nonlinear relationships inherent in their large scale, scope, and complexity. Advanced by Professor Herbert Simon (1978 Nobel Prize in Economics), this "principle of bounded rationality" suggests even the best human judgment and mental analysis when applied to large, complex problems simply cannot account for all the interactions that will affect and determine outcomes.[3] Compelling evidence from theoretical investigation and the empirical record of actual experience clearly reveals that the behavior and performance of large scale, global supply chains must indeed be characterized as "complex, dynamic systems."

These defining features—large-scale, complex, dynamic, tightly coupled, feedback, and nonlinear—are summarized in this paragraph to illustrate their relevance to supply chain behaviors, including oscillation, amplification, and phase lag, described previously in chapter 4. *Large scale* implies that the system is composed of a large number and variety of interdependent components. *Complexity* exists as a consequence of these interdependent components having cascading impacts on other aspects of a *tightly coupled* system that can yield counterintuitive effects. The system is *dynamic* with the cumulative impact of market-based cycles, multiple delays, error corrections, and unexpected changes creating short-run responses to perturbations that may be different than long-run response. Interactions abound due to internal linkages with causal connections causing *feedback*, tight coupling, and cascading effects. Cause-and-effect relationships do not have simple, proportional relationships and, for systems easily affected by outside conditions, result in high-synergy, *nonlinear* behavior.

Unless these feedback mechanisms and their interactions can be anticipated, standard optimization methods will underestimate the impact of changes, often dramatically. Fortunately, an alternative approach that explicitly focuses on capturing the structural dynamics and complexity of such systems has been developed and refined.

System dynamics, more than other formal modeling techniques, stresses the importance of nonlinearities in model formulation while also possessing highly evolved guidelines for model construction, including proper representation, analysis, and explanation of the dynamics of complex technical and managerial systems. While traditional mathematical programming tools are useful when dealing with *combinatorial complexity* in projects that have multiple parallel and sequential activities, system dynamics better deals with the *dynamic complexity* created by the interdependencies, feedbacks, time delays, and nonlinearities typically found in large-scale projects.[4] One of the original, foundational beliefs underlying system dynamics was that complex management systems could be modeled using the same concepts of feedback control that apply to engineered systems. A central feature of systems dynamics, especially when enabled with computer simulation, is its ability to illuminate and explain seemingly counterintuitive results and effects commonly found in complex organizational and social systems.

These observations suggest that large-scale, transformational endeavors are much more than conventional "construction" engineering efforts.

They represent a major human enterprise where effective managerial decision making requires a thorough understanding of the evolution and dynamics of the change undertaken. New software tools now make it possible for managers to actively participate in the development of these system dynamics models, so-called management flight simulators, which have become the basis for learning laboratories in many organizations.[5]

Army Logistics Transformation would benefit enormously from such an application. Within a supply chain management context, system dynamics modeling and analysis would explore how various policies interact; would they interfere or cause diminishing returns? Ideally, the aggregate sum of their effects and benefits would be greater than their individual policy impacts, but what are the sources of synergy to create such results? Since supply chain behavior often exhibits persistent and costly instability, a "stock management structure" (Figure 43) is used to model and explain these effects. Because this structure involves multiple chains of materiel stocks and information and financial flows, with resulting time delays, and because decision rules often create important feedback loops among the interacting operations of the supply chain, system dynamics is well suited for modeling and policy design. As explained previously, it is important to understand the "optimal sequencing" of a wide array of possible policy initiatives to fully capitalize on their collective potential benefits.

Much of the management literature in business process reengineering emphasizes finding, then relaxing, major bottlenecks in the existing manufacturing or operations process.[6] This is the fundamental philosophy behind "theory of constraints," described in chapter 9 in the context of improving depot repair operations management and productivity. Focusing improvement effort on the current bottleneck immediately boosts throughput, while effort on nonbottleneck activities is wasted. However, relaxing one constraint simply enables another to develop as time progresses. Obviously, waiting for each successive bottleneck to occur would prolong and retard rather than accelerate continuous improvement. The value of system dynamics modeling is accelerating this understanding by exploring the implementation of different sequences in a synthetic (simulated) environment. By using the model to anticipate and accelerate this shifting sequence of bottlenecks, a *prioritization* scheme for these many initiatives can be developed.

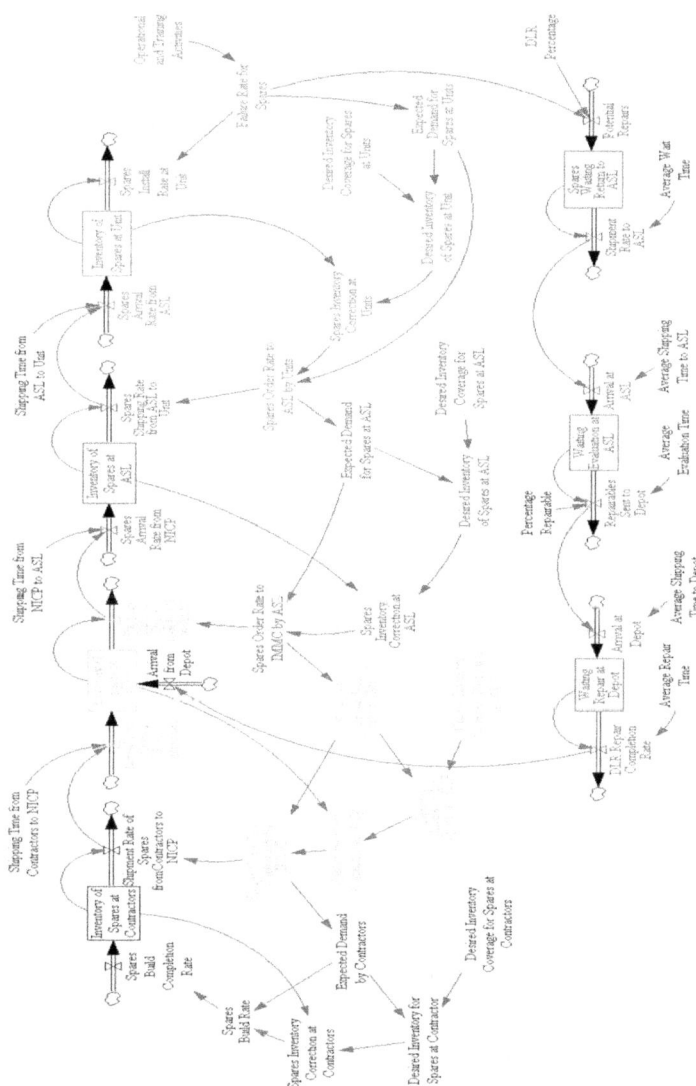

Figure 43. Stock management structure: System dynamics model.

This process redesign method, referred to as "sequential debottlenecking," enables potential chokepoints in the actual system to be anticipated, understood, and eliminated, using the system dynamics model, before they become binding constraints on throughput. When applied to commercial supply chains, this approach has enabled faster growth, lower volatility, and greater value creation for organizations that have used it.[7] For the army, a system dynamics model of the supply chain has the potential to guide and help accelerate Logistics Transformation by optimally sequencing and synchronizing the vast array of initiatives that have been, and will be, suggested for implementation. Previously, in chapter 4, we highlighted use of this modeling approach to demonstrate aviation supply chain vulnerability to the bullwhip effect.

Decision analysis, the second major analytical component in the evolution of DSP, enables structuring the combination of system dynamics–enabled design choices so they can be made in stages as a system evolves over time. Cost-effective options can be evaluated to determine the best pattern for system development depending on how uncertainties, both within the system and external to it, are resolved over time. Thus DSP defines an optimal *strategy* or policy rather than a fixed plan. It is the designer's responsibility to determine this (resilient) strategy rather than merely pick a single (fragile), "optimal solution" from a menu of choices.

The most recent DSP improvements have focused on incorporating methods to evaluate and build "flexibility" into designs. These include "real options" and "robust design" methods that enable calculation of the value of flexibility that was not previously considered. Consequently, flexibility was neglected as an attribute of engineering systems design. "Real options," applied to "real" physical systems, is an adaptation of "options analysis," which was developed for and has been applied extensively in financial markets. Recent and ongoing applications of this newest aspect of DSP indicate the approach leads to substantial improvements in design. Embedding flexibility into existing systems already optimized for performance under traditional engineering design concepts is also leading to substantial savings in many cases.

Inserting flexibility into the design of technological systems using real options enables managers to better react to unanticipated events, significantly increasing versatility and overall performance. This represents a fundamental shift in the engineering design paradigm, from a focus on fixed specifications to a concern with system performance under a broad range of situations that could occur. Massachusetts Institute of Technology engineering systems professor Richard de Neufville, internationally renowned for both innovative concepts in engineering education and their successful application in complex engineering systems, states, "Designing flexibility into projects increases their value significantly. It reduces the maximum possible loss, and increases both the maximum possible and expected gains."[8]

An illustrative national security application of DSP was the original development of an army strategic resource planning capability in 1996–1997. Initially developed to support the national defense strategy during the first Quadrennial Defense Review (QDR), this dynamic strategic resource planning capability was also intended to guide army resource planning in subsequent QDRs as defense strategy adapted to changing geopolitical trends and military requirements.[9]

Statistically based models for "robust design" should also be included for a comprehensive DSP capability. Two are described in greater detail here: statistically based experimental design methods and multivariable testing (MVT). Design of experiments (DOE) are descriptive models to statistically evaluate multiple initiatives and their dynamic, interacting effects. For experimental research, typical applications are conducted "off-line" in a controlled setting such as a laboratory. In actual systems and operating environments, MVT can be used to identify cause and measurable effect "online" within the existing organization.

Achieving continuous performance improvement requires a process of guided learning through scientific research. In contrast to spasmodic, utopian efforts where everything is indiscriminately attempted at once and it is impossible to learn what works and what doesn't, experimental design methods recognize that some equally plausible interventions work and others won't. Searching for interventions that work and then verifying what works with scientific evaluation are needed for learning to take place.[10] This process of learning can be depicted as a feedback loop in which discrepancies between data and hypotheses lead to discovery, learning, and the gaining of knowledge.

This iterative statistical model–building process requires significant trial and error in data gathering and experimental design. As the scientific investigation proceeds, more and more is learned about *which* variables should be considered, the *scale* in which they should be measured, and the *degree of complexity* needed in the model. The object of statistical methods is to make this process as efficient as possible.[11]

Any scientific investigation must begin with some structure or plan. This structure defines the entities or variables to be studied and their relationship to one another. Some of the basic concepts for experiments include independent and dependent variables, measurement and error, reliability, validity, randomization, and control. Most experimental designs in practice have several independent variables and are designed to assess their combined effects on the dependent variable in question. These "factorial designs" can identify where interactions provide more explanatory power than main effects alone. Although the use of multiple regression for factorial designs can illuminate which main effects and interactions are significantly related to the dependent variable, one complication is that the effects in the equation may not be independent, that is, the independent variables might be correlated. When this occurs one must take care interpreting the results. One method for analyzing correlated terms involves sequentially adding or deleting effects in the analysis, or "stepwise regression."

Multivariate designs have also been developed to address complex phenomenon that cannot be reduced to single measures and where measurement is not well developed for complex, multidimensional phenomenon. Further enabled by the growth in computing power for data analysis, an important advantage of including multiple dependent variables is that it allows determination of complex relationships that would be ignored by univariate approaches.[12]

In contrast to the highly controlled environmental setting in a research lab for DOE, MVT deliberately uses the organizational environment in an operational setting for both its idea generation capacity and the experimentation process. MVT is designed to test many business improvement solutions simultaneously to identify those solutions that help, those solutions that make no difference, and those solutions that actually degrade performance.[13]

As complexity in large organizations increases and genuine understanding yields to perception, apparent solutions can become deceiving and real solutions increasingly counterintuitive. And of course, process change is especially resisted if it is exclusively driven by top-down mandates. However, if new concepts are tested and evaluated in workplace operational settings to visibly demonstrate added value, old habits can be discarded and new ones institutionalized more rapidly. All too often ideas are tested one at a time, and results are measured with (perhaps) all other conditions held constant. Unfortunately, this method has some severe shortcomings: it is highly inefficient, it cannot identify synergies between ideas or processes, and test results often cannot be consistently repeated.

MVT traces its roots to the early days of operational research (OR) during World War II. When the British desperately needed to improve the accuracy and lethality of their antiaircraft artillery fire to better protect London from German bombing raids during the Battle of Britain, Winston Churchill gave the challenge to a special British military OR unit. Two mathematical statisticians, R. L. Plackett and J. P. Burman, found a way to quickly test both different types of projectiles and multiple variations on different components to find the best combination. They devised screening experimental designs that allowed them to test 30 to 40 variables at a time and were successful in developing a projectile design that greatly improved antiaircraft effectiveness. After the war, they published their work in an influential paper describing their new system, "The Design of Optimum Multifactorial Experiments."[14] This concept—now known as Plackett-Burman fractional factorial designs—has been used and refined over the decades in a wide variety of applications, from factory designs to the petrochemical industry and from manufacturing to nuclear weapons design.

MVT adheres to a two-phase, 12-step process, essentially using "screening" experiments followed by "refining" experiments. The initial screening phase assesses many combinations of ideas with only a few tests. Using advanced statistical and mathematical concepts, only a small portion of the many potential combinations of ideas are selected for testing. Screening experiments provide insight into potential large-magnitude synergies or interactions by calculating what is referred to as *quasi-interactions*. Then, standard statistical displays including Pareto charts and quadrant analysis are used to identify and prioritize improvement ideas. This initial phase also determines the right size and duration of the experiment, whether some tests are to be repeated, and the logistics of running the tests. Then analysis is conducted on the screening phase results. Typically, about 70% of the total improvement ultimately generated by the MVT process is revealed by this initial screening phase of the process.

The second phase in the MVT process, "refining" experiments, is then used to optimize results. Most of the techniques that are used here can be described as classical DOE. The difference is that the ideas now being tested have already shown that, as a result of the screening phase, they can quantifiably improve results. About 30% of the total improvement achieved from the MVT process is obtained through these MVT refining experiments.

This "practical" application of DOE in organizational environments has evolved, benefiting from other statistical methods including the Taguchi Method, and has been widely applied in over 1,300 projects testing 150,000 ideas across a thousand companies of various sizes over the past 25 years in the corporate sector. The method has a strong track record for consistently delivering measurable improvements, often yielding surprising and counterintuitive solutions. Results show for the improvement ideas that worked, about 80% of them are changes that did not require any capital expenditure or increase in operating expenses.

MVT can be compared and contrasted with Lean and Six Sigma management methods as well. In comparison to Six Sigma, the MVT experience shows that only about 10% of the total process improvement in a project can be attributed to process variation reduction efforts, with the remaining 90% accounted for by other experimental testing methods. However, there have been many situations where MVT has been combined very successfully with Six Sigma efforts, and in these instances results have been impressive. MVT, when applied to manufacturing companies that had previously adopted Lean manufacturing techniques, has been able to increase throughput over and above what the company had already accomplished.

Since a great deal of inertia exists in most bureaucracies, positive cultural change and workforce environment improvements are more likely to be achieved as a consequence of, rather than as the source for, improved organizational performance. MVT provides focus for busy, complex organizations by scientifically narrowing the range of business options to a few of the best ideas on which management needs to focus. Management can then stop directing resources, organizational energy, and time to other issues and use fact-based decision making to focus on promising ideas rather than letting judgment calls, opinions, instincts, clichés, or best guesses influence the future. MVT has also been shown to indirectly impact organizational culture by improving morale and promoting and increasing innovation. Given the army's recently initiated Lean Six Sigma "campaign," these results suggest that next steps for continuous performance improvement in operational organizations should include MVT.

Finally, in addition to experimentation and operational testing, a strong predictive modeling capability is needed to complement statistically based analyses for "robust design" and a comprehensive DSP capability. These longitudinal, or time-dependent, models simulate the extended life-cycle effects of decisions and policy options over time to gain a long-term perspective and appreciation for fleet-wide dynamic trends and performance in complex supply chains. Three such models, with varying degrees of sophistication and data requirements, that are currently available include the Army Supply Chain Simulation (ASCSim) developed by the Army Materiel Systems Analysis Activity; the Aircraft Total Life Cycle Assessment Software Tool (ATLAST) developed by Clockwork Solutions, a private company supporting military aviation communities; and the Defense Sustainment Chain Operational Readiness Evaluator (D-SCORE) developed by the Logistics Management Institute.

Each of these modeling capabilities has the capacity to demonstrate how changes to policies (e.g., RBS), processes (e.g., improved retrograde), and engineering parameters (e.g., component reliability)—and especially the interacting effects of combinations of all three—effect weapon system readiness and life-cycle costs over extended periods of time in various operational environments. These modeling approaches effectively combine the high fidelity needed for multiechelon, multi-item, multi-indenture supply chains using discrete-event simulation technologies and the efficiency of closed-form, analytic solutions. Various hybrid methods, including heuristic and genetic algorithms, are used to overcome the inherent challenges of combinatorial complexity and its associated computational time.

These modeling capabilities can provide accurate and credible comparative assessments by simulating new, perhaps untested policies and processes in parallel with the old to accumulate enough evidence, support, and learning so that the need for proposed changes become visible, compelling, and apparent to all. This is the idea behind cross-sectional time series experiments for operational testing and evaluation and for policy analysis. All of these models are available today and have been evaluated, in addition to several others, as part of this project. Yet none of them are routinely used by the army. Consideration should be given to incorporating their systematic use for both "simulation-based supply chain learning" and dynamic strategic planning.

CHAPTER 17

Operational and Organizational Risk Evaluation

Whenever substantial risk is involved, the best approach to systems design involves a strategy.
—Richard de Neufville, professor of engineering systems, Massachusetts Institute of Technology, from *Applied Systems Analysis*

One of the most difficult tasks that is least addressed in the systems analysis literature is knowing how to model a system.
—Yacov Haimes, professor of systems and information engineering, University of Virginia, from *Risk Modeling, Assessment, and Management*

Uncertainties inevitably enter into complex problems from several sources: process variability, lack of knowledge, and human error. To some, "uncertainty" implies an absence of knowledge whereas "variability" or variation is considered a distinct form of uncertainty. Statistical uncertainty can be classified into one of two sources reflecting its meaning and nature: aleatory or epistemic. Aleatory uncertainty is found in physical and natural variation, which cannot be reduced given new information, data, or knowledge. Epistemic uncertainty is due to lack of knowledge but can be reduced by increasing sample size, gaining new information (e.g., Bayesian methods), or subjective elicitation from experts. A third category, error, refers to (human) mistakes, such as numerical miscalculations or misinterpretations. These uncertainties—natural variability, lack of knowledge, and error—can be associated with different types of risk: strategic uncertainty (e.g., unknown responses by a reacting enemy) and both operational and organizational risk described in this chapter.

In conjunction with dynamic strategic planning (DSP), a wide variety of analytical methods should also be used to understand, evaluate, and reduce risk during Logistics Transformation. Risk assessment, when viewed as the likelihood and consequences of failure, incorporates realism into the development of a strategic plan. "Risk" can take on different connotations depending on the application. Accordingly, we address two concepts here: (a) operational risk faced by the logistics system responding to various shocks, supply chain disruptions, and mission requirements that may not have been anticipated; and (b) organizational risk to the U.S. Army logistics community, including the combination of investment, or programmatic, risk associated with new project undertakings and the larger impacts induced by transformation uncertainties associated with organizational change at a difficult and challenging time.

Operational risk, in this decision analysis context, consists of assessing both the likelihood of a particular adverse outcome as well as the consequences of that outcome. One of the most important steps in this risk assessment process is the quantification of risk. Yet the validity of the approach commonly used—expected value—is fundamentally flawed. Expected value metrics fail to represent the true risk of "safety-critical" systems for which the consequences may be catastrophic, even though the probability of such an event may be low. This occurs because the expected value approach essentially equates events of high consequence but very low probability of occurrence ("extreme events") with those of low consequence yet high probability, perhaps frequent occurrence. Thus extreme events with low probability are given the same proportional importance regardless of their potential catastrophic and irreversible impact. Such systems should not be measured solely by the standard expected value metric, especially when the consequences are unacceptable.

Theoretical advances in modeling and assessment have addressed the risk associated with extreme events and the fallacy of the expected value approach. One particular technique, the partitioned multiobjective risk method, explicitly captures the value of extreme events. Then, using a risk filtering, ranking, and management methodology, these risk elements are ranked based on severity and then systematically addressed through a risk mitigation process. The mitigation process includes relevant scenario-based analyses in conjunction with risk reduction methods including redundancy (backup components to assume functions of those that have failed), robustness (insensitivity of system performance to external stresses), and resilience (system ability to recover following an emergency).

Another more recently refined technique that should be considered includes an adaptation of the Leontief input-output model. This new technique provides for a comprehensive risk assessment and management framework designed to ensure the integrity and continued operation of complex critical infrastructures. The theoretical derivation and supporting application principles for some of these analytically based risk management methods have been developed by the University of Virginia's Center for Risk Management of Engineering Systems and are presented and explained by Professor Yacov Haimes in *Risk Modeling, Assessment, and Management*.[1]

Practical management frameworks, incorporating the advances described previously, have recently been developed to systematically identify supply chain vulnerabilities, assess risk, and then formulate strategies to reduce those vulnerabilities and mitigate risk. Various sources and potential causes of disruption are then bundled into associated risk categories.[2] Analytical "tool kits" can be applied to examine specific effects and larger consequences for these risk categories and then supply chain modeling and simulation is used to analyze, evaluate, and compare alternative operational strategies and their respective costs.[3]

Those strategies that reduce disruptive risk and enhance supply chain resilience, *while simultaneously improving both efficiency and effectiveness*, are ideal candidates for accelerated implementation. Two practical risk mitigation strategies that impact all three supply chain system performance objectives—efficiency, resilience, and effectiveness—were provided in chapter 13: (a) the readiness-driven supply network that reduces buffer inventory, improves readiness, and provides tactical agility; and (b) theater-level "decoupling points" to enhance operational agility and flexibility by providing, respectively, "slack inventory" for short, specific mission surge needs (e.g., humanitarian noncombatant evacuation operations) and, when necessary, "slack capacity" for long-term increases in demand to sustain in-theater operations (e.g., Aviation Classification Repair Activity Depot for sustained combat operations).

To address organizational (rather than operational) risk for Army Logistics Transformation, a variety of virtual, constructive, and live simulation methods, especially analytical demonstrations, field testing, and experimentation, can identify early on which technologies or new methods warrant further consideration. This process enables differentiating those appropriate or sufficiently mature for implementation from those that are not. In this context, organizational risk consists of the combined effects of both uncertainty of outcomes—simply not knowing the impacts of various alleged improvements on the logistics system—and also the uncertainty of future costs incurred as a consequence of either adopting, or failing to adopt, particular courses of action.

A recent example of this accelerating, crawl-walk-run approach is the sequence of experimentation and testing adopted by this project to first demonstrate, through rigorous analytical experimentation using the UH-60 aircraft in the 101st Airborne Division, the potential value of adopting readiness-based sparing as aviation retail stock policy; these insightful, positive results then provided impetus for and enabled further, more widespread field testing with several aircraft types in an operational training environment at Fort Rucker.

Confidence and credibility in a new, different method have been gained through experience while significantly reducing the uncertainty initially surrounding the new initiative. And return-on-investment results clearly reveal reduced investment costs while still meeting or exceeding aircraft training availability goals. A graphical display to conceptually portray these several analytical contributions to reducing organization risk is provided in Figure 44.

The MITRE Corporation has further extended risk management to "enterprise systems engineering," where the goal is to identify and mitigate

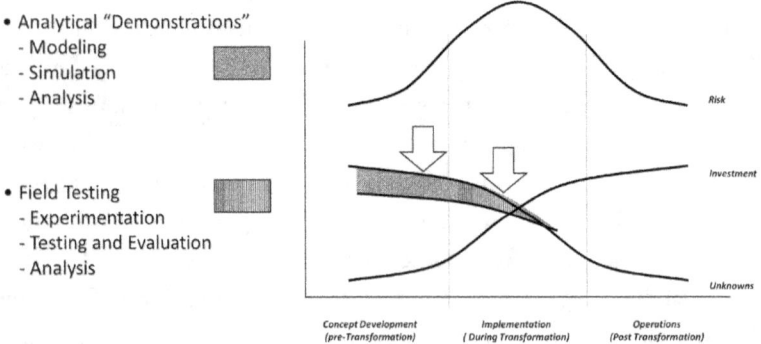

Figure 44. Reducing organizational risk: Analytical demos, field tests, and experimentation.

or resolve risks, their potential consequences, interdependencies, and "rippling effects" both within and beyond enterprise boundaries. Whereas risk in traditional systems engineering typically addresses impacts on cost, schedule, and technical performance, enterprise risk management broadens the scope of this consequence space to address higher-level effects requiring critical decisions for enterprise-wide resource allocation and management. Analytical frameworks and computational models have been developed to assess and measure risk in large-scale, complex enterprise systems. These include risk management methods for "capability portfolio clusters" and analytic methods to identify and measure critical, multiconsequential impacts and dependencies across enterprise-wide capabilities.[4]

Finally, the Global War on Terror has illuminated a wide range of vulnerabilities in commercial global supply chain operations.[5] Among several research projects addressing these challenges is the "Supply Chain Response to Global Terrorism" project recently initiated by the Massachusetts Institute of Technology's Center for Transportation and Logistics. This project is highlighting the "dependence of corporate supply chains on public infrastructure and systems coordinated or affected by the government [that] represents new vulnerabilities for businesses now more heavily dependent on the government than previously recognized."[6] Using assessments from recent terrorism effects on supply chain disruption as well as other historical observations, both natural and man-made, several common failure modes have been identified. The current research focus is on developing cost-effective methods and classifying various responses for reducing vulnerabilities by improving both the internal security and organizational resilience of these global networks. The army logistics community should actively participate in this project.

CHAPTER 18

Logistics System Readiness and Program Development

The U.S. does not effectively program or manage defense spending... It manages it through failure... The real issue is not to seek ways to reduce defense costs or resources, but rather to determine what levels of spending are actually needed and provide them.

—Anthony H. Cordesman, Center for Strategic and International Studies, in *U.S. Defense Planning: The Challenge of Resources*

The fourth and final enabling analytical component includes the development, refinement, and use of econometric and transfer function models for future-focused, capability-oriented, "early warning" systems. This capability is needed so that Office of the Secretary of Defense (OSD) and Headquarters, Department of the Army–level budget planners and resource programmers can relate budget and program investment levels with associated performance effects, including future capability needs and desired readiness outcomes. New impetus for this long-recognized need is now provided by Department of Defense (DoD) Directive 7730.65, which requires developing and implementing a new Defense Readiness Reporting System (DRRS). This new DRRS

> shall provide the means to manage and report the readiness of DoD and its subordinate Components to execute the National Military Strategy... The DRRS [will] establish a capabilities-based, near real-time readiness reporting system... identify critical readiness deficiencies, develop strategies for rectifying those deficiencies, and ensure they are addressed in program/budget planning and other DoD management systems... The Secretaries of the Military Departments shall develop Service mission essential tasks in support of their responsibilities to Combatant Commanders and functions as prescribed in [Title 10, United States Code, as amended]."[1]

In general terms, these Title 10 "functions" include manning (e.g., recruiting), equipping (e.g., weapon system procurement), training (e.g., Basic Combat Training [BCT] and Advanced Individual Training [AIT], unit training, noncommissioned officer education system [NCOES], etc.), and sustaining (e.g., logistics) forces in each of the military departments. The armed services, as "force providers," generate and maintain military capabilities that are then provided to the regional combatant commanders to accomplish specified missions. Each Title 10 function consists of significant institutional resources, organizations, and programs that collectively define "systems." Hence, a measure of each system's ability to achieve its respective goal can be defined as its "readiness" (e.g., logistics system readiness).

Application of this systems approach using supply chain management concepts will help to identify constraints and "weak links" that are inhibiting desired readiness output (e.g., operational availability, or Ao) thus reducing the overall strength of the logistics chain. Marginal investment resources should then be spent on strengthening these weak links. OSD and the armed services are pursuing many logistics initiatives, but as the supply chain structure is improved and refined, the logical next step is to understand and report the ability and capacity of the chain to generate output commensurate with its purpose.[2]

New supply chain management concepts are incorporating geospatial sensors and AIT to enable total asset visibility and the transition toward adaptive supply chains. In particular, radio frequency identification (RFID) is expected to significantly reduce transaction error rates while also providing near-real-time, high-volume data. Although these new technologies hold great potential, it is unlikely that legacy software and enterprise resource planning (ERP) systems will be able to provide improved decision support and fully extract all of the potentially useful information contained in these high-volume data streams.

Traditional forecasting methods typically use conventional *linear* regression models (CLRMs) that assume that unexplained variance is *homoskedastic,* implying that the error term in the model is constant (and normally distributed). However, complex supply chains exhibit *nonlinear,* dynamic qualities due to the interactions, delays, and feedback effects across multiple stages of materiel, information, and financial flows—the bullwhip effect as previously described. Not only does CLRM fail to capture the volatility inherent in the process but as data streams magnify in volume and accelerate in time due to RFID, the error term becomes increasingly *heteroskedastic* (the error term itself is stochastic and varies with time), rendering forecasts that are less rather than more accurate.

Recent forecasting advances for financial markets (including a Nobel Prize in Economics), which exhibit similar volatility, have yielded improved, more accurate and precise results.[22] These models, described as *generalized autoregressive conditional heteroskedastic* (GARCH), are able to significantly reduce the error term by better quantifying interaction and lag effects among the explanatory variables and time series within the model. As the volume of data increases, the ability of GARCH techniques to better disentangle and explain cause-and-effect relationships *while reducing forecasting error* (unexplained model variance) improves (Figure 45). One project initiative involves examining the application of GARCH to RFID-generated supply-demand data for units engaged in ongoing military operations in Iraq. Early results are promising, indicating that GARCH is yielding order-of-magnitude improvements for predictive performance compared to standard CLRM methods.[3]

As these new, powerful forecasting tools are refined and improved to provide near-real-time, enterprise-wide visibility into demand variability and volatility at the points of consumption, they can be combined with emerging agent-based modeling approaches, which will replace existing

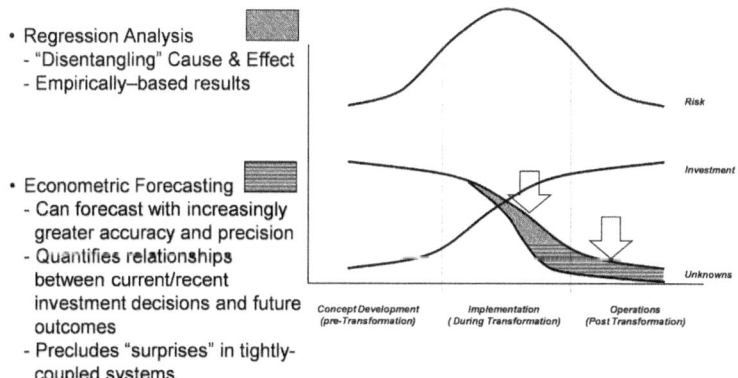

Figure 45. Reducing organizational risk: Systems analysis, management information (MIS), and decision support (DSS).

equation-based models currently used in legacy and ERP systems.[4] These innovative technologies, when fully developed and implemented, will ultimately enable the transition to adaptive value networks in the commercial sector and, for DoD, a genuine capacity for autonomic sense and respond logistics.

In the near term, however, driven by the new DRRS mandate and enabled by supply chain concepts, econometric modeling, and dynamic forecasting to understand, measure, and monitor army logistics as a readiness-producing system, a conceptual framework has emerged for a "Logistics Readiness and Early Warning System." The purpose is not only to assess and monitor supply chain capacity to efficiently and effectively support current requirements but also to anticipate its ability to responsively meet a range of future capabilities-based requirements. The objective is to overcome what has historically been a funding-induced cycle of instability manifested in periodic "boom-and-bust" cycles.

As Figure 46 portrays, three elements would interact in a "feedback-alert-warning" cycle. Automated Monitoring continuously tracks and forecasts both fleet-wide tactical readiness (e.g., Ao) and supply chain parameters and then signals an alert if there is a decline in projected readiness or adverse trend in metrics. Management Assessment then validates an alert, quickly evaluates the potential problem, and assesses the impact of current and planned resource allocation as well as other technical initiatives that might mitigate or improve the logistics projection. After HQDA-level policy analysis and review, Policy Response acts to prevent a shortfall while minimizing recognition and resource response

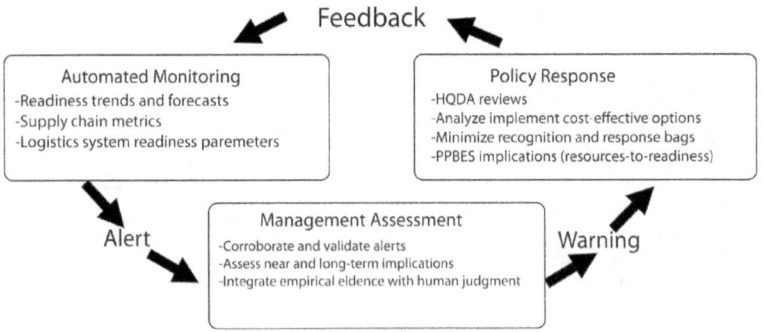

Figure 46. Logistics readiness and early warning system.

lags. This responsive link to program development is absolutely crucial to an adaptive demand network. Historically, however, this response has significantly lagged or been missing altogether causing boom-and-bust cycles in resource programming, thus precluding viable resource-to-readiness frameworks for management decisions.

As cause-effect relationships are better understood, and as model parameters, decision variables, and elasticities are refined to reduce forecasting errors and improve model "calibration," this capability will help to quantify high-impact investments and the differential effects of various logistics "drivers" on readiness outcomes. Our purpose is to both improve performance execution and refine requirements-planning abilities using leading indicators to anticipate, diagnose, and then preempt potential supply chain failures using analytically based decision support systems. As part of this project, a modeling capability is being developed to support performance-focused strategic resource analysis and logistics program and budget development.[5]

Further developed and refined over time, these forecasting models can increasingly be used for future capability forecasting, program requirements determination, and readiness prediction. Forecasting is used to proactively anticipate and get ahead of the problem; planning to evaluate a range of alternative solutions; and then forward budgeting to allocate program resources to dampen, and ideally eliminate, future boom-and-bust cycles. These models should constitute part of a "Logistics Readiness and Early Warning System" contributing toward the DoD mandate for a larger DRRS by linking army PPBES (resource planning system) to operational planning systems (capabilities).[6] The goal is to relate planning guidance, funding decisions, and execution performance in meaningful ways, all of which are informed by this supply chain "health monitoring and management" concept.

CHAPTER 19

Accelerating Transformation

An "Engine for Innovation"

> Our transformation process focuses not only on technological innovations; we are looking equally critically at changes to current doctrine and organizational processes that will enable Transformation. Change must occur quickly, and accelerating change requires extricating ourselves from antiquated cycles and processes.
>
> —General Paul Kern, commanding general, Army Materiel Command

If innovation can be characterized by the disruptive consequences resulting from the synergistic effects of multiple inventions converging in time,[1] then how can this process be better understood and then accelerated in a controlled way to minimize disruption?

Several agencies and organizations with logistics modeling and supply chain simulation capabilities should be pulled together, just as this new army aviation–focused logistics readiness project has attempted to do.[2] They should now be integrated, even if loosely, into a more formal research consortium to better coordinate their efforts and reinforce their respective strengths. This synergistic effort will facilitate properly sequenced field tests, experiments, and evaluation with supporting modeling, simulation, and analysis. Furthermore, these organizations should form the nucleus of an "engine for innovation" for Logistics Transformation.

There are several commercial applications and academic sources of expertise that should also be included. One possibility is to create, as the U.S. Navy has done, a dedicated organization consisting of a partnership with both academia (for creative, cutting-edge concepts) and the corporate world (for existing commercial applications) working in conjunction with a new navy-led, congressionally funded logistics readiness research center.

Another recently proposed partnership concept for the army is creation of a Center for Innovation in Logistics Systems (CILS). The purpose of the CILS is to harness and apply the power of modeling, simulation, and analysis to "post–Milestone C" logistics and supply chain challenges facing the army, including product support integration for performance-based logistics (PBL), supply chain optimization, and logistics system readiness. The enabling catalysts described in previous chapters, including the "readiness equation," mission-based forecasting, and readiness-based sparing (RBS) can be tested using modeling to better forecast requirements using predictive analytic methods in scenario-based simulations. Decision support concepts, including a Logistics Readiness and Early Warning System, would be developed, tested, and refined to better link resource investment levels to readiness-oriented outcomes and required capabilities. Use of supply chain enterprise simulation models would enable creation of synthetic environments—microworlds—to better understand and measure the combined, synergistic effects of fully integrating the various catalysts for innovation. The impact of replicating the tremendous success of RBS at Fort Rucker across other major training installations, and also extending multiechelon RBS to tactical army locations, could be evaluated and quantified. The CILS would also generate and evaluate methods to "connect" condition-based maintenance to the supply chain to improve inventory management and supply performance.

The center would also serve as a virtual test bed by providing a synthetic environment for experimentation and evaluation of innovative ideas and concepts. As an integrating focal point for several ongoing yet fragmented research efforts, the center could guide and accelerate Logistics Transformation along a cost-effective path for the army. By helping to integrate existing yet highly fragmented logistics organizations and technology initiatives, the CILS would provide the "analytical glue" to enable PBL to succeed. It would, in essence, serve as an "engine for innovation" to steer and drive Logistics Transformation. Furthermore, it would align well with both army business transformation and AMC life-cycle management command objectives.

The CILS organizational construct consists of three components that essentially comprise the core competencies (mission essential tasks) for the center:

1. An R&D model and supporting framework to function as a generator, magnet, conduit, clearinghouse, and database for "good ideas"

2. A modeling, simulation, and analysis component that contains a rigorous analytical capacity to evaluate and assess the improved performance, contributions, and associated costs that promising "good ideas" might have on large-scale logistics systems and global supply networks
3. An organizational implementation component that then enables the transition of promising concepts into existing organizations, agencies, and companies by providing training, education, technical support, and risk reduction and mitigation methods to reduce organizational risk during transformational phases

These three components do the following:

1. Encourage and capture a wide variety of "inventions."
2. "Incubate" those great ideas and concepts within virtual organizations to test, evaluate, refine, and assess their potential costs, system effects, and contributions in a nonintrusive manner.
3. Transition those most promising into actual commercial or governmental practice.

Hence the term "innovation" is deliberately in the center's title to express the notion of an "engine for innovation" to support major transformation endeavors in the government and private sectors driven by an increasingly recognized necessity for change. These organizational components and their relationships (Figure 47) are defined next.

The "R&D Model and Framework"—(1) in Figure 47—provides a generalized structure for supply and value chains enabling the development of a research model. The model enables our current understanding of endogenous and exogenous factors influencing the performance of logistics organizations and also indicates where existing theory and research are inadequate. The logistics research model also yields an association between various subject matter expertise (organizations and individuals) and the manifold elements that compose the research model. These organizations include academia, federally funded research and development centers, research offices and companies in the corporate world, and both federal and state government agencies.

A consortium will be established consisting of representatives from these research organizations to share recent research information, define

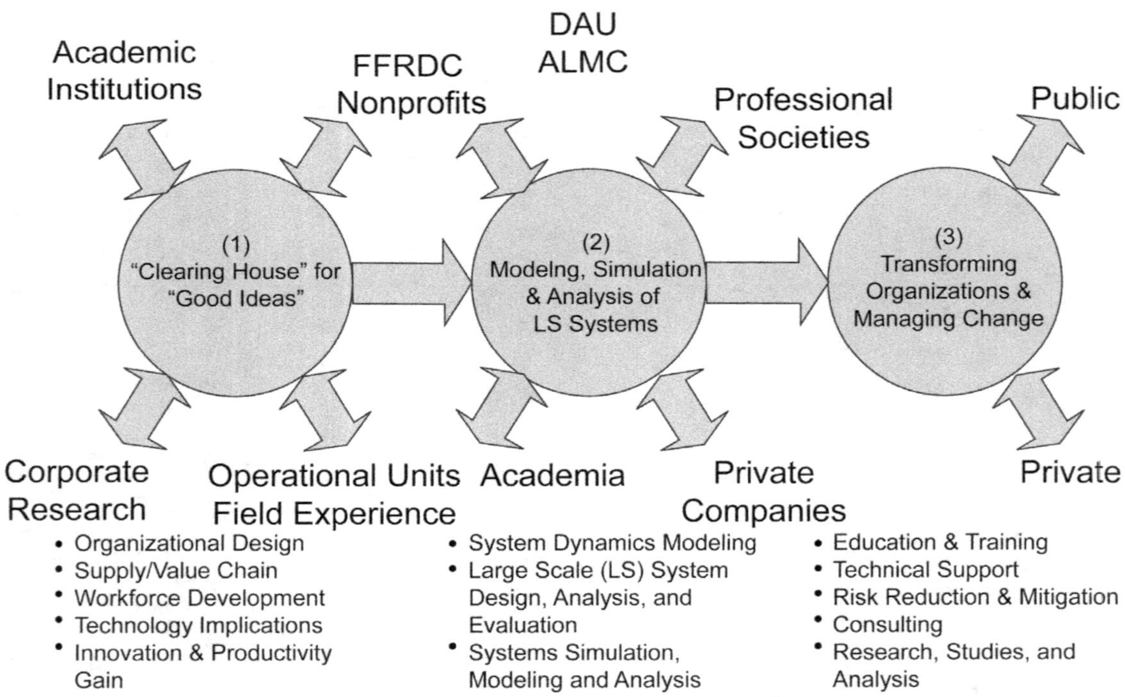

Figure 47. *Center for innovation in logistics systems.*

and clarify gaps and opportunities in current theory and research, partner on research development projects, periodically refine and adjust effort, and generally guide the advancement of the logistics research model. The objective is to improve the understanding of supply chain behavior, management, and design. This collaborative effort is intended to drive the "engine for innovation" with "good ideas" generated from a focused, solid research program and supporting research campaign plan. It could also further the interests of private sector companies wishing to offer their creative concepts to further scientific scrutiny and greater visibility. This enterprise constitutes the logistics research "strategic outreach" program to promote and encourage innovation thereby enabling a continual process of improvement in practical application.

The "Large-Scale Supply Chain Management and Logistics Systems Analysis, Modeling, Testing and Experimentation" component—(2) in Figure 47—rigorously examines the implications of good ideas generated by the research consortium. Using comprehensive modeling, simulation, and testing capabilities, it provides a virtual, or synthetic, laboratory for innovation and transformation. The disciplines involved and methods applied should include the following:

- Industrial and systems engineering
- Engineering management
- Market research and cost analysis
- Workforce implications of sociodemographic, psychographic, and labor economic trends
- Organizational design and social psychology
- High-performing systems theory
- Inventory theory, supply chain management, and design
- System dynamics and large-scale, high-resolution systems simulation
- The integrating power of systems analysis, operations research, and management science

The purpose of this extensive modeling and analysis effort is to thoroughly understand not only the likely immediate and isolated impact of adopting new and different concepts and initiatives but also their potentially broader implications for the larger value-producing enterprise over time. Concepts warranting further evaluation from these analytical demonstrations, which use constructive and virtual simulation and modeling approaches, would then be assessed in a "live" environment using pilot tests, field testing, experimentation, and evaluation.

The final CILS component, "Implementing Organizational Change"—(3) in Figure 47—provides the means to accelerate the "transition to market" phase of the larger innovation process: commercializing good ideas and inventions into successful applications in both the public and private sectors. Effective training, education, and technical support are indispensable to ensuring the success of leaders and organizations committed to and about to undertake major changes in traditional practices, processes, procedures, and especially their organizational culture.

The development of strategic planning and management frameworks are also essential to enable learning within organizations. The identification of organizational risk, including investment costs and anxiety-causing unknowns, can illuminate the need for and value of applying analytical methods to reduce and mitigate these various elements of risk for organizations embarking on major transformations (Figure 48).

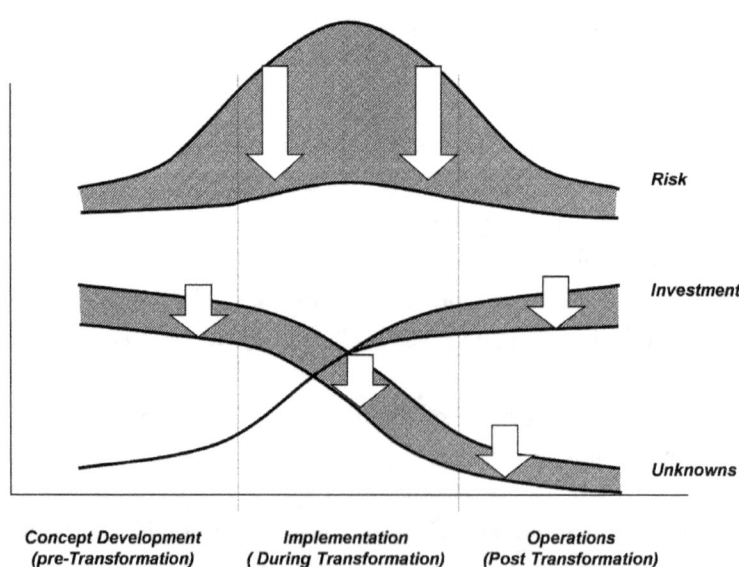

Figure 48. Reduced Transformation risk: Using analysis to disentangle cause and effect, reduce cost and uncertainty.

This provides crucial feedback to the other two CILS components. These feedback "loops," central to a "learning" organization, establish the connection to real-world challenges and results, thus refining and guiding the research model by providing necessary adjustments and enhancements, grounded in empirical evidence, to improve the accuracy and predictive power of systems simulation models. These feedback loops provide for a repository of lessons learned as well.

These four modeling approaches—multistage optimization, dynamic strategic planning, risk management, and program development—should be used in unified and complementary ways to constitute a dynamic strategic logistics planning (DSLP) capability. DSLP can take, as input, both the empirical evidence of ongoing operational evidence (real-world results) and also the potential contribution of new opportunities derived from an "engine for innovation" (experimental results) such as CILS, and then guide—as output—Logistics Transformation toward strategic goals and objectives: an efficient, increasingly effective, yet resilient global military supply network. Collectively, they constitute the "analytical architecture" needed to sustain continual improvement for Logistics Transformation (Figure 49).

One implementation option is to start with the Team Redstone community, leveraging and incorporating local organizational competencies and technology expertise.[3] Then, as subsequent success warrants, CILS capabilities and support could be expanded army-wide. A phased approach could progress as follows:

- Phase 1: Establish the CILS initially with sufficient resources to conduct "local" (e.g., aviation and missile) pilot tests, field experiments, empirically based modeling and simulation, and case studies to provide local program manager and U.S. Army Aviation and Missile Command (e.g., G-3, Integrated Materiel Management Center, G-8) customer support and to generate compelling analytical arguments for policy and business process changes.

- Phase 2: Pending demonstrable and significant results, expand CILS analytical core competencies and capacity to provide army-wide support across all PEOs and life-cycle management commands.

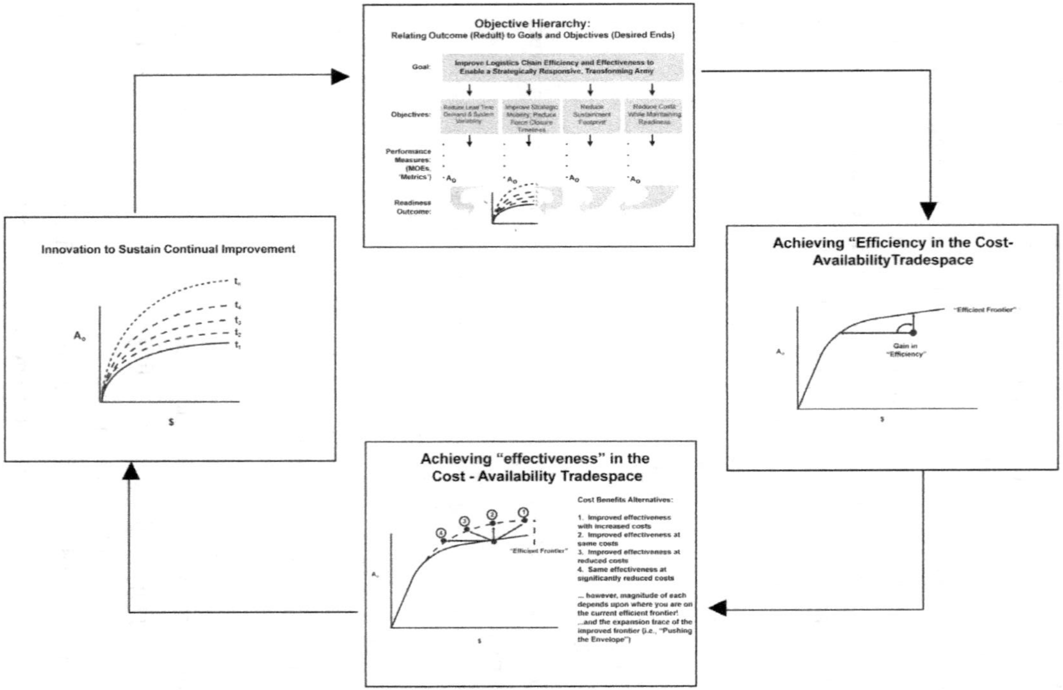

Figure 49. Sustaining innovation while linking execution to strategy.

- Phase 3: As momentum builds, success becomes widespread, and demand for CILS capabilities grows, expand further to support joint agencies and commands (e.g., MDA, U.S. NORTHCOM), and other U.S. government organizations (e.g., NASA, DHS).

The *2007 Army Modernization Plan* describes the need for institutional adaptation of the generating force, including a goal to "foster a *culture of innovation* to greatly increase institutional agility."[4] Nonetheless, since the army logistics community is a bureaucratic, highly complex social system, this laudable objective will likely remain empty rhetoric until sources of innovation exist for the culture to embrace. Together, CILS and DSLP provide a source for *management innovation* by building a capacity for low-risk, low-cost experimentation. This can be achieved using a synthetic environment where analytically rigorous cost-benefit analyses can be performed to differentiate between desirable objectives and attainable (affordable) ones that can actually be implemented. The purpose of this deliberative, cyclical process is to sustain continuous improvement through technology and *management innovation* achieved through experimentation, prototyping, field testing, and, especially, rigorous analysis.

Recently published research on institutionalizing innovation outlines the need for three key elements necessary to drive continuing improvement: (a) blueprints for growth, (b) innovation engines and systems, and (c) mind-sets. Funding innovation can be compared to managing investment funds comparing different types of projects with varying levels of risk. Creating the growth engine requires setting up a screening and development process to reduce uncertainty and an innovation structure that helps oversee high-potential, high-risk projects. Unless these elements are in place, new ideas tend to be modified to look like things the organization has done in the past, undermining the ability to pursue highly differentiated new strategies.[5]

Although admittedly ambitious, the approach outlined throughout these chapters in part IV aligns well with the three key elements of innovation success noted in the previous paragraph. When aggressively implemented, institutionalizing innovation for the army's supply chain enterprise becomes possible: (a) a "blueprint for growth" is provided by these analytical architectures and DSLP; (b) the "innovation engine" is the CILS capability to accelerate *management innovation*; and (c) a strategic culture, or mind-set, for embracing a genuine learning enterprise can be encouraged and developed as just described and further elaborated next in part V.

PART V

Management Concepts for Transformation

There is no lack of hi-tech, R&D vendors offering a quick fix, or consultants bombarding corporate offices to sell their services for guiding change. Yet in today's unsettled environment of confusion and anxiety there is a general lack of understanding of what needs to be done and how to accomplish it . . . You cannot visualize the future if your imagination is out of focus.

—Shoumen Datta, research director and cofounder, Forum for Supply Chain Innovation, Massachusetts Institute of Technology

Chapters

20. Organizational Redesign for Army Force Generation
21. Contributions of (Transactional) Information System Technology and (Analytical) Operations Research
22. Performance-Based Logistics and Capabilities-Based Planning for an Expeditionary Army
23. Financial Management Challenges to "Business Modernization"
24. Human Capital Investment for a Collaborative Enterprise
25. Strategic Management Concepts for a Learning Organization
26. Final Thoughts

Strategy is fundamentally about dealing with change—it represents the heart of management. Today, however, an honest appraisal suggests existing U.S. Army organizational structures, relationships, and logistics processes are collectively the product of decades of short-term work-arounds, ad hoc solutions, and periodic management fads but mostly inertia rather than disciplined strategic thinking. This pattern has been accompanied by archaic management policies, ossified organizational procedures, and persistent failure to challenge predisposed paradigms. Under increasing organizational pressure, the tendency toward reactive, ad hoc crises management has completely supplanted long-term strategy. Army logistics *management* has become sclerotic.

As with any complex, large-scale engineering systems challenge, key enabling concepts will be essential for successfully initiating, coordinating, and managing change. These concluding chapters address several organizational, analytical, information technology, cost accounting, and workforce-related strategic management issues and concerns that confront the army's ambitious, but absolutely essential, Logistics Transformation endeavor. Individually and collectively, they should all be guided by a clear understanding of the ultimate purpose for which the enterprise exists, an organizational vision for the future, and a supporting strategy to realize the vision (Figure 50).

This strategy must focus the effects of transformative change on capabilities-based, readiness-oriented outcomes. For logistics, the "ends-ways-means" strategy paradigm has not been routinely applied. Sporadic efforts have attempted to compensate for perceived inadequacies in means (resources) and ways, instead yielding reactive, narrowly focused responses attempting to Band-Aid yesterday's problems rather than focusing on the "ends"—generating mission readiness, which is the reason the entire enterprise exists.

"Management innovation as a strategic technology" (MIST), introduced in the preface as the fourth purpose for the book, is a new concept

Figure 50. Logistics transformation framework: Linking strategy to measurable results.

for transformational change in large-scale, complex, interdependent organizations that comprise an extended enterprise. Developed to provide a strategic management means for performance-driven organizational transformation in public sector and government institutions, the three conceptual building blocks for MIST include the following:

1. Data-driven, operations research–based, decision support systems
2. A transformational, rather than incremental, approach to strategic planning that is guided by an "engine for innovation"
3. An "integrated" management science to increase the likelihood for successful transformative change by enabling, rather than impeding, organizational implementation

The chapters in parts II and III, which derived and explained several catalysts for innovation oriented on three materiel enterprise performance objectives for efficiency, resilience, and effectiveness, addressed the first MIST building block. The chapters in part IV then developed both "dynamic strategic logistics planning" and an engine for innovation (CILS) as key enablers for transformational strategic planning—the second building block for MIST. These next chapters in part V now address the third building block for MIST, those enterprise implementation challenges including organization, information, financial, and workforce development considerations, which must all be "aligned" in the management of change process for Logistics Transformation.

Transformation will indeed require adjusting existing cultural paradigms, causing an inevitably disruptive period of significant change. Nonetheless, and despite the inexorable advance of technology, *it will be improved management and decision support systems that ultimately enable innovation potential to be realized.* Finally, this endeavor should embrace that of a learning organization. This will be a crucial enabler for sustaining continuous improvement.

CHAPTER 20

Organizational Redesign for Army Force Generation

We have increased the capacity of the Army, but it is being consumed as we build it.
—General Peter Schoomaker, Chief of Staff, Army, 2003–2007

The Department of Defense must take a hard look at every aspect of how it is organized, staffed, and operated.
—Robert M. Gates, Secretary of Defense, 8 May 2010

An honest and forthright postmortem begs the question: "Why has the state of army logistics become what it now is?" Two responses are offered here. First, external factors that are usually credited with driving significant change in business world supply chains during the past decade or more are not apparent, at least to the same degree, within the Department of Defense (DoD) logistics system. These external factors include greater competition resulting from both deregulation of business structures and increasing globalization; the adaptation of information technologies to new business process needs and opportunities; the so-called Wal-Mart effect causing a shift in the distribution channels toward tailored logistics, value-added services, alliances, and partnerships resulting in "everyday low prices"; and, of course, the increasing empowerment of the consumer.[1]

In contrast, while these same external factors were not forcing DoD, and the public sector more generally, to change as the private sector was changing, there were no compelling internal factors mandating change at the time either. Following the end of the Cold War and then the dramatic, lightning-quick Gulf War, the U.S. military was universally acknowledged and recognized as "top dog." There has been no incentive to change because, until recently, there was no clear evidence of either imminent or evident failure.

A second, complementary rather than competing explanation argues that, in retrospect, the military drawdown during the decade of the 1990s decimated the existing analytical brain trust of logistics-focused, military operations research/systems analysts within Army Materiel Command (AMC). Officer operations research/systems analysis authorizations (FA 49) declined from 55 in FY1989, including five colonels, to none by FY2000 and have remained at zero since then (Figure 51). Army civilians (GS 1515) also took a disproportionate share of cuts as well, declining from almost half of army-wide authorizations in FY1990 to less than a third by FY2002 (Figure 52). Nearly all of those who remain, however, are providing matrix customer support to program management offices as cost analysts.

In the case of the U.S. Army Aviation and Missile Command (AMCOM), no dedicated resources to support outsourcing logistics systems analysis, research, or studies had existed for over 5 years until this project was initiated. Even this effort was initially funded through working capital and competed directly with underfunded spare part procurement needs. Organizing the army logistics community for success must start with an appropriate investment in "analytical reconnaissance."

The organizational design for the operational army is now undergoing significant change, more than at any other time during the past half century. This ongoing transition from traditional division-based operations toward a "modular" brigade-based design has been given increased impetus due to multiple overseas deployments for both active and reserve land force units engaged in Global War on Terror operations. This sustained, high demand for army and U.S. Marine Corps units—in an era now characterized as "persistent conflict"—obviously was not foreseen or expected during the 5 decades of the Cold War. If major combat between global superpowers had occurred then, it was expected to be initially conventional and intense, possibly escalating to nuclear weapons, but then resolved in a relatively short period following a horrific, spasmodic clash of titans. The "tiered readiness" organization construct served us well during the Cold War by providing a structured basis for allocating constrained resources. Its limitations, however, have now become apparent given the sustained stress on ground forces during this "long war." So in addition to developing the modular brigade force structure, the army is simultaneously transitioning from tiered readiness to a "rotational

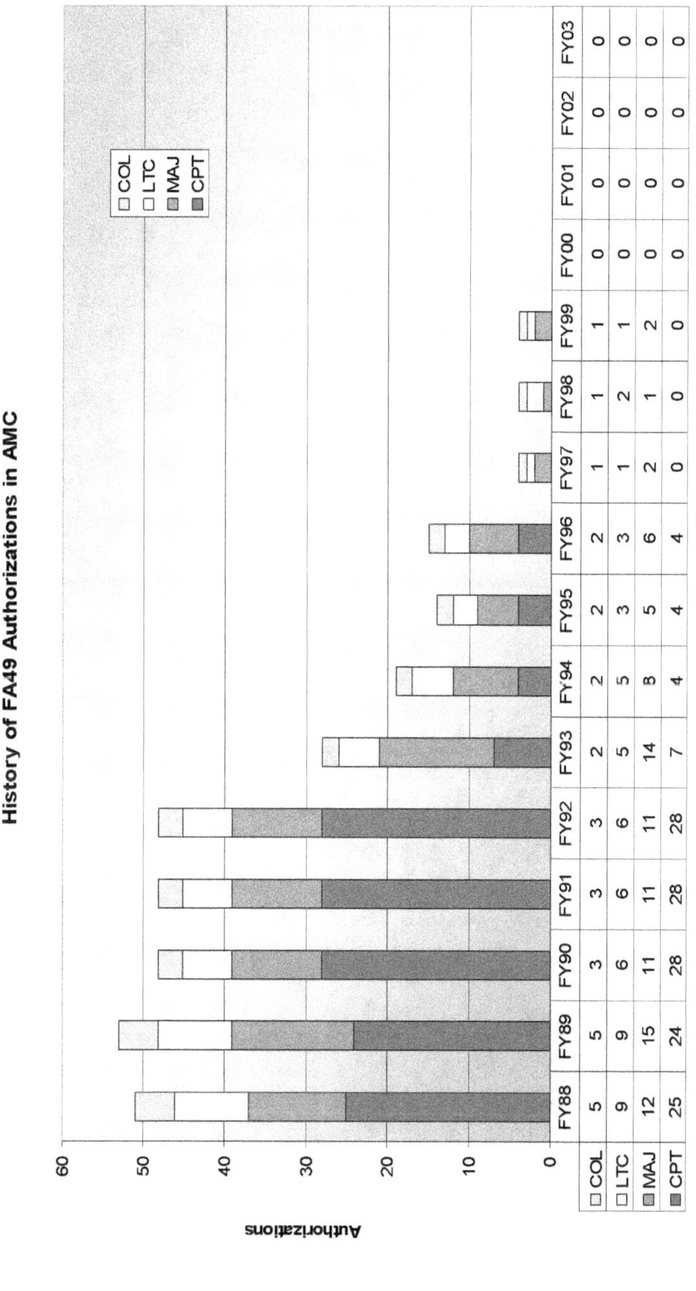

ORGANIZATIONAL REDESIGN FOR ARMY FORCE GENERATION 173

Figure 51. Officer ORSA Strength in Army Materiel Command (AMC).

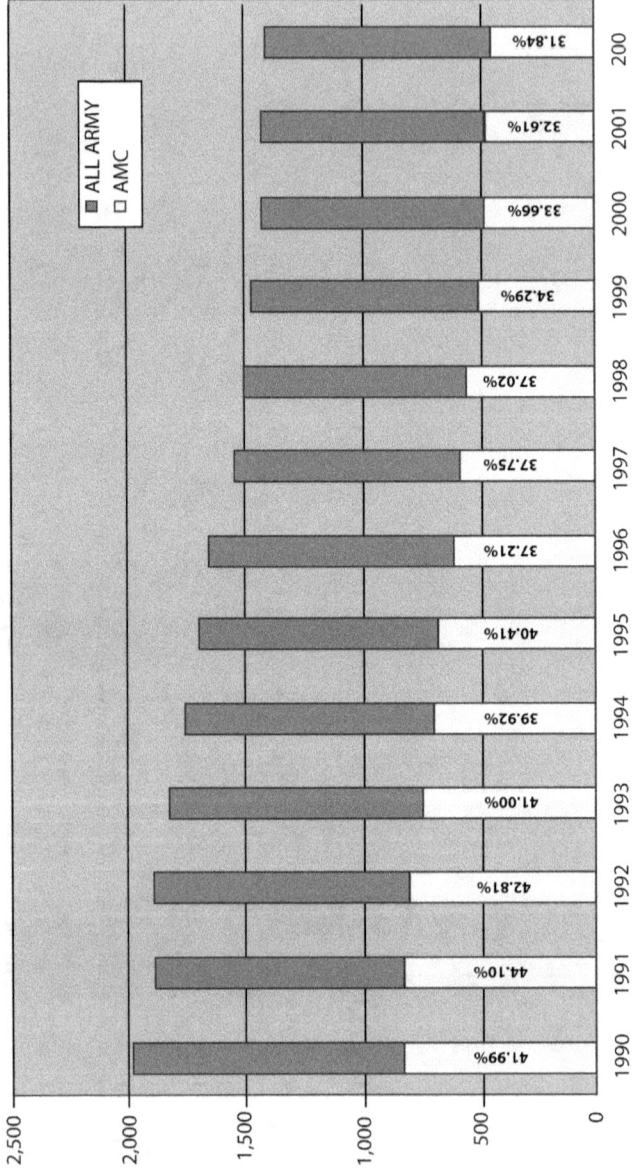

Figure 52. Civilian ORSA Strength in AMC.

readiness" force management concept described in recent years as the Army Force Generation (ARFORGEN) model.

The *2007 Army Modernization Plan* describes ARFORGEN as

> the structured progression of increased readiness over time, resulting in recurring periods of availability of trained, ready, and cohesive units prepared for operational deployment in support of combatant commander requirements. The goal is to achieve a sustained, more predictable posture to generate trained and ready forces, tailored to meet Joint requirements more effectively and efficiently. These operational requirements drive the ARFORGEN training and readiness process which, in turn, supports the prioritization and synchronization of institutional functions to resource, recruit, man, equip, train, sustain, source, mobilize, and deploy cohesive units.[2]

ARFORGEN is also guiding the transition of the reserve component (the U.S. Army Reserve and the Army National Guard) from a strategic reserve to an operational force. The modular design and cyclical management concept of the generating force are critical components of the overall army transformation strategy. Increasingly, ARFORGEN is viewed as a "control policy" for managing and regulating the recurring, cyclical life cycle for operational forces.

At the same time, efforts are underway to better align the institutional army (the generating force) to support the operational army (the operating force). The importance of clearly understanding the readiness equation and implementing readiness-based sparing (RBS) becomes even more critically important under ARFORGEN. Requirements to incorporate both the Army Recapitalization Program and RESET initiatives into the ARFORGEN process, and the need to allocate and shift resources based on unit mission priorities and deployment schedules, are all major challenges that will require, and benefit tremendously from, comprehensive analytical capabilities. Such a capability will become increasingly essential to enable leaders and managers to effectively manage and synchronize these very complex activities.

Previously, in part II we identified several "catalysts for innovation" emerging from the root-cause analyses to reduce supply-side variability and demand uncertainty—the proximate causes of the notorious "bullwhip effect." These include the "readiness equation" (chapter 5), "mission-based forecasting" (chapter 6), "readiness-based sparing" (chapter 7), and "readiness responsive retrograde" (chapter 8). These "catalysts for innovation" can now be combined to create "integration opportunities" for the materiel enterprise. For example, combining the "readiness equation" with RBS and MBF can provide a means for aligning and synchronizing logistics support consistent with the new ARFORGEN force management process (Figure 53).

So far, examining isolated contributions from each of these catalysts, we have seen significant potential for improvement that, extrapolated across the army, could likely yield hundreds of millions of dollars in efficiencies while simultaneously achieving more cost-effective operations. However, in addition to linking logistics support to operational forces in order to produce desired, mission-focused readiness outcomes, combining these catalysts can yield synergistic effects where the efficiencies resulting from their implementation become multiplicative rather than merely additive across the materiel enterprise. And with new integrated management practices, such as DSLP described in part IV, the potential magnitude for improvement is truly dramatic—tens of billions of dollars in further savings are likely, and more importantly, it becomes possible to relate investment levels to current readiness and future capabilities.

The emerging need to better align the institutional army to accommodate the operational army's transition from tiered-readiness to rotational readiness under ARFORGEN has resulted in several new logistics support organizations and concepts. These include the recent creation of AMC's Army Sustainment Command (ASC) and the reorganization of U.S. Army logistics support activity into support "channels." The purpose of ASC, operating through its subordinate theater support commands (TSCs), is to provide improved integration and logistics support for deployed, deploying, and training forces and to better link the "industrial army"—the civil-military sustaining base—to the "operational army."

Additionally, the ongoing effort to merge previously separate acquisition program management offices (which report by law to the army acquisition executive—the Assistant Secretary of the Army for Acquisition, Logistics, and Technology)—with sustainment commodity commands (which are subordinate organizations in AMC) into new life-cycle

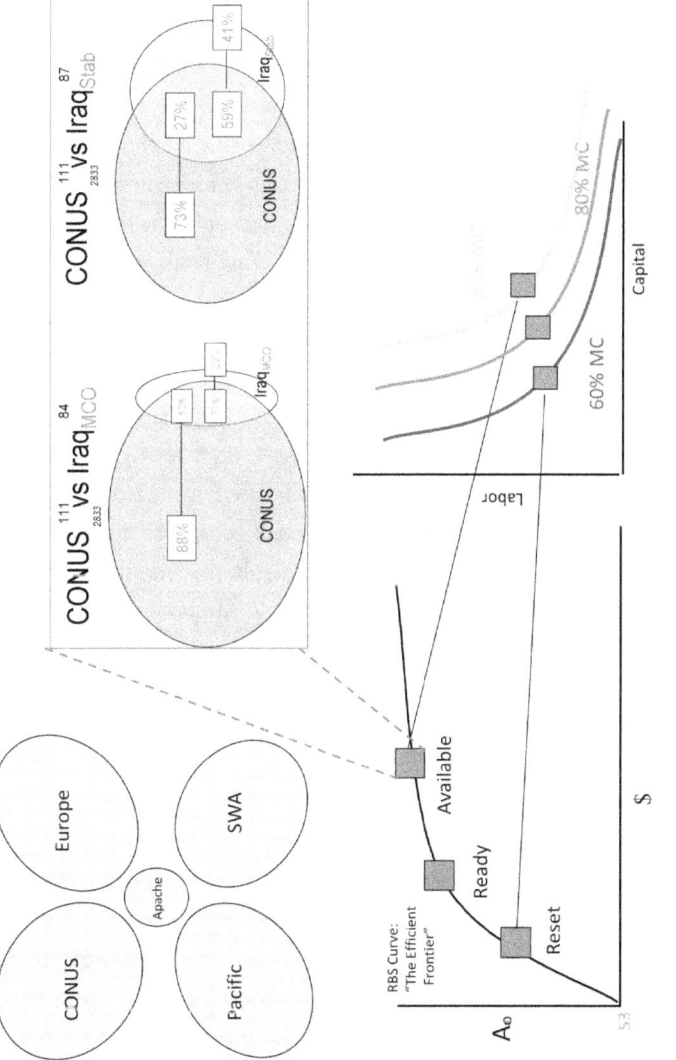

Figure 53. ARFORGEN Synchronization using RBS and MBF.

management commands (LCMCs) better supports the as-yet-unrealized concept of "life-cycle management."[3] Transforming existing materiel management centers from managing supply levels for individual items to managing readiness for weapon systems would be consistent with, indeed necessary for, implementation of a multiechelon RBS approach.

Consequently, previous objectives that emphasized managing individual items to supply-side interface metrics, such as supply availability and fill rate, can now be replaced by *managing the entire supply system to weapon system readiness-focused output.* Additionally, this would better enable performance-based logistics by realigning organizational structure toward the desired goal of relating policies, investment levels, and management focus at the wholesale and retail levels to readiness-oriented outcomes. In a system where there has been *no* accountability for enterprise-wide performance, this is a significant step toward bringing together previously separate, diverse groups to form collaborative teams with a shared purpose driving toward common goals.

The shortfall in depot-level reparable surge repair capacity in the existing Aviation Classification Repair Activity Depot (AVCRAD) organizational design and mission concept, discussed previously in the wholesale-stage section in chapter 9, is now both evident and recognized. A new capabilities document for a "Mobile Aircraft Sustainment Maintenance Capability" (MASMC) was recently processed through the Joint Requirements Oversight Council validation and approval milestones. This new concept emphasizes the versatility for both a sea-based and land-based capacity to better and more responsively support an expeditionary capability, especially during the initial deployment phase when seaports or airports may not exist or become available.

In fact, historical precedent exists for this sea-based concept: U.S. Naval Ship *Corpus Christi Bay* was used as a floating aviation maintenance and repair platform off the coast of Vietnam from 1966 to 1975. And the U.S. Marine Corps, traditionally an expeditionary force, maintains two aviation logistics support ships for aviation maintenance and repair support to the Marine Expeditionary Forces (MEFs). Resurrecting such a concept today would also be consistent with our evolution toward more robust sea-basing as a practical response to the growing number of nuclear-armed regional powers where mobile offshore logistics support can better be defended against possible theater ballistic and cruise missile attacks.

As the new MASMC concept is reviewed and evolves, consideration should be given to adopting a force structure for the supporting multipurpose aviation sustainment brigades (the replacement AVCRADs) similar to the U.S. Army Special Forces concept. Both active and reserve special forces groups are similarly organized but then tailored, trained, (e.g., foreign language training), and then deploy to conduct support operations in specific regions of the world. In the case of the MASMC, the concept of operation would associate each of five MASMC brigades with the five corresponding regional combatant commands: U.S. European Command (and the new U.S. Africa Command), U.S. Pacific Command, U.S. Southern Command, U.S. Central Command, and the newly formed U.S. Northern Command (NORTHCOM).

Given the current pace of global operations, this concept would enable habitual association and command relationships to develop. Again using the special forces model as a concept of operation, special expertise, modifications to MASMC brigade organization (which should be table of organization and equipment [TOE] rather than table of distribution and allowances [TDA] as the AVCRADs are), and capabilities peculiar to the operating conditions or special challenges faced by aviation support operations within each unified command can better be accommodated.

In the case of NORTHCOM, both the homeland defense (NORTHCOM itself) and homeland security (Department of Homeland Security) missions will continue to require National Guard aviation support requirements that have imposed additional demand that could not have been anticipated in the original Aviation Depot Maintenance Roundout Unit-AVCRAD concept, which dates to 1979. This MASMC concept of operation would then provide for more immediate and sustained support to each of the regional combatant commands and a dedicated brigade to support the increased demands of homeland defense and security. Additional flexibility and capacity would then be available within nondeployed brigades to support sporadic surge requirements or other deployed brigades in either a rotational or reinforcing mode to sustain extended operations.

Finally, yet particularly urgent, creation of a chief knowledge officer (CKO) and supporting office of resource managers, logistics systems analysts, operations researchers, and strategic planners would provide the knowledge and talent base to develop, measure, and monitor programs with supporting metrics that link strategy to measurable results. To fully comprehend the effects of promising new technologies and methods on the existing logistics system, the current system's previous path, defined by history, organization, process, and culture, along with its directional momentum—the "hysteresis" of the system—matters and must be understood.

While vision drives organizational goals, objectives, and missions ("Where are we going?"), core competencies heavily influence both organizational processes and structure ("How do we function and organize to get there?"). For army logistics, this crucial core competency, logistics systems analysis, is central to understanding what is happening, what is likely to happen, and why. Knowledge must be continually extracted from the system's hysteresis to encourage innovation and sustain organizational improvement.[4]

Within existing military organizational structures, this source of information collection, analytical capability, and knowledge creation is sometimes found in program analysis and evaluation organizations and, within joint staff (J-staff) and army general staff (G-staff) structures, in J-8 or G-8 high-level staff directorates. This logistics systems analysis capability, if viewed as a core competency, could also reside in a separate army center of excellence. For supply management policy, the nucleus for such a center once existed in the form of the original Army Inventory Research Office, which was abolished in the early 1990s as an early victim of the post–Cold War drawdown.

The proposed Center for Innovation in Logistics Systems (CILS), described in chapter 19, could resurrect and extend this much-needed competency. At last three different organizational constructs could be considered: (a) a public-private partnership, (b) a "distributed" model, and (c) an "enterprise transformation" concept. One option is to follow the navy's lead. In 2005, congressional funding was provided to establish a new Naval Logistics Readiness Research Center. The organization is a navy public-private partnership with both academic institutions and commercial firms and is focused on resolving many of the longstanding Government Accountability Office–noted deficiencies by developing new models, systems, and approaches to enhance and improve readiness affordability, including implementation of multiechelon optimization applications for the naval supply system. For the army, the nucleus of such a partnership could be the existing Army Materiel Systems Analysis

Activity (AMSAA) within AMC's Research, Development, and Engineering Command (RDECOM).

A second, distributed construct would be to create requisite CILS capabilities using assets and resources from within existing army organizations. Under this concept, supply chain simulation, modeling, and analysis expertise could be developed within RDECOM's subordinate research and development centers for their habitually supported acquisition program offices and commodity commands. For example, in the specific case of the army's aviation and missile communities, this construct would include (a) the Aviation and Missile Research, Development, and Engineering Center (AMRDEC) for scientific and technical support in modeling, simulation, and analysis; (b) the program management offices under both PEO Aviation and PEO Missile for system life-cycle management; and (c) the AMCOM IMMC, G-3, and G-8 for functional logistics, cost analysis, and resource management expertise. AMSAA could also provide augmentation as needed in a "reachback" capacity. This construct integrates well into the new LCMC concept and further extends the traditional relationship that program managers have had with research, development, and engineering centers on the "front end" of the life cycle (concept design and engineering development "pre–Milestone C") into the sustainment phase of the life cycle, or "post–Milestone C."

A third organizational design option would be to create a new analytical Center of Excellence as a separate agency reporting to HQ, AMC, but also aligned under the new Army Business Transformation Office. This option would accommodate recent congressional mandates to establish "Chief Management Officers" in DoD to improve and transform "business operations" while also aligning with the army's newly configured "enterprise" management concept consisting of four core enterprise operations which correspond to the Army's Title 10 responsibilities: human capital, materiel, readiness, and services and infrastructure. This Materiel Enterprise center for analytical excellence and innovation could also serve as a prototype for organizational design, integration, and collaboration for each of the other core enterprise endeavors as well.

Alternatively, if logistics systems analysis is recognized as needed but not deemed a core competency it could be "outsourced." If this view prevails, then an option would be to create a responsive and durable, mutually convenient relationship with a consortium of partners and expertise that could be utilized as needed. The air force has very effectively followed this construct over the years with strong relationships between the Air Force Logistics Management Agency, the Logistics Management Institute (until recently a federally funded research development center, and now a not-for-profit organization), and the Air Force Institute of Technology (co-located with the air force's materiel and logistics support command at Wright-Patterson Air Force Base in Dayton, Ohio).

While many of the structural barriers to integrated supply chain management are organizational, limiting Logistics Transformation to these planned and suggested redesigns of current organization and force structure, while necessary, will undoubtedly prove insufficient. Both organization *and process* must follow strategy.

CHAPTER 21

Contributions of (Transactional) Information System Technology and (Analytical) Operations Research

We need to alleviate the collection of useless data and information. Too many bureaucratic layers managing unnecessary information continue to exist because "that's the way we've always done it." We need to collect only that information that adds value to the decision making process.

—General Paul Kern, Commanding General, Army Materiel Command

What matters most is what the data means . . . Information is most certainly not wisdom . . . The transformation of information into knowledge has in fact represented an intractable and almost unsolvable problem that has not significantly improved over the past half-century. Masses of information tend to obscure what commanders need to know.

—Major General Robert H. Scales, former commandant,
Army War College, from *Yellow Smoke*

Operations Research has also gradually lost much of its original empirical focus; modeling is now chiefly a deductive undertaking, with little systematic effort to test deductive claims against real world evidence.

—Stephen Biddle, *Military Power*

The historical record reminds us that the basic principles of the conduct of OR are enduring.

—Sir Keith O'Nions, chief scientific advisor, United Kingdom Ministry of Defence

Obviously, military supply chain management is extremely complex and there is no simple or cheap "solution" to the many challenges and issues illuminated in this book. For many businesses in the corporate world, efforts to install and implement enterprise resource planning (ERP) systems have proven unexpectedly difficult, costly, and time-consuming. Their experience suggests that the army should also be cautious when pursuing so-called information technology (IT) solutions. It is crucial to differentiate between the purpose and functions of operations research (OR)—which comprises knowledge-based decision support systems (DSS)—and transaction-based ERP technology that is concerned with acquiring and processing raw data and the compilation and communication of reports. While effort required to replace a legacy management *system* may be considerable, overcoming barriers to legacy *thinking* about supply chain decision making—the "analytical" component—is a more difficult and challenging task, since it requires overcoming cultural and organizational barriers to achieve fact-based decision making.[1]

Basically, an ERP system is a grouping of software modules that interface with a common database. The purpose of these modules is primarily oriented on monitoring routine transactions, making an ERP a sophisticated, responsive accounting system. However, ERP "solutions" were increasingly advertised and sold as a panacea for all kinds of corporate decision-making processes. Nonetheless, they lack the analytical capabilities needed to optimize the efficiency of those transaction-oriented processes.[2] While ERP systems provide considerable visibility into "what just happened?" they provide very little insight into "why?"; even less about "what is likely to happen?"; and certainly nothing about "what should happen?" if current conditions either continue or change. As Massachusetts Institute of Technology Professor Jeremy Shapiro has observed, "Enterprise Resource Planning (ERP) is really a misnomer because it fails to provide insights into decisions affecting 'resource planning.'"[3]

As numerous case studies have noted, ERP implementations expose problems with existing organizational processes. All too often, disaster is courted (and occurs) when ERP "solutions" are undertaken without a comprehensive understanding of these outdated or even inappropriate underlying processes. The clear lesson drawn from these many case studies is that an ERP implementation is first and foremost an organizational management challenge to create *new* business-process designs and only secondarily to install software systems to support those new designs.[4] In the Army's case, the focus of ERP implementation to date has been on replicating current management approaches and processes rather than using information systems in ways that facilitate strategic change.

In contrast, OR has been defined as the "science and technology of decision making." Its historical roots can be traced to multidisciplinary teams applying several scientific methods to military operations during the early years of World War II. The term "operational research" was actually invented in 1937 by a team of British scientists who were then assisting UK Ministry of Defence military leaders, including Air Chief Marshall Hugh Dowding, Head of Fighter Command for the Royal Air Force (RAF). Subsequently, they also supported RAF Coastal Command and the British Army's Anti-Aircraft Command.[5] Their purpose was to gain the maximum possible benefit from applying newly invented radar to the detection of aircraft during the Battle of Britain early in World War II after the fall of France. In these nascent years, historians referred to OR as "a revolution in management science, risk assessment, and military planning."[6]

For several years following World War II, the British Operational Research Society defined OR as

> the application of the methods of science to complex problems arising in the direction and management of large systems of men, machines, materials and money in industry, business, government and defence. The distinctive approach is to develop a scientific model of the system, incorporating measurement of factors such as chance and risk, with which to predict and compare the outcomes of alternative decisions, strategies, or controls. The purpose is to help management determine its policy and actions scientifically.[7]

Later, OR gradually became recognized as the discipline of applying advanced analytic and modeling frameworks for dealing with complexity and uncertainty, especially in large-scale systems and organizations. Utilizing principles from mathematics, engineering, business, computer science, economics, and statistics, OR has developed into a full-fledged academic discipline with practical applications in business, industry, government, and the military. Its purpose is to assist managers and executives with their decision-making processes by furnishing insight and guidance on complicated management issues using advanced analysis to interpret information and create knowledge. In essence, it is about the creation and management of productivity gain and thus has been described as the "productivity gain engine" used to help organizations achieve their full potential.

A recent article published by INFORMS, the professional organization for OR and management science, describes OR as follows:

To raise the question of improvement in an organization's productivity without taking full advantage of all that OR offers would be analogous to pursuing a required improvement in one's health while ignoring the entire medical community. The realm of OR is productivity gain.[8]

Hopefully, this medical analogy, introduced at the beginning of chapter 1, is evident in both the use of supply chain concepts to help "diagnose" root causes, offer a set of genuine "prescriptions" to cure the underlying "illness," then fully heal army logistics. As this medical analogy would suggest, it is very difficult to treat a disease if it is misdiagnosed or confused with its symptoms: If misdiagnosed, then the wrong illness is treated; if the symptoms that are masking the underlying causes are treated, then a cure cannot be affected. And importantly, a defining feature of OR is its strong advocacy of multidisciplinary approaches, recognizing that no one scientific discipline is adequate to effectively deal with the complexity inherent in real-world problems.

Recently, the phrase "the science of better" has been adopted by INFORMS. Its professional conferences and workshops continue to focus on a worrisome trend occurring in large-scale, complex organizations. Without reengineering business processes using the analytical, integrative power of OR, the growing obsession with IT may result in increasingly complex systems that exceed the interpretive capacities of the organizations responsible for developing and using them—an example of an "ingenuity gap" that is described later in chapter 24. IT "solutions" now have ubiquitous appeal with enormous investment levels to substantiate this growing, widespread trend. Driven by increasing awareness and recognition that effective management of the entire supply chain can lead to sustainable competitive advantages in the corporate sector, it is nonetheless remarkable how small the percentage of such successful firms actually is.

One recent major research effort focused on attempting to better understand what may be causing this result and to identify those supply chain transformative strategies that differentiate the few successful firms from the many that are not. This research, involving case studies of 60 companies and 75 different supply chains, attempted to determine whether or not there is a direct correlation between business process "maturity," IT infrastructure and investment levels, and supply chain performance. The experimental design was unique in that it enabled empirical results to differentiate cause and effect: Could financial performance results be attributed to improvements in business processes, IT investment levels, neither, or both? The research was designed to empirically determine the characteristics that enable high-performing businesses to consistently outperform their peers over the long term.

The results, not surprisingly, indicated those companies with existing appropriate, mature business processes (directly related to the firm's long-term strategy and business objectives) that invested in IT "solutions" enjoyed significant operational performance improvements and financial profitability. Amazingly though, this result occurred in less than 10% on the companies evaluated. Conversely, those companies that focused on reengineering business processes without implementing associated IT "solutions" were not nearly as successful as those who did yet still improved performance by more than 25%. Finally, the truly illuminating and surprising result from these commercial case analyses was the realization that those companies that tended to substitute IT "solutions" as surrogates for necessary business process reengineering not only failed to achieve returns on their IT investments but also *declined* in relative performance as well (Figure 54).[9]

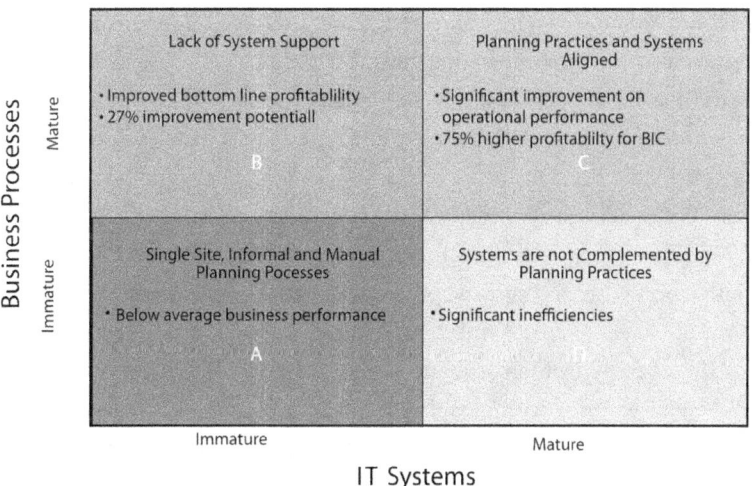

Figure 54. Linking processes and systems with operational and financial performance.

Numerous efforts are also underway to transform supply chains within the government. One relatively successful effort involves the $2.3 billion defense medical logistics community, which has been ongoing for nearly 15 years. In addition to considerable success and several accolades, including the Hammer Award in 1998, several challenges have been documented as major concerns and lessons learned. Although business process reengineering was officially a prime objective from program inception, it was not clear who had ownership of the effort. According to case study results, many managers tended to allow technology to drive the reengineering effort or were tempted to simply automate existing processes rather than improve the process *before* applying the best technology. Several program managers were pressured to produce results quickly and only performed cursory business process reengineering (BPR) efforts, and risk-averse managers were reluctant to invest in outcomes they would then be obligated to achieve within a bureaucratic organization with diffuse responsibilities.[10] These observations are indeed instructive for the Army Materiel Command today, given the enormous investment in the Logistics Modernization Plan and the larger Single Army Logistics Enterprise initiatives.

Driven by various forms of information systems and decision technologies, the accumulating evidence from supply chain transformation experiences is now clear. Empirical studies have consistently shown that supply chain improvement projects, even when implemented with the best information systems tools, have not produced desired or expected results without accompanying business process changes. The business world has come to realize that investments in new IT systems, without first examining and implementing needed business process changes, simply automate existing inefficiencies resulting in negligible benefits. Process "rationalization" initiatives (discrete reengineering efforts) and IT integration, when combined for example in ERP "solutions," *may* reduce transaction costs and provide other logistics savings. Conversely, they are far more likely to create "information glut."

Increasingly in the corporate world, the term "business intelligence" (BI) is used to encompass both "analytics" and the data processes and technologies used for collecting, managing, and reporting decision-oriented information. The BI architecture is an umbrella term for an enterprise-wide set of systems, applications, and governance processes that enable sophisticated analytics by allowing information and analyses to follow to those who need it, when they need it. "Analytics," as a subset of BI, refers to the extensive use of data, statistics, and quantitative algorithms for descriptive (explanatory), predictive (forecasting), and prescriptive (optimization) analyses essential to drive decisions and actions for fact-based, "analytic" management.

As Thomas Davenport and Jeanne Harris observe in their popular book, *Competing on Analytics: The New Science of Winning*, analytic management is often impeded by organizational pathologies: Conventional wisdom crowds out critical thinking; high-level managers fail to demand rigor and dispassionate analysis; and organizations lack the capacity for empirical work. What is needed is an analytical process that leads to insight, refinement, and better decision-making capacity.

Nonetheless, since the idea of "competing" on analytics is relatively new, the theoretical development and empirical studies needed to link comprehensive analytical approaches to business performance as a whole is still relatively immature. Two comprehensive studies of large organizations using ERP systems completed in 2002 and 2006 revealed that better decision making was the primary benefit sought. The focus on managing data became increasingly important as huge data sets were becoming available from information systems such as ERP and point of sale (POS), and later from Internet-based transaction systems. Consequently, by the time the 2006 study was completed, "analytics" was the technology most sought to take advantage of the ERP data.

Vision and analytics should not be seen as mutually exclusive paradigms. Rather, analytics should link organizational vision to operational results by defining and monitoring metrics that are tied to strategic enterprise objectives and aligning incentives with business objectives. We should also be wary of so-called IT solutions, as well as ERP modifications and "custom code" to replicate outmoded and obsolete business models—these are all common failings. Rather, ERP and POS management information systems (MIS) must be "connected" to "analytics," or analytically based decision support system capabilities. What is needed is a symbiotic—not merely complementary—relationship between DSS and MIS to fully capitalize on the promise of BI.

Hence, for large-scale complex organizations, the greatest return on investment is derived from the creation and implementation of new decision support systems incorporating analytically based forecasting, planning, and optimization technologies. Ultimately, it is this *management innovation* approach that will enable senior leaders and managers to generate knowledge and better decisions from the growing amounts of information and improved situational awareness made available by advances in information systems technologies. Thus as mounting evidence suggests, the source of real advantage is not obtained merely by procuring information technology "solutions" (e.g., ERP) but in the business model itself and organizational ability to convert information into insight and actionable decision options (Figure 55).[11]

Author and London Business School professor Gary Hamel, in his recent book *The Future of Management*, observes that although modern management was invented to solve the problem of *in*efficiency, our progress to date has been constrained by our bureaucracy-based paradigm:

> Much has been written on why companies are slow to change, and how bureaucracies stifle new thinking. The real challenge, though, is not diagnostic but rather therapeutic. We know a great deal about why large companies are incompetent at certain things, yet

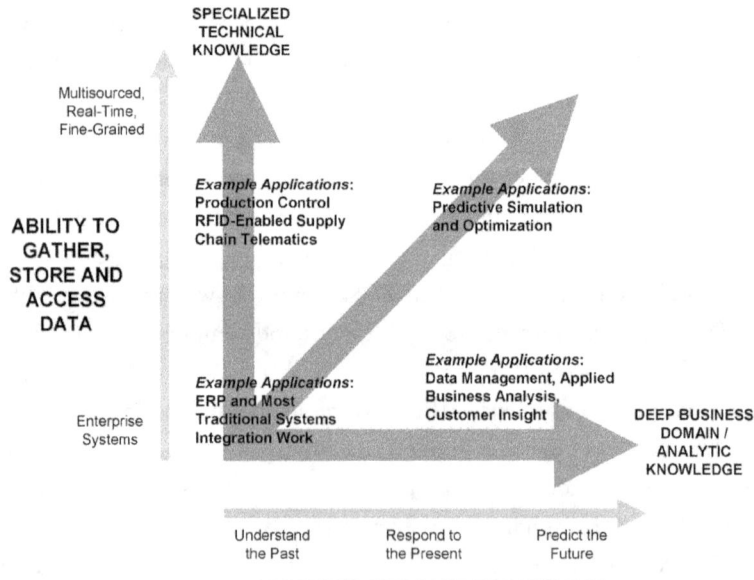

Figure 55. The evolution of insight.

despite this abundant advice and admonition, few seem to have overcome these limitations. *What's lacking is truly bold and imaginative alternatives to the management status quo.*[12]

In summary, army logistics policy makers and supply chain managers have not yet properly conceptualized management modernization efforts to genuinely reflect a performance-oriented focus. What has been lacking is a comprehensive strategy and implementation plan incorporating effective decision support analytical tools (OR) *with* the appropriate IT required to enable and provide the decision support needed to achieve cost-effective, performance-oriented results. The goal should be effective integration of analytics into organizational decision making.

Certainly crucial to this analytically based, decision support capability is the need for an IT-based infrastructure to provide real-time visibility into the relevant data flows and information transactions throughout the network. An effective DSS must also include solution algorithms that are fast and responsive to changes across the global logistics network and that illuminate actionable decision options. This DSS capability must be linked (e.g., using application program interface technology) to an underlying transaction-based IT ERP. This enabling, "knowledge-based" DSS would be capable of providing feasible, meaningful decision options by incorporating those system-wide objectives described previously: efficiency, resilience, and effectiveness (Figure 56).

Recognizing these needs and then developing the capacity to achieve them are the first steps toward *management innovation* for the U.S. Army materiel enterprise.

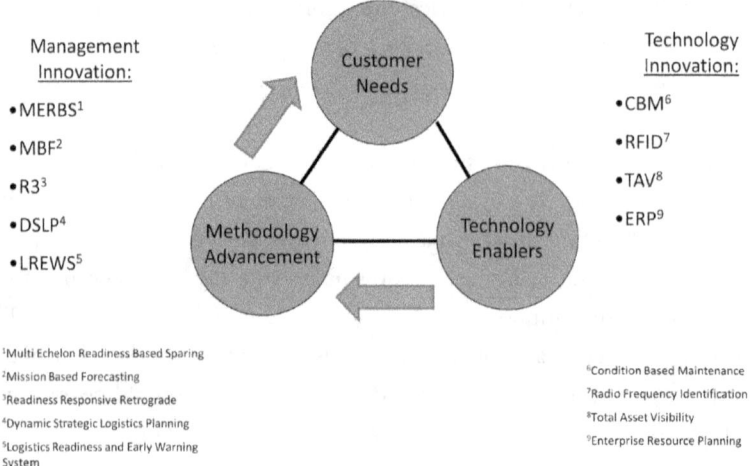

Figure 56. *Management innovation for improved decision-making.*

CHAPTER 22

Performance-Based Logistics and Capabilities-Based Planning for an Expeditionary Army[1]

In Performance-Based Logistics, forecasting is everything.

—Ray Figueras, director for product support, The Boeing Company

Spanning nearly a half-century now, the genealogy of Department of Defense (DoD) acquisition reform movements is extensive. Among those many management initiatives focused on improving system support performance and reducing costs have been integrated logistics support, value engineering, design-to-cost, total quality management, contractor logistics support, focused logistics, enterprise resource planning, and most recently for the U.S. Army, Lean Six Sigma. While the objective has been fairly constant over recent decades—efficient allocation of resources to sustain readiness objectives—methods for achieving this result have varied but remain disappointing.

For example, the Defense Logistics Agency's Business System Modernization program is the sixth attempt in the last 20 years to change organizational business processes. Nonetheless, operations and support cost growth has continued to plague all the armed services, especially the army where billion-dollar shortfalls in obligation authority have caused component and part shortages resulting in reduced readiness for many major systems. Furthermore, tactical user community distrust with the supply support system leads to labor-intensive work-arounds and local "solutions" that, over time, induce even greater complications, inefficiencies, and costs. Finally, military logistics supply chains are inherently complex with overlapping functions—material, information, and financial flows—spanning several independently operating organizational stages that collectively compose the logistics support structure and system (Figure 5).

With so many organizations and agencies having authority over their respective functions and operations, accountability for integrating system-wide performance across all these "jurisdictions" has been nonexistent. As a former Army Materiel Command commanding general observed, "No single manager performs the oversight, anticipatory, integrative role as a fleet manager."[2] The following perspective is representative, insightful, and relevant to these ongoing challenges:

> We have gone through Total Quality Management, reinvention and reengineering, downsizing and rightsizing, along with the revolution in information technology. Now people are asking us to take on process improvement, performance management, balanced scorecards, knowledge management, and who knows what else? We face so many conflicting demands we need to figure out what our focus and priorities should be. How can we make sure all of this effort is headed in the right direction?[3]

The resulting consequence of this chronic lack of accountability, described in this quote, has been an inability to generate an adequate sense of urgency for institutional change. This inability to build momentum for positive improvement has resulted in bureaucratic paralysis. However, this effect should not be confused with "risk averse" behavior that is frequently attributed to senior officials who have lengthy, significant investments within their institutional environments. In contrast, by failing to change they are actually incurring greater risk, certainly not less. Since they do not have the analytical tools needed to generate the compelling arguments for change needed to illuminate and reduce risk, paralysis sets in. This result commonly afflicts large, complex, hierarchical organizations. It is also consistent with bureaucratic "inertia," which has proven difficult to overcome or redirect when crises occur and failures, sometimes catastrophic, loom imminent.

It might also be argued that continuing with the tried and true is usually safer than attempting the new and untested. But this argument incorrectly equates "newness" with "riskiness." Risk is a function of uncertainty and its consequences, whereas newness is a function of the extent to which an idea lacks precedent or counters existing convention. However, novelty implies nothing about risk. This persistent failure to distinguish between new ideas and risky ideas also reinforces the tendency to "overinvest" in the past.[4]

The most recent official response to address these challenges is the concept of performance-based logistics (PBL), which was recently mandated by DoD Directive 5000.1 in May 2003. PBL, a management approach that encourages outsourcing logistics support functions, endeavors to prescribe and fix accountability to a single system fleet manager (the program manager, or PM) by focusing on system performance outputs and readiness goals (rather than inputs and interface metrics), and reduce system life-cycle costs. Fundamentally, PBL emphasizes the proposition that the private sector, given appropriate incentives, can outperform government agencies in managing activities that are of a fundamentally industrial kind, hence not "inherently governmental." In the private sector, the term "product support" has been used to describe a similar management philosophy of providing cost-effective maintenance and repair parts support to customers. PBL attempts to engage industry more completely throughout the life cycle of managing systems support and sustainment by giving industry partners a financial stake and incentive to maintain required readiness at minimum overall cost.

If PBL can be successfully implemented, then DoD and the armed services may have found a way to fix accountability for sustainment performance (i.e., the "post–Milestone C" phase of the acquisition life cycle). The belief is that by using commercial and organic logistics providers who are now working for PMs, performance agreements can be developed and implemented that effectively align logistics provider incentives to PM readiness-oriented goals. In so doing, the goal is to both fix accountability and improve performance—objectives that have been elusive despite the long genealogy of DoD reforms and initiatives mentioned earlier.

However, developing appropriate metrics and meaningful incentives for PBL-based performance agreements constitutes a new venture for DoD. As the army transitions from traditional support methods to PBL, program managers and supporting life-cycle management commands need to continuously monitor supply chain performance to ensure policy and process changes achieve desired results. Currently, however, inadequate analytical capacity exists to relate different investment levels, policy initiatives, and innovative processes to capabilities-based performance outcomes.

The challenge is one of crafting and selecting incentives for the logistics provider within a contract logistics support (CLS) contract so that both buyer and seller objectives can be met. The buyer—the army's PM—has a constrained budget within which global, fleet-wide system readiness and performance goals must be met. The seller—the commercial logistics support provider—is obligated to achieve results specified in the contract but must do so while also making a profit. Thus the CLS provider has a contract-based incentive to maximize profit while the PM must meet or exceed readiness requirements and performance objectives for his weapon system. To accommodate both objectives, the CLS provider's profit maximizing conditions must be aligned with the PM's readiness objectives in the performance agreement specifications.

Since profit is maximized for the logistics supplier where total revenues exceed total costs by the greatest amount (or where marginal cost equals marginal revenue), the challenge is to align this condition as closely as possible to the readiness and performance goals required by the PM. In so doing, the gap between profit motive and readiness targets will be reduced. While derivation of the cost function—measured in dollars—is relatively straightforward and can be estimated with accuracy, establishing the "production function" in terms of readiness and performance (e.g., operational availability, or Ao) is difficult to quantify in dollars. Some method of converting "readiness" into value that can be equated to dollars is needed. This difficulty is reflected in current PBL performance agreements where, typically, very complicated scoring regimes have been developed to quantify value as output in dollar terms. Not surprisingly, measures chosen tend to reflect what traditionally has been used. Accordingly, heavy emphasis has been placed on "interface metrics," especially fill rate. This approach may enable comparisons of PBL contract performance with traditional base case supply performance metrics, including fill rate, but it precludes focusing on system output performance to capitalize on the promise and inherent advantage of PBL.

This disconnect between logistics supplier performance (profit) and PM buyer objectives (readiness) is a direct consequence of the metrics used in the scoring regime. In this (typical and actual) case, only 30% of the metrics chosen actually related to readiness performance parameters (non-mission-capable supply [NMCS] and Ao) while the remaining 70% were all related to supply performance interface metrics (Figure 57). The CLS provider did, in fact, achieve the mandated 85% fill rate goal that reflects precisely what the preponderance of the scoring regime incentives (the award fee) encouraged. Although a high fill rate (85%) yielded maximum profit, the disparity between seemingly good supply performance interface metrics and actual supply system readiness outcomes (Ao and NMCS) is truly dramatic (Figure 58).

Incentives have a major impact on how performance is determined. Under current rules, various stakeholders often find it in their interests to stock inventory levels that would not otherwise be found in a centrally stocked supply chain managed toward readiness-focused outcomes. Contract agreements that include performance-based incentives—based on fleet capabilities and readiness—with appropriate risk and cost-sharing mechanisms must be adopted.

Although the emphasis so far has been placed on weapon system readiness (Ao) as a performance objective in PBL, there are other key performance objectives as well, including reducing battlespace support "footprint" and reduction of growth in both operating and life-cycle costs. A lesson for future conflicts, demonstrated in both Operation Enduring Freedom and Operation Iraqi Freedom, is limiting the physical presence

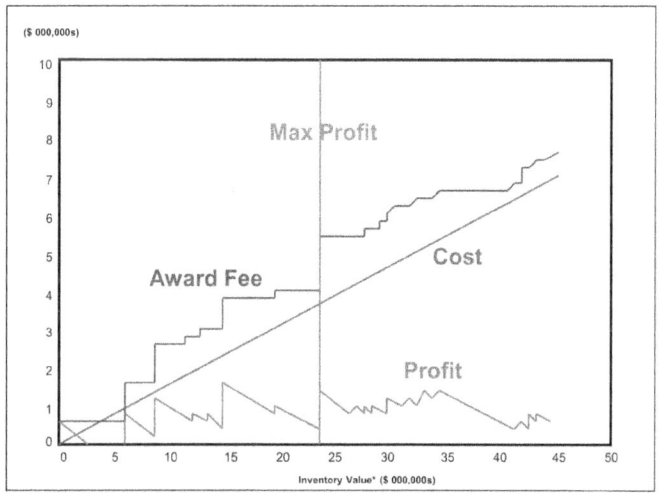

Figure 57. PBL contract scoring regime results.

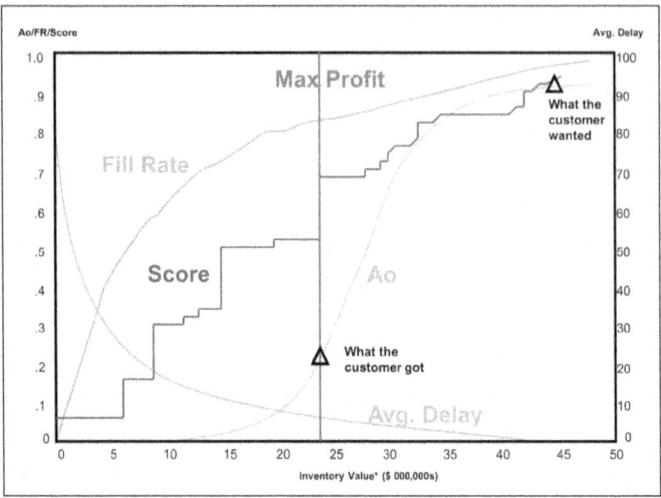

Figure 58. The fallacy of "Fill Rate" as an incentive for supply chain performance.

of support forces and materiel. This improves force agility by reducing deployment times, intratheater lift requirements, and force protection resources. The desired effect is to minimize the logistics footprint within the battle space while maintaining effective sustainment. This can best be achieved by adopting "readiness-driven supply networks" that require sparing-to-availability and mission-based demand forecasts. These methods should explicitly be incorporated into PBL contracts, since they are resource-efficient methods of achieving effective results.

PBL also has the potential to overcome confrontational relationships that have traditionally characterized contracts between the government requiring services and the commercial provider supplying those services. What is now needed to accelerate and ensure success for this new management paradigm is a trusted agent: an objective, neutral, mutually respected, analytically oriented, third party that can negotiate performance agreements with confidence between both buyer and provider. The challenge confronting successful implementation of PBL as a new operating principle and management philosophy is analytically "aligning" the incentives within the contract to achieve readiness outcomes and performance results so that there is a transparent, mutually understood, objectively derived way of generating performance agreements that link price, cost, and incentives to readiness and performance.

The analytical methods, logistics, and supply chain simulation models necessary to do so are actually available today, though not currently used by army logistics analysts or PMs. The army should adopt this approach expeditiously. Once implemented, PMs will rely on this trusted third party to generate performance agreements with appropriate metrics and the ability to "see" the impact on readiness and performance by allocating their resources under different incentive scoring regimes. CLS providers, likewise, would depend on a mutually trusted third party to analytically determine best methods and innovative approaches to improve logistics support, meet contract performance goals, and maximize profit. This third party thus becomes the honest broker and "analytical glue" that enables PBL to succeed, proliferate, and become a dominant sustained standard practice across the army and DoD—potentially a first in the long genealogy of defense acquisition reform initiatives.

The objective is to combine the use of sound theory with empirical data to take the guesswork, politics, and emotion out of major decisions. Knowledge of logistics systems and supply chain behavior will be essential to design effective incentives needed to achieve performance goals. If these new approaches are not adopted, then, in words recently expressed by one corporate defense official with long experience as a professional army logistician, PBL could become just another "monument to passing fancy."

CHAPTER 23

Financial Management Challenges to "Business Modernization"

We don't know what the lifetime cost of operating a single weapon system is. No one person is accountable. The Program Manager is responsible for the design, development and fielding of the weapon system [then] the system gets thrown over the fence to somebody else to sustain it over its lifetime.

—Diane K. Morales, deputy under secretary of defense for logistics and materiel readiness

We plan budgets two to five years out but do not have adequate funding for contingencies that arrive today. We then rely on supplemental funding and pay unfinanced requirements out of current operations . . . We try to minimize financial risk at the expense of operational risk . . . This system must change, enabling our nation to be better prepared for contingencies that are predictably unpredictable . . . We simply do not put enough money into the sustainment mission until we are in a crisis.

—General Paul Kern, commanding general, Army Materiel Command

Mr. Secretary, DoD needs a new financial system.

—Representative Neil Abercrombie, D-HI, comments to Secretary of Defense Robert Gates during House Armed Services Committee hearings on the FY2009 president's budget proposal for DoD, February 6, 2008

Simplicity is the ultimate sophistication.

—Leonardo da Vinci

Long-standing financial management problems and budget processes contribute to U.S. Army logistics shortcomings and further compound persistent supply chain problems. As with Department of Defense (DoD) inventory management since 1990, the Government Accountability Office (GAO) has also been calling on DoD to address its financial management challenges as well. In fact, "defense financial management" was added to its "high-risk" series of reports in 1997.[1]

Financial management linkages to policy-planning guidance have long been inadequate. Current management practices and accounting processes obscure the ability to track costs to their purpose, e.g., associating support cost levels needed to maintain weapons systems at desired readiness levels. These financial challenges are manifested at multiple organizational levels.

At the DoD level, the department continues to struggle with monumental accounting problems that are truly incomprehensible. For example, the DoD inspector general (IG) reported the existence of $1.1 *trillion* in unsupported adjustments to the DoD FY2000 books, out of $4.4 trillion in adjustments overall. This problem is so large that full audits by the DoD IG have been discontinued until DoD management is able to report that department books have become sufficiently reliable to justify the expense of another attempt at a full audit. DoD has not yet been able to achieve this.

At the service level, improvements in support-system performance promised when the new Defense Business Operating Fund (DBOF) was established in 1991 have not materialized. For example, in the U.S. Air Force, overall non-mission-capable supply (NMCS) rates steadily rose from FY1991 (8.6%) to FY2000 (14.3%). This occurred even as real costs of air force depot-level repairs rose 25% from FY1994 to FY2001 and as inflation-adjusted prices air force customers had to pay for spares rose 14% from FY1992 to FY2001.[2]

And at the operational level where thousands of supply transactions occur daily across DoD, financial management processes and policies face structural problems that call for new approaches. For example, the "full cost recovery" pricing practices in working capital fund (WCF) activities are sending incorrect pricing signals to customers leading to counterproductive effects.[3]

The idea that it should be possible to run DoD support activities "like businesses" is almost as old as the department itself. Following World War II, the National Security Act of 1947 established the DoD, created the Office of the Secretary of Defense OSD), and charged the new secretary with reorganizing the military services to "eliminate duplication."[4] Within two years, responding to recommendations of the first Hoover Commission (1947–1949) and some of its committees, the Congress amended the 1947 act and authorized the secretary to establish "revolving funds" for industrial and commercial-type activities providing "common services" within the department. The presumption was that the customer-provider relationships that characterize the revolving fund approach would lead to more "businesslike practices" in the provision of such common services, thereby helping to reduce the duplication of services and other inefficiencies that had grown up during the war.[5]

More recently, DoD business management "modernization" can trace its evolution directly from congressional passage of the Chief Financial Officer (CFO) Act of 1990 and its requirement to produce externally auditable financial statements. The fact that producing auditable financial statements has been and continues to be a primary objective may be an understandable development. Nonetheless, it is also unfortunate, unrealistic, largely irrelevant, and probably unattainable.[6]

A core assumption of DoD's business management modernization efforts, consistent with the CFO Act of 1990, is that *financial accounting* can add value in government activities. Accordingly, a primary DoD objective, mandated by the law, has been to produce auditable financial statements necessary to achieve CFO compliance in DoD's five "business domains" (acquisition, financial management, human resources, installations, and logistics). The fatal flaw of this assumption and fallacy of its supporting objective are that none of DoD's support activities operate in competitive markets. Pressures in the private sector to continually make enterprises more effective and efficient do not exist in the public sector setting of DoD, and efforts to generate surrogates for them simply have not worked.[7] Even if auditable financial statements could eventually be produced, they cannot be expected to have the same effects on defense support activities as they do on real businesses in the private sector. Where competitive forces in the market place help to create shareholder value, no comparable external pressures exist within DoD.

The DBOF was officially established by a high-level defense management decision—Defense Management Report Decision (DMRD) 971—following recommendations from the president's Blue Ribbon Commission on Defense Management (the Packard Commission) in 1986. The DMRD's stated purpose in establishing the DBOF was "improving the performance and lowering the costs of the support establishment." However, this has not been achieved. In fact, ever-increasing operations and support (O&S) real-cost growth indisputably shows that support costs have grown while performance has declined. This trend has persisted despite considerable effort to contain and reduce such costs over recent years using, for example, OSD program analysis and evaluation's (PAE) Visibility and Management of Operating and Support Costs program.[8]

Previously, these supplies and maintenance services were funded by direct appropriations. Under DBOF, however, the premise has been that DoD's central support activities will work more efficiently and effectively if they are funded by a cash account that is replenished by "customers" with appropriated funds who must "pay" for the goods and services they receive. This "revolving fund" financing concept has a long history in DoD. In 1949 the Hoover Commission effectively established the premise as received wisdom in the department when it recommended that revolving-fund financing be used as the way to "improve the delivery of common services" to the Military Department, arguing that revolving-fund financing would promote the use of "sound business practices" that would help reduce the "duplication of services" and other inefficiencies that were a consequence of World War II.[9]

Yet efforts to force military logistics financial systems to conform to these "business" approaches, including the perceived need to match sales revenues with operating expenses, have led to enormous increases in labor-intensive, transaction-oriented bookkeeping without adding any value.[10] Indeed, distorted practices and confused behavior have now created an environment where supply managers believe it is their job to balance these revenues with expenses, even if the level of spares support falls below that needed for weapon system materiel readiness. Growing recognition of unrealized DBOF goals have now resulted in at least five efforts to "reform" the DoD working capital funds over the past 15 years.

The army in particular has a very limited ability to associate military dollar and personnel costs with specific, institutional outputs.[11] This inability to accurately relate "resources to readiness" is further hindered by the rigidities of the budget allocation and financial management processes that, coupled with the chronic lack of analytical capacity for logistics systems analysis and supply chain management, paralyze logistics improvement efforts.

In the congressional budget process, "investment" funds consist of research, development, test, and evaluation (RDTE) and procurement. Allocating appropriate amounts of these funds to sustainment engineering (system sustainment and technical support, or SSTS funds) could potentially yield significant O&S cost reductions. However, SSTS competes in funding categories with other major acquisition programs. In a rational process, these budget "stovepipes"—different "colors of money"—would not inhibit capital investments to reduce future costs and improve performance. Nonetheless such "investments" find few supporters, since the competition for available investment funding traditionally has favored improved capabilities (new weapon systems) over reduced operations support and manpower costs.

Additionally, the Army Working Capital Fund (AWCF) actually precludes, rather than encourages, efficient behavior. Over the past 2 decades, installation and tactical commanders have been forced to use local, lower-cost repair and supply sources, often without adequate quality control and acceptance testing. This "work-around" has led to lower reliability and reduced quality as well as reduced demand for organic repair facilities and maintenance depots. In turn, this has created artificial excess capacity in organic repair sources and higher costs for both commercial and organic repairs. As a result, repair costs have been rising precipitously for a decade, and outrageously high prices for parts have been charged to the customer, adversely affecting readiness.[12]

Periodic cost reduction pressures in the army have resulted in sustainment engineering funding levels that are inadequate to adopt many of the improvements needed for increasingly aging fleets. In private industry these improvements would be considered prudent capital expenditures with "return on investment" payback expressed in greater time between component failure and unit replacement, resulting in fewer requirements for component removals and repairs, lower costs, and fewer maintenance man-hours. In chapter 10, this concept was referred to as "reliability design to readiness." However, no such mechanism or incentive is available within the army due to the inherent structural limitations of the appropriations and financial management processes. Furthermore, potential savings generated by innovative investments cannot be transferred across RDTE and operating (operations and maintenance, army [OMA]) accounts. So even where surrogate incentives for commercial "market" pressures might exist to reduce life-cycle costs, existing financial management constraints preclude them from being acted on. And finally, these underlying problems are masked by the illusion that tactical repair services—army mechanics in combat organizations—constitute a "free good" to perform labor-intensive work-arounds necessary to compensate for an inadequate supply support system.

By design, the AWCF's largest "customers" are within the army itself: tactical units. Moreover, these customers are captive to the AWCF because they usually have no other place to go to obtain the goods and services (e.g., weapon system spares) that they must buy to maintain weapons system readiness. The survival and viability of the AWCF enterprise therefore ultimately depends on army appropriations, *not on market forces* supposedly created by having AWCF mechanisms in place.

If, for whatever reasons, enough appropriated dollars (OMA) are not available, then the AWCF will suffer a loss for that particular year. Even when they are available and in the hands of customers, they might not be spent and thus do not flow into the AWCF in sufficient quantity to cover AWCF expenses for a given year:

> The inventory management process has been frequently disrupted by transfers of "cash" (revenues from sales of components to operating forces) to pay other service bills not related to product support, leaving the inventory management process without funds to replace depleted inventory . . . [This] causes overall costs to grow even faster than inflation . . . Each of the services has run into billion-dollar shortages of obligation authority—which have led to shortages of components and lower system readiness for some major systems.[13]

These annual losses have become so common that they now regularly occur. Furthermore, this *market-like* DBOF effort collides with the planning, programming, budgeting, and execution system (PPBES) *central-planning* process every year. This conflict between central planning and market-based approaches has become much more apparent.[14] Central supply and maintenance facilities must project their future costs just as appropriated activities must do. Additionally, they must predict what their customers will actually be spending to avoid losses to the underlying WCFs on which they rely to pay all their projected operating costs. The inability to determine exactly how tactical unit buyer "purchases" and AWCF "sales" are supposed to be "matched" over time is one of the reasons OSD PAE has had great difficulty every year, when evaluating service program submissions, in determining whether or not sufficient funds have been allocated to customers for the goods and services they will consume when they execute their programs.

The unavoidable fact is that DWCF activities in DoD do not operate in freely competitive marketplaces, so they are not subject to the same marketplace forces that lead private-sector businesses to work at becoming more effective, efficient, and profitable. Unlike real businesses in the private sector, WCF activities *must* continue to exist as part of the national security capability. Unlike real businesses, the AWCF cannot use some of its "profit" to grow or expand; to improve; or to set money aside for future downturns, bonuses for employees, or dividends for shareholders. Of course, WCF activities have never been able to achieve true "businesslike" performance or success because there is no "profit."[15]

The DBOF philosophy uses unit cost principles to focus management attention on the total cost of a product as the basis for full cost recovery. According to the DoD comptroller, the purpose of unit cost resourcing was to "enhance visibility of costs and contribute to better management of resources." Unit cost was introduced DoD-wide in 1989, and in 1991 the supply management and distribution depots were the first functional areas to receive unit cost budgets. Then, with the establishment of the DBOF in 1992, all five of the DoD "business domains" received unit cost budgets in 1992.

Since the WCF pays the salaries and other management expenses of its staffs to comply with the "full cost recovery" policy, the price to the customer includes not only the cost of the item supplied by industry or the defense repair center but also a "surcharge" to cover this defense inventory management process overhead. This full cost recovery pricing policy also requires those activities to include a surcharge for recovery of *past* losses as well. This is necessary to ensure the continued solvency of its underlying funds so that it can continue to function. Not only does this policy require that prices be set to recover losses over which the customer has absolutely no control or real influence but also that the customer to pay those prices one way or another—not exactly consistent with traditional free-market economic theory and the notion of an elastic demand curve for prices. Throughout the decade of the 1990s, the ever-increasing costs of excess overhead of both workforce and facilities had to be covered by a decreasing volume of products and services sold to a diminishing number of unit customers as military force structure was drawn down following the end of the Cold War. The result, of course, was outrageously high prices to the customer.[16]

A significant body of defense economic research over the past 15 years has pointed out these problems with the WCF full cost recovery method of pricing, arguing that prices should be set based on incremental, or marginal, costs rather than full cost recovery. Under the DBOF full cost recovery pricing policy, the depot-level reparable (DLR) exchange price must also include additional "cost recover elements" that may or may not be related to the repair and replacement cost. This policy forces exchange prices to be higher, often much higher, than what normally would be considered "marginal" repair and replacement costs.[17]

Recall that DLRs are capital assets that are "used" (actually "borrowed"), periodically returned via retrograde when they become unserviceable—the reverse pipeline—for repair and upgrade at maintenance depots, and then distributed through the forward supply chain for reuse by tactical units. Many of the problems with DLRs that arose in the early days of DBOF implementation—cost control, cost recovery, cash management, inventory accounting, financial accounting, customer behavior, customer funding, and material readiness—are as serious today as they were then. Indeed, this is one of the reasons the GAO has also listed DoD inventory management on its "high-risk" list as well. The fact that so many problems still exist in so many different areas, after 2 decades of effort, suggests that "business improvement" effects that were supposed to materialize under DBOF and WCF concepts have not occurred, are not likely to occur, and in fact have gotten worse.[18]

When designing an optimal price and credit policy, it is important to keep in mind that the army should be attempting to achieve readiness objectives while minimizing the real costs of supporting weapon systems, such as repair, procurement, and overhead costs. Prices and credits are simply accounting transactions, the purpose of which is to create financial incentives for logistics customers and suppliers and to reduce real costs. The army could considerably reduce financial planning uncertainty and the number of financial transactions by using an exchange pricing system for these DLRs. Under an exchange price system, OMA customers pay the difference between the price and the credit when a purchase is accompanied by a return. Credits can be thought of as reflecting either the value of a serviceable or unserviceable asset to the army or the cost of returning an asset to a serviceable condition and making it available to another customer. If the unserviceable asset is not returned within a fixed time limit, then the customer is penalized the amount of the credit. OMA customers can also receive credit for unmatched returns or pay full price for a purchase without a return.

Both the navy and air force currently use exchange pricing, which is mandatory policy by current DoD regulation.[19] However, the army annually requested a waiver from this policy because it lacked an accurate system for tracking assets that would allow it to penalize units that did not return unserviceable DLRs within the allotted time. Customers were required to pay full price for a purchase and then received a separate credit transaction for the matched return. The army is now developing the necessary asset visibility capabilities that could then be used to help implement an exchange pricing system.[20]

The financial management "system" also undermines efficient and effective program management for weapon systems, aircraft, and equipment fleets. As a former AMC commanding general explained,

> The present process is a complex bureaucratic concoction that is frustrating and wasteful—a perverse incentive for effective, efficient support . . . Current complexities are major impediments to providing needed product support to combat forces. Simplifying financial processes for [sustainment] will be essential for progress.[21]

Under recent DoD guidance (DoD Directive 5000.1) intended to establish responsibility for the sustainment phase of the life-cycle ("post–Milestone C" accountability), weapon system program managers (PMs)

> shall be the single point of accountability for accomplishing program objectives for *total* life-cycle systems management, including *sustainment* . . . PMs shall consider supportability, life cycle costs, performance, and schedule comparable in making program decisions. *Supportability*, a key component of performance, shall be considered throughout the system life cycle." [Emphasis added]

However, while PMs continue to receive RDTE and procurement funds for acquisition, they have not been given AWCF obligation authority or OMA funds for procuring sustainment support. Thus they do not yet have funding authority commensurate with their new total life-cycle responsibilities.

This current funding allocation leaves PMs with inadequate means to manage the product support phase—"post–Milestone C"—of their life-cycle responsibilities. To execute their responsibilities for system research and development and acquisition, PMs have RDTE and procurement funds. For their recently acquired life-cycle sustainment responsibilities, PMs have neither WCF obligation authority to purchase spares or component repairs nor sufficient OMA funds to obtain contractor support or other resources necessary to provide the direct support and customer units with the support they require. This lack of sustainment resources undermines the new policy of PM life-cycle management responsibility. Without this funding authority, PMs have no real directive power to influence life-cycle support, and it becomes difficult to see how they can be held accountable to achieve the objectives of this new DoD policy.[22]

Today, sustainment funding and AWCF obligation authority are still managed and controlled by AMC's commodity commands. Now with the new DoD mandate for PM life-cycle responsibility, a new challenge is creating organizational relationships—referred to as "life-cycle management commands" (LCMCs)—by merging AMC commodity commands with supported acquisition organizations and processes that enable PMs to more effectively manage the entire life cycle of their programs, especially the postacquisition sustainment phase. Once these organizational and funding authority issues are resolved, however, PM life-cycle accountability, enabled by performance-based logistics (PBL) support contracts, may offer opportunities to "bypass" many of the dysfunctional and paralyzing effects of the current financial management system.

"Outsourcing" takes these commercial "business" expectations to an extreme, yet seemingly logical, conclusion. A growing emphasis on various forms of public-private partnerships, outsourcing, and privatization has occurred over the last 2 decades. Both businesses and government have been eager and ready to tackle complex policy problems using modern technology and the creative spark of private enterprise to improve government performance. The National Performance Review and

Reinventing Government Act provided legislative impetus along with two broad trends that were also occurring, one in government and the other in the private sector.

Increasing senior leadership turnover in the public sector was creating growing organizational turbulence as newly appointed leaders rotated in, focused on the latest corporate business "best practices," and sought to impose the latest management philosophy that may have worked for them as corporate managers. At the same time, middle management had become adept at standardized processing routines for applying rules and regulations but lacked the critical skills necessary for business process reengineering and creating visions for agency "transformation." These discontinuities were becoming prescriptions for failure rather than public sector "solutions." Additionally, for many government agencies, especially at the local and state levels, separate capital budgets did not exist, making investment difficult for what otherwise could have been innovative and cost-effective strategic plans.

Simultaneously, in the commercial world, three developments help to explain how public sector outsourcing gained momentum. The rapid expansion of information technologies and growth of digital platforms enabled consolidating data sources, making them more accessible. Private sector partners with their experience as network integrators, combined with advanced decision support systems employing algorithms to quickly analyze large amounts of data, helped public sector organizations to identify their problems and structure individualized solutions.

Although these outsourcing notions are certainly seductive, what happens when the idea is carried too far? Across the federal government, the original goal was to contract out nearly a million civilian employees. However, this emphasis produced tensions with Congress over the effectiveness of private sourcing. For example, in 2003 the army contracted with a commercial lead systems integrator (LSI) for the future combat systems (FCS) because of the program's ambitious goals and the army's belief that it did not have the acquisition workforce capacity to manage the program. Nonetheless, if the army outsources systems engineering, integration, and management support services (as in the case of the FCS program with Boeing and Science Applications International Corporation [SAIC] as FCS LSIs), then the army clearly needs to be able to independently comprehend and evaluate the quality and worth of those services as they are provided. However, it is increasingly evident that the army lacks this capacity. Growing congressional concerns have been expressed over the close working relationship between the army and LSI, increasing the burden of oversight and accountability for program outcomes.[23]

Prompted by insufficient capacity across a range of critical skills, aggressive outsourcing by the army has resulted in performance shortcomings in other areas as well, from contract interrogators at Abu Ghraib to living conditions for recovering soldiers at Walter Reed Army Medical Center. Of course, outsourcing difficulties are not confined to the Army. Other government agencies, from the Internal Revenue Service to the Department of Homeland Security, have been struggling with public-private partnership relationships as well.

Outsourcing has also caused a centrifugal force on government. Effective outsourcing requires the capacity to oversee, yet this capacity is increasingly limited in government due to workforce reductions spurred by downsizing initiatives and an aging civil service. This shortage of government employees to oversee outsourced functions has a cumulative effect. It pushes the government even further in the direction of contracting out and increases the need for oversight. Indeed, some government agencies have been forced to contract out the duty to oversee those jobs already contracted out. Quality control, oversight, and accountability are bound to suffer as supervision is lost and public management becomes ineffective. One recent example is the public assertion by the under secretary for policy in the Department of Transportation (DOT) that the lack of contract oversight is at a "crises" level now for DOT.[24]

Although the practice of using private contractors to perform these necessary functions in the military and civilian sectors of government has been increasing, defining and interpreting what constitutes an "inherently governmental" function—work that is too important, or too public, to be done by contractors—has become controversial. Even if agreement is attained on an "inherently governmental" function, what happens when government turns out not to be very good at inherently governmental work?[25] On the other hand, a separate legal concern is whether practices for competitive sourcing and contracting out under OMB Circular A-76 (so-called A-76 studies) impinge on the constitutional premises of government.[26] Nevertheless, given government workforce pressures and skill capacities today, practical implementation concerns seem less about which sector to employ than about the availability of the requisite skills and decision support technologies.

Thorough analysis enables and supports sound decision making. To decide well, government officials need the analytical capacity to generate and effectively judge alternative courses of action. Although reasoned decision making remains an elusive concept, outsourcing provides the temptation to delegate analysis to commercial providers. Yet since thinking through the problem before action is taken is essential to rational decision making for which the government is accountable, then this capacity represents a function that should not be delegated. That is, official accountability for public decisions cannot be delegated to agencies outside the government. Given the aging of our bureaucracy and difficulty in finding qualified replacements, maintaining significant analytical and decision support capacity in-house will be crucial to the preservation of a competent civil service corps.

As a leading scholar in administrative and regulatory law, Paul R. Verkuil explains in his recent book *Outsourcing Sovereignty*,

> Privatization may demonstrate efficiency principles, yet it also encourages the outsourcing of governmental decision making where accountability is a countervailing principle. Of course, efficiency and accountability need not be in opposition—they can and do coexist. But when efficiency dominates, as is the case with outsourcing important aspects of public sector decision making, it clashes with accountability and can undermine important democratic values. Outsourcing of management functions undermines government performance . . . by weakening or atrophying government's power to perform these functions in the future.[27]

A growing imbalance is occurring between those in government who should oversee and those in the private sector who need to be overseen. Increasingly, accountability is lacking. The *Wall Street Journal* asks a provocative question: "Is government 'outsourcing' its brain?"[28] If beleaguered agencies such as DoD, by far the largest government contracting agency, are ever to perform competitively, then it will be as a result of an effective civil service corps rather than an army of consultants.

This government capability will cease to exist if not exercised. And so after many years of infatuation with the idea of privatization, the potential downsides of contracting out government functions are now being closely examined.

The existing financial management system encourages behavior inimical to organizational effectiveness and, ultimately, tactical unit readiness. Distortions caused by the WCF system detract from combat unit training and operational effectiveness and are largely a consequence of system-induced tactical unit incentives to find ways to conserve operating (OMA) funds. For customers, it has made DLRs very expensive, motivating many of them to delay or avoid DLR purchases whenever possible, even when they shouldn't. For providers, recurring and serious cash-flow problems in their underlying funds persist when DLR sales have failed to generate sufficient cash to cover current expenses, as they have done on a regular basis. But even beyond the problem of customer dissatisfaction about DLR prices they don't understand and provider frustration by losses they cannot control, there has been a steady deterioration in readiness, as reflected in higher NMCS rates for major weapon systems across all the armed services.[29] "Customers"—in this case, army combat organizations and their readiness—ultimately bear all the consequences and risks of this dysfunctional system.

Congress must enact legislation that supports rather than inhibits acquisition reform, one example being restrictions and boundaries defining where and how appropriated dollars may and may not be spent. These "stovepiped" funding processes preclude generating "honest" budgets and programs, and associated "color of money" restrictions prevent spending where it makes the most sense.[30] One conspicuous example, as Boeing general manager Jay Kappmeier recently observed, is the high expectations for and current emphasis on PBL that, nonetheless, "is increasingly on life support because of 'color of money' problems . . . DoD cannot really buy 'performance' because they are not programmed to do so."[31]

Trust and credibility must be established and reinforced by building analytical capacity to credibly relate funding levels to readiness outcomes. Roger Kallock, former under secretary of defense for logistics and materiel readiness, suggests this "blindness to true demand" results in a very "high cost of low trust." And as Moshe Rubinstein, UCLA's distinguished professor of engineering and organizational systems, has observed: "There is no survival without trust."

DoD "business modernization" needs to be fundamentally reoriented. The recently established Defense Business Systems Management Committee (DBSMC, which replaced the Business Management Modernization Program [BMMP] in February 2005) and new DoD Business Transformation Agency, created in February 2006, have been established to "advance the development of world-class business operations in support of the warfighter." This new governance structure now has a chance to review and reevaluate, from first principles, what "business modernization" in DoD should be all about. The goal of such a review should be to determine where and how changes in basic financial and operational policies would help to clarify incentives, improve cost visibility, and relate those costs to intended outcomes while simultaneously simplifying financial accounting.

First, emphasis must be shifted away from externally auditable *financial* accounting for "business modernization" to internally accurate *managerial cost* accounting focused on readiness and capability performance requirements. Second, corresponding changes must be made in what are now viewed as necessary accounting policies because of current "business practices." For some activities, this should require a return to direct funding and traditional, public-fund budgetary accounting. For example, DLR aviation components should be treated as capital assets that are "used" rather than as inventory held for sale to be "consumed" and DLR transactions restructured accordingly. Finally, and most importantly, DoD should pursue what in all likelihood the Congress intended and wanted the DoD to pursue when it passed the CFO Act in the first place: sensible, responsible, and honest *internal managerial cost* accounting that will lead to more effective and efficient support operations in the department.[32]

As described earlier, PMs currently have RDTE and procurement funds to execute their responsibilities for system development and acquisition. Yet even though they are now responsible for the entire life cycle, they have neither WCF obligation authority to purchase spares or component repairs nor sufficient O&M funds to obtain contractor support for sustainment. This lack of sustainment resource authority undermines the new policy of PM life-cycle management responsibility.

This flawed policy should be replaced by a life-cycle "ownership" doctrine for PM fleet readiness responsibilities. This new philosophy, as envisioned by AMC's former commander, General William Tuttle, would assume that the armed services "own" these systems rather than subordinate commands. Fleets are dynamically allocated to tactical organizations that serve as custodians for these systems. This allocation can be altered as necessary to accommodate changing operational requirements for joint and combined operations. Under this service ownership concept, PMs can then be designated as "agents" for managing these fleets. All funds for maintaining system fleet readiness and capabilities would be allocated to the PM, thereby providing funding authority commensurate with "post–Milestone C" sustainment responsibilities. The budgeting process would allocate O&M funds to PMs based on the readiness requirements for supported units under the new Army Force Generation management concept now being implemented.

Additionally, under this new "ownership" policy, and consistent with the army's new Single Stock Fund, PMs would be responsible for all fleet DLRs. These reparables would then be managed by direct exchange, since they are capital assets used, rather than consumed, by tactical units. This new "ownership" doctrine would also remove the burden of financial accounting for product support from operating forces and allow them to focus on operational missions and training.[33]

In addition to better aligning performance agreement metrics to readiness and capability focused outcomes (described in chapter 25), recent research also illuminates important relationships between alternative types of contracts, asset ownership, and control. Historically, the government has procured spare parts using fixed price or cost plus materiel contracts. Consequently, traditional incentives for suppliers have not considered readiness performance. Rather, suppliers generate revenues by selling more spare parts to the government. As long as OEMs and suppliers can pass on the higher logistics costs of today's logistics structure and contracting habits to their customers, they have little incentive to reduce the number of expedited orders or to change their service parts management policies. Performance-based contracts are intended to reverse this through risk sharing and outcome-focused (e.g., readiness) incentives.

Management "reform" in DoD has consisted predominately of imposing "businesslike" *financial* accounting practices and other efforts to induce "market-like" behavior. The consequences of adopting this commercial orientation and "transplanting" it into DoD have been considerable "rejection." Another consistent historical reform theme has been the penchant for technology-based "solutions" manifested now in the enormous investment levels in information technology (IT) to replace legacy management information systems. Yet an equally clear and disconcerting pattern is that neither IT "solutions" nor "business reform" have proven adequate to the challenges of transforming DoD business operations.

Why is this?

An objective assessment reveals that repeated efforts at reform over the decades have fundamentally failed to understand the central purpose for which these DoD "business domains" exist. And regardless of the persistent efforts over the years to make them so, these organizations and agencies are neither profit driven nor do they operate within market economies where prices are determined by the familiar dynamics of supply and demand. These supporting organizations, and the capabilities they provide, all exist to enable tactical units—"customers" in the commercial business model lexicon—to generate the capabilities and readiness levels required to conduct assigned operational missions.

As government agencies are charged "to provide for the common defense," they should do so responsibly, both effectively and efficiently. However, blindly adopting private sector management notions for business modernization, demanding (stock) market-oriented financial accounting statements, and mandating to financially "break even" by limiting "customer" (combat unit) sales to balance AWCF operating expenses have proven counterproductive. These efforts at reform have disconnected the supply chain's functional mission, operational performance metrics, incentives, and, indeed, organizational culture from the real purpose for which the enterprise exists in the first place. "Business modernization" has proven to be a misguided pursuit.

For certain, comprehensive approaches will be needed to overcome systemic, long-standing problems. And as the GAO recently noted in its 2007 "high-risk series" update, DoD future success in supply chain management is closely linked with its defense business transformation efforts, improvements in financial management, and completion of an integrated logistics strategy.[34] Common sense is needed to reconnect organizations to their purpose so that resources can be related to near-term readiness and investments to future capabilities. Technology innovation (IT or otherwise) cannot be expected to provide a silver bullet for what is fundamentally a cultural challenge. Furthermore, beyond the need to address *managerial cost* (versus *financial*) accounting for business modernization in DoD as mentioned previously, in the larger sense of "defense reform" what is needed is *management innovation.*

Management innovation can be induced by analytical capacity and encouraged by appropriate incentives rather than, as with technology innovation, the autonomous result of advancements in science and technology alone. The scientific foundation and necessary analytical methods for management innovation exist today. Yet their capacity to guide innovation within the army has not yet been developed, integrated, and institutionalized to enable supply chain transformation for the army's materiel enterprise. And so while much of the science and engineering expertise for model development, systems simulation, and rigorous analysis exists today in the Army Research Lab and AMC's newly established Research, Development, and Engineering Command, this extensive capability has not yet been organized to focus on the "post–Milestone C" phase of lifecycle management.

However, once this analytical capacity has been harnessed and is in place, resource investment levels and new management polices and technology initiatives can be correlated with operational outputs. Various support activities will better relate to one another and understand how their respective outputs ultimately contribute to operational performance. Improved alignment between the institutional army (the generating force) and operational army (operating force) can be achieved. And the long-perceived need, addressed with enormous effort over the decades, to create "businesslike" efficiency for financial management reform can be superseded. It becomes possible to relate resources to performance and to develop accurate budgets for near-term readiness and credible programs for future capabilities.

CHAPTER 24

Human Capital Investment for a Collaborative Enterprise

Institutions are grounded in culture and culture changes very slowly.
—Thomas Homer-Dixon, *The Ingenuity Gap*

You can't transform logistics without transforming logisticians.
Randy Fowler, director, Curricula Development and
Support Center, Defense Acquisition University

One military logistics analyst noted that "supply chains for contingency operations are complicated by the dynamics, risks, and uncertainties of these operations, which make it particularly difficult to establish metrics for logistics functions."[1] In addition to the challenges posed by executing contingency operations while also transitioning toward the adaptive network concept of sense and respond logistics, opportunities for accelerating innovation provided by the infusion of major new technologies during a time of significant geopolitical turmoil will inevitably lead to disruptive change. Managing workforce expectations for organizational performance during such a period of transformative change requires strong, determined leadership. Common directional understanding throughout the organization must be generated by shared vision and a strategic implementation plan.

"Change," frequently undertaken without an analytical foundation and guiding process, can easily create initiative overload and organizational chaos. Attempting to orchestrate unmanaged change leads to cynicism and burnout as "good ideas" proliferate and the workforce becomes burdened with increasingly disconnected efforts. In the absence of a change management process, the organization has no ability to subsequently explain the consequences of the many initiatives allegedly contributing to either success or failure. It becomes impossible to disentangle cause and effect, and the gap between workforce expectations and actual organizational performance grows. Employees dismiss the next initiative with growing skepticism—another "flavor of the month"—and managers lose credibility. Since the evidence indicates more than two-thirds of these new initiatives actually fail, it is no surprise that so-called change management programs seem to be decreasing in popularity.[2]

What is needed is this "analytical architecture" as a foundation for a credible transformation strategy so that resources can then be allocated to meet appropriate expectations.[3] The history of innovation suggests the reality of change is, all too often, a failure to plan, resulting in expectations of performance that simply cannot be met. This occurs especially during the period of disruption when historical performance normally declines, although only temporarily for those organizations that are ultimately successful (Figure 59).[4]

Currently, the workforce providing logistics support to the armed services and other Department of Defense (DoD) organizations includes over a million people. Within DoD this workforce averages 50 years of age. As of 2001, nearly 20% of the U.S. Army's acquisition workforce was eligible to immediately retire and 50% could do so within the next 5 years.[5] Certainly, as well, the psychological effects on the remaining, predominantly civilian workforce of more than a decade of repeated downsizing, realignment activities, and personnel "cut drills" cannot be discounted. Common themes expressed during project interviews with army logistics officials are that "work-arounds" are endemic, "ad hocism" has become routine by necessity, and "intense management" is the standard reaction to compensate for chronic system and organizational inadequacies.

These converging trends are making it increasingly burdensome to manage a compliance-focused, transaction-intensive system with an aging, declining workforce. This surviving, very dedicated, and professional workforce is struggling valiantly to compensate for an archaic system that is increasingly failing them. Although the DoD logistics enterprise has historically been manpower intensive, durable human capital investment strategies have not existed. Finally, despite assurances to

HUMAN CAPITAL INVESTMENT 221

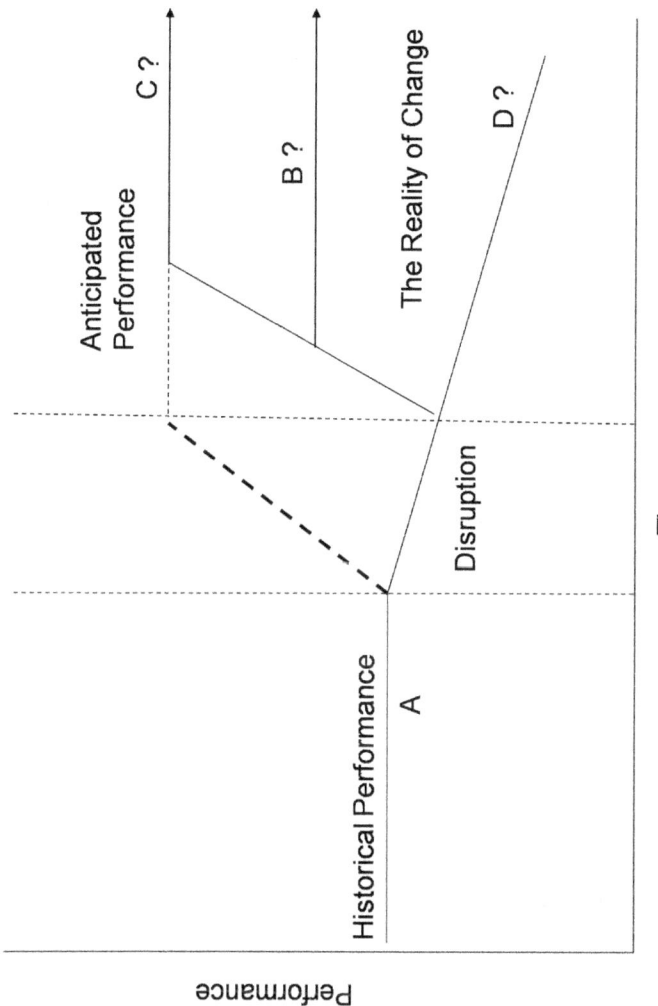

Figure 59. *Common expectations and the reality of change.*

the contrary, a false premise seems to persist suggesting that manpower is overhead to be cut or outsourced rather than capability to be developed.

An essential yet typically underappreciated and therefore undervalued aspect of major organizational reengineering endeavors is the adequacy of investment in and attention to human capital. The current "techno-centric" approach in DoD is based on a presumed information technology–driven revolution in military affairs (RMA) that is reflected in our transformation lexicon: "system-of-systems"; "network-centric operations"; "smart" weapons; global, space-based "total situational awareness" enabling an "information/surveillance/reconnaissance precision strike complex" to achieve "full spectrum dominance." The consequence of this RMA has recently been described by one defense analyst as "an ability to bomb any target on the planet with impunity, dominate any ocean, and move forces anywhere to defeat just about any army."[6]

While this may be true, ongoing operations nevertheless reveal existing DoD-wide force structure to be extraordinarily expensive yet increasingly inadequate to sustain current missions. While a major premise of "transformation" is that speed, agility, and precision can take the place of "mass," the unfolding reality of the Global War on Terror is that eradicating the root causes of contemporary ("unconventional") aggression requires a completely different skill set.[7] Furthermore, it is becoming apparent that current U.S. military force posture is at odds with the emerging strategic environment.[8] For example, we have more fighter aircraft than we have infantry squads in the active component. As a respected military historian and former Army War College commandant bluntly stated, "Soldiers and marines are paying the price today for our collective neglect of the centrality of landpower in modern warfare."[9]

More than any other deficiency, the initial shortage of troops in Iraq, and more recently in Afghanistan, hampered the U.S. response. Numbers clearly matter in counterinsurgency far more than they do in conventional warfare where technology can substitute for manpower. Historically, a harsh "human-centric" arithmetic seems to correlate with success or failure for internal stability operations.[10] Why is our incredibly expensive military chronically short of people? And so in this "network-centric," precision strike, technology-focused, defense "reform" era, we should remember that power ultimately takes its meaning from the values and purposes it serves.

Regardless of the relevance (or even existence) of this heralded RMA, the army is currently burdened with disconnected, outdated, and inefficient legacy logistics systems that cannot keep up with new operational war-fighting concepts. And at the other extreme, the institution is challenged to absorb very sophisticated systems being developed by our remarkable scientific communities. Indeed, an "ingenuity gap" may be developing—a growing inability of leadership, management, and the larger DoD workforce to fully understand and cope with complex, tightly coupled engineering and information systems.[11] The following is an illustrative and relevant example:

> One of the key reasons for the failure of distribution-based logistics to work in operations as massive as OIF [Operation Iraqi Freedom] is the incredible complexity of the system . . . Failure in any one of the component areas of distribution-based logistics will cause problems. Failure in multiple areas, or in the case of OIF in nearly all areas, can be disastrous. This complexity is manageable, but only if the system is established and is viable.[12]

Although its extent may not be well defined, this growing ingenuity gap is further exacerbated within the military, especially the army, when placed within the context of the recent decline in the appreciation, use, influence, and contributions of operations research (OR).

Following its introduction and operational focus in the early stages of World War II and then broad postwar acceptance, OR was incorporated and institutionalized within a wide range of army organizations and functions, including resource planning, land warfare analyses, combat developments, force structure design, manpower and personnel, acquisition, test and evaluation, and logistics. OR, in these earlier decades, using the words of one of its most experienced and distinguished contributors

> relied heavily on experiments, tests and analysis of empirical data to develop a thorough understanding of processes being modeled . . . [These] *experiments were designed for learning*. Unfortunately, the Army today does "demonstrations," not experiments as they did in [earlier decades] . . . Relative to 1960–1995 the Army has now reduced the use of model-based analyses to address

system, force design/structure, and operational concept/doctrine issues and is relying more on large field exercises and "subject matter experts" in a gaming context. It remains to be seen if OR and model-based analyses will play *any* role in designing the versatile [transformed] force.[13]

Today, for example, the army is struggling to organize and man small OR teams to support operational deployments for army combat units (divisions and corps). At the same time OR support to the "institutional" army, which includes the Title X functions of manning (e.g., recruiting), training, equipping, and sustaining (e.g., logistics), has also significantly declined during the past decade. In fact, a recent "state of army OR" article published in a prestigious army professional journal now excludes logistics systems analysis (LSA) altogether as a domain for army OR.[14] Given the lack of *any* uniformed military OR expertise within the command responsible for LSA now (Figure 51), this would not appear to be an oversight by the authors. Rather, it is an accurate perception of the dramatic and regrettable extent of the decline of operations research within the institutional army. Indeed, the Office of the Deputy Under Secretary of the Army (Operations Research) was disbanded in 2005 with supporting staff functions eliminated or scattered to disparate organizations across the army.

Nor, today, does there appear to be any compensating trends in our *logistics* professional education and training programs. For example, in our professional military education we do not currently emphasize strategic logistics,[15] and our advanced civil schooling programs do not yet include supply chain design, management, and analysis concepts.[16] It is also noteworthy that all of the armed services classify their civilian logisticians—occupational code 346—as an "administrative" rather than "professional" category.[17] In army technical courses, the emphasis is on the operating mechanics and administrative requirements associated with existing logistics information systems (e.g., commodity command standard system, requirements determination and execution system, standard army retail supply system, standard army maintenance system, unit level logistics system, etc.) rather than understanding inventory theory, supply chain dynamics, and ways to address current challenges to improve performance.[18] For an organization that justifiably boasts the world's most effective military leadership development programs—across all ranks—this lack of a comparable civilian logistics professional development program is truly perplexing.

These current army-specific trends are further exacerbated by looming national workforce trends in the civilian labor market. Demographic shifts in our population are creating a workforce phenomenon where employers are increasingly losing significant talent, expertise, and manpower relative to projected future demand that potential growth opportunities provide. Our aging workforce is now interacting with other educational patterns, population dynamics, and technology trends, causing a growing gap between workforce supply and demand.

One immediate effect is the imminent "obsolescence" of both federal and state government labor forces due to age-induced retirements combined with the sustained effects of severely limited hiring actions during the past 3 decades. The U.S. Bureau of Labor Statistics estimates that there are now two retirements for each new person entering the workforce. With the aging and mass retirement of the baby boomer generation, this trend is expected to continue with projections of a 10-million-worker shortage by the end of this decade, causing employers to face a growing competition for employees—the so-called war for talent.

Simultaneously, as recent studies including the Hart-Rudman "Commission on National Security Strategy for the 21st Century" clearly emphasize, our educational production capacity and enrollment into the science, engineering, and management disciplines are increasingly inadequate to sustain what historically has been a competitive edge for the United States. Above all, despite our cultural proclivity for, and increasing reliance on, technology for "solutions," we must constantly remind ourselves that a less skilled military is a far greater liability than less advanced technology.[19]

The challenge then, especially for recognized high-tech regional "clusters," is to find, create, and retain highly educated and skilled employees while keeping wage pressures under control. Thus an important element of an "engine for innovation," such as the Center for Innovation in Logistics Systems described previously, is a coordinated, *collaborative* effort with various training, certification, education, and professional development programs. Elements of this "human capital production function" include various programs, courses, and delivery means. Training and education initiatives could range from narrowly focused continuing education courses and certificate-producing seminars to undergraduate, graduate, and postgraduate education programs.[20] For the local and regional levels this effort could produce the crucial talent pool needed to better meet future supply chain management and logistics workforce demand.

At the same time these sociodemographic trends are straining organizational workforce manning capacity and capability, the organization itself, as a structural entity, is undergoing a major evolutionary change.[21]

The modern evolution of organizational forms extends from the industrial-age bureaucracy to a new, information-age "collaborative enterprise." This evolution from the industrial age to the information age has seen organizational management challenges transition from deconfliction to cooperation and now to integration; from centralized then to decentralized bureaucracies and now to the collaborative enterprise; and from compartmented and independent to interdependent matrix organizations with integrated product teams and now to "networked" organizations capable of "learning."

During the late 19th century, German sociologist Max Weber helped German agencies pioneer modern administration. In *The Theory of Social and Economic Organization* he asserted that the defining characteristic of a bureaucracy should be an institutional ability to apply general rules to specific cases, thereby making the actions of government predictable and fair. This efficient, rational, and honest system soon replaced practices inherited from the Middle Ages owing loyalty to the king, dukes, and the church. Indeed, the bureaucratic coordination of the actions of large numbers of people has become the dominant feature of modern organizations. Key principles include the application of laws and regulations within fixed, jurisdictional areas; hierarchy and levels of graded authority where lower offices are supervised by higher ones; and management following rules prescribed by official documents, such as standard operating procedures.

Shortly after Weber's pioneering efforts, a century ago, self-made industrial engineer Frederick W. Taylor in *The Principles of Scientific Management* sought to centralize knowledge from the industrial production process in the organization's managers and engineers. His goal was to maximize value by making behavior in bureaucratic organizations entirely routine—"scientific management." Yet the major thrusts of changes in work over the past few decades have been to diffuse knowledge more broadly throughout the organization by encouraging production workers to improve their work, bringing development labs into the core of business activities, and encouraging salespeople to take initiative and responsibility in dealing with customers.

Gradually the weaknesses of the bureaucratic mode of organization have become apparent. As we have experienced with army supply chains, the inevitable result of isolating functions and failing to communicate across functional boundaries is suboptimization. Though the bureaucratic design is excellent for control and the development of expertise, it is cumbersome, highly compartmented, and structured inwardly to perform internal routines. As a result, different levels within the organization exhibit friction across boundaries (e.g., irrelevant interface metrics), require supervision for direction, and cannot sense and react to the external environment. All too often these weaknesses culminate in a common bureaucratic pathology: individuals perform in a perfectly rational and competent manner yet produce an irrational result.

A major challenge is to develop channels for sensing environmental change and link this information back to coordinating and planning mechanisms that steer the organization as a whole. These pressures for responsiveness and innovation imply an increased need for systematic learning. The bureaucratic model of system learning required information to flow upward so that managers could see and understand what was happening. Learning was then codified in structures or rules, which became the "memory" of past experiences. This is one reason why bureaucracies tend to move in a direction of creating more rules and levels of control.

Today it seems increasingly the case that formal organizational lines—between hierarchical levels and functions—serve as barriers preventing connections needed for learning. The strategic and operational views, in effect, are not connected in a way that would allow the organization to effectively deal with emerging opportunities.

Two dimensions—vertical and horizontal, or command and association—are common to all organizations. Most familiar and studied is the vertical or hierarchical dimension involving superiors and subordinates. Weber's analysis of bureaucracy in the late 19th century focused on how legitimate authority is applied, the resulting pathologies from excessive span of control, and the effects of inadequate autonomy for subordinates. But even the most structured bureaucracy cannot deal with everything through stacked boxes of hierarchical accountability. Vertical connectivity must be supplemented by an ability to communicate across functional boundaries and levels when necessary. This represents the horizontal, or associational, dimension of organizations.

The common way of treating these two dimensions has been to portray the hierarchical one as "formal" and the horizontal one as "informal." In bureaucracies, associational relations are structured by informal ties such as water-cooler conversations, personal relationships, and peer pressure. This "informal" organization was first discovered by the Hawthorne studies conducted by Western Electric in the 1930s. More recently, there have been growing efforts to overcome the strict division of labor and tasks built into bureaucracy and to achieve more flexible ways of combining different forms of knowledge and expertise.

The long-term trend has been toward a formalization of the mechanisms of association. What used to be done by the "informal organization" is now increasingly being performed by organized systems outside the hierarchical structure. This is the significance of the tremendous growth of seemingly "ad hoc" organizational constructs (e.g., task teams; quality circles; process management; integrated product teams; and now, most recently, "X-Teams"[22]) as companies struggle to bring people together in a coherent and planned way around tasks, without losing control of the organization.

Research has also shown that organizations differ considerably depending on whether they operate in stable or rapidly changing environments. In stable environments, organizations can specialize in routine activities with strict lines of authority and distinct lines of assigned responsibility. In contrast, "organic" forms of organization are preferred in a changing environment where flexibility, innovation, and adaptation are needed.

Thus the most effective way to organize is *contingent* on conditions of complexity and change in the environment. Recently developed, "contingency theory" argues that there is no one best way to organize. It is important to have a good "fit" between the organization's structure, its size, technology, and requirements of the environment. Organizations whose structures are not fitted to the environment will not perform well and will fail. Organizations facing complex, highly uncertain environments typically differentiate so that each organizational unit is facing a smaller, more certain problem. Accordingly, the organization should design its structure, leadership style, and control systems to be adaptive to the prevailing situation. Organizational design features must relate structure and design to the environment and identify the exact nature of interdependencies and their impact on managerial style. Classical bureaucracy can be contrasted with contingency theory by observing that the former moves toward greater order, standardization, and predictability, while the latter tends toward greater openness, sharing, creativity, and individual initiative. One "tightens" the organization up; the other "loosens" it.[23]

Recognition that there are different "species" of organizations that adapt to different environments also helped establish the metaphor of the "organism" as a modern approach to organization theory. This perspective emphasizes environmental dependence, technology as a transformation process, and structural adaptation as strategies for organizational survival.[24]

Most classical and many modern approaches to social structure fall into the category of static models. Dynamic models, on the other hand, focus on how the organization changes over time and with changing circumstances. This evolutionary perspective is represented by Larry Greiner's life cycle theory that depicts organizational growth as a sequence of evolutionary periods punctuated by revolutionary events. Sooner or later centralized decision making becomes a bottleneck for action. The solution to the crisis results in delegation, the next phase, the point at which formalized bureaucracy appears. Eventually "the crises of red tape" follows that has given bureaucracy its bad name. To emerge from the red tape crisis, bureaucracies must then undergo a qualitative change in organizational form—a "collaboration" phase. Greiner argues that failure to achieve this renewal inevitably results in organizational lethargy and decline.[25]

So what is this emerging organizational concept—referred to as the "collaborative enterprise"—that potentially replaces bureaucracy?

The "enterprise" is defined as an interdependent collaborative network of diverse contributors. *Cooperation* refers to local, stable teams and relations, whereas *collaboration* refers to the operation of extended, dynamic, and diverse systems of interaction. Collaboration makes it possible to connect responses directly to environmental stimuli. And to increase organizational responsiveness, extended collaboration can increase the organization's ability to continually improve processes and routines—to learn.

Communication channels in bureaucracies can carry significant information but at the cost of greatly restricting the number of links. Markets, on the other hand, have many connections and links but carry limited information, mainly price. Ideally, collaborative enterprise eliminates both restrictions. As with markets the number of links is potentially infinite; as with bureaucracies the content of the information can be extensive. The difficulty is in keeping this incredible explosion in information growth from devolving into organizational chaos.

Consequently, the structure of extended collaboration is far more complex than that of bureaucracy. Bureaucracy works in large part by sharply restricting the number of possible connections; collaboration multiplies them. The former has only one upward connection and a few downward ones; in the latter, this restriction is lifted and anyone can reach out to wherever needed capabilities can be found. An essential reason why collaboration is potentially the more powerful system is this ability to organize diverse resources far more efficiently.

The growth of collaborative systems is also reflected in the explosion of interest in "network theory" inspired by Metcalfe's Law. Nonetheless, both the theory and practice of "postbureaucratic" organizations are in their infancy. As Yale University's distinguished professor of management and political science, Paul Bracken, admonishes,

> We should not make the mistake of equating better horizontal integration with a network organizational structure . . . The unbridled substitution of networks for hierarchies will create organizational chaos, not efficiency. Higher organization involves a mix of strategy, people, and structure.[26]

The central concept of extended collaboration involves diversity of skills and perspectives, open boundaries, and especially a strengthening of the "horizontal" or associational dimension of organizations. From this perspective, the collaborative enterprise represents the first social system in which important kinds of diversity are not merely tolerated but actually embraced as a part of interactive dialog. Good project teams work not in spite of but because of the fact that they involve people with differing points of view and knowledge. This central principle of collaboration is that people with relevant viewpoints should work together to share and pool their knowledge and experience. Therefore it brings together, in an unprecedented way, people from different functions. And as these interdependencies increase, mechanisms for horizontal coordination must also increase to preclude devolution into chaos as Professor Bracken warns.

The "stability" imposed by organizational culture frequently impedes innovation, especially in large-scale bureaucracies such as the military. Every transformation is faced by obstacles rooted in the "old" system where mind-sets or cultural patterns are buried deeply in an array of habits and relationships that are hard to disentangle. And the process of change often creates distorted group reactions of defensiveness with a highly emotional charge. As a result of these stabilizing and dampening effects of existing culture, two basic types of organization change processes have evolved: incremental and transformative. Pursuing one or the other is largely dependent on the external pressures and immediacy of threats, or perceived opportunities, faced by the organization. In either case, the restraining effects of organizational culture will have a controlling influence on the pace of change that the organization can absorb. Although transformative change typically requires simultaneous shifts throughout an entire system and feels to participants like massive confusion accompanying a sudden "leap," the actual evolution of successful transformative change in large organizations and complex systems is long and complicated.

From this short theoretical summary of the evolution of modern organizational design, what arguments can be made about their practical impact on (or reflection in) evolving army supply chain organizational structure? Two thoughts are offered here.

First, a gradual transition toward a more collaborative enterprise *is* clearly evident in several of the organizational and policy changes that are now occurring across the army's logistics and supply chain communities. Some obvious examples of these include: the Army Materiel Command's (AMC) creation of the life-cycle management commands to improve horizontal integration with program executive offices (PEOs), especially for "post–Milestone C" sustainment challenges; the creation of the new Army Sustainment Command to better connect the industrial base to operational army needs and the new Army Force Generation force management concept; the adoption of the "single stock fund" to mitigate organizational "ownership" issues and better enable multiechelon solutions; improved asset visibility and information sharing eventually available through the Single Army Logistics Enterprise set of enterprise resource planning systems; and the extensive use of AMC and contract logistics assistance representatives (front-line technicians) for sensing, monitoring, and responsive reaction to the "external environment."

A second, but less obvious, observation is the truly remarkable similarities between the new "collaborative enterprise" design principles described previously and the original organizational forms and purposes that created OR initially in England during the Battle of Britain, and that were used shortly after by the U.S. Army, during the early years of World War II three-quarters of a century ago. The idea for, and practical implementation of, a "system of teams" with multidisciplinary expertise across a wide range of scientific and military disciplines, using empirical evidence from ongoing military operations in conjunction with creative scientific models for rapid learning, defined OR at its inception. Working closely with, trusted by, and responsively advising high-level commanders and leaders, all while operating under extraordinary pressures—indeed the fate of Western Civilization was at stake in those early years—was the hallmark of OR.

While the army moves toward a more collaborative structure, characterized by some of the trends mentioned in the first and most evident observation, it is the need for resurrecting and significantly expanding the second—OR—that will provide the organizational "glue" needed to coordinate, orchestrate, and pull the enterprise together to keep it focused and continuously learning, precluding chaos during a period of transformational change.

CHAPTER 25

Strategic Management Concepts for a Learning Organization

Organizations manage what they measure, and they measure what their leaders tell them to report on.

—David Kilcullen, from *Counterinsurgency*

Managing by anecdote is no better than managing by averages . . . [and] managing by averages leads to below average performance.

—Arnoldo Hax, former deputy dean, Massachusetts Institute of Technology Sloan School of Management, from *The Delta Project*

The modern corporate world has been routinely buffeted by competing, sequentially adopted management philosophies that periodically appear, gain popularity, and then recede. Despite these evanescent fads, or perhaps because of them, chronic gaps persist in strategic planning capacity resulting in systemic failure to develop concepts relevant to emerging realities. Data deficiencies frequently conspire with analytic challenges, making it nearly impossible to determine effective approaches. All too often, focus and effort have been confined to existing system constraints and current metrics instead of concentrating on what truly needs to be done.

Within the U.S. Army, tactical units are renowned for pioneering and refining the After Action Review concept as a continuous learning method to surface, diagnose, and correct deficiencies to improve and sustain operational excellence. Yet comparable diagnostic effort has not been prevalent at strategic levels within the institutional army bureaucracy. Since analytically rigorous "autopsies"—"dissection" for root cause diagnosis, understanding, and response—on management issues are not routinely performed to uncover "ground truth" and learn from mistakes, reactive "firefighting" seems to be the persistent response to visible symptoms.

When confronted with significant organizational stress, an analytical framework is needed to address tough issues, define direction, and guide sustained improvement amid the "cacophony of current crises" that inevitably seems to dominate the present. Recently, in contrast to these episodic and ephemeral management fads, an emerging school of thought suggests an alternative concept fundamentally consisting of three simultaneously operating and complementary approaches. The goal is attainment of an integrated management science where these *analytically based* approaches are derived from a larger, more comprehensive and scientific framework. Decisions on strategic choices and management options need to be made within a reasonable, ends-means architecture focusing on the ultimate purpose for which the organization exists. This concept is one which enables emergence, then sustainment, of a durable "learning organization."[1]

These three approaches serve different purposes within this framework, yet they all relate to organizational effectiveness and durability and should ideally be used in a complementary and unified way. Each approach emphasizes different perspectives on the organization:

1. Internal efficiency, which is the need to evaluate the current capacity of the organization's ability to transform resources into products, service, or both to generate an appropriate level of short-term performance
2. Demand flexibility, which is a more comprehensive perspective that incorporates near-term dynamic patterns and longer-term trends, endeavoring to understand cause-and-effect relationships among the several "flows"—physical, information, and financial—both within the organization and in relation to external factors, most notably customer demand, that evolve over time and may subtly effect, or abruptly shock, the organization
3. Innovation (including, for example, product development) and the need to clearly define purpose, provide goals, and nurture culture to encourage long-term growth and improvement while situating the organization within a larger, competitive environment

Supporting each of these organizational performance perspectives are corresponding analytical methods:

1. Logical yet circumscribed, statistically based techniques including Six Sigma, Lean, and the theory of constraints that emphasize the physical aspects of process improvement by focusing on improved process efficiency and output quality within the current boundaries of the organization
2. Market research, organization theory, and the domain of systems sciences including the disciplines of systems simulation and analysis, control theory, adaptive networks, and system dynamics, which focus on analyzing and modeling both internal integration and external adaptation to dynamic processes and conditions that interact to affect and influence organizations
3. The more creative field of strategic planning that, nevertheless, has distinct quantitative aspects that require development of objective hierarchies

Strategic architectures for analysis, management, and planning (STA-AMP) have been developed to visually portray relationships between system-wide goals, supporting objectives, and strategies intended to pursue these various objectives. These analytically based, strategic architectures establish and relate meaningful performance trends to the larger objectives, goals, and vision of the organization. Aligning execution and measures associated with organizational performance to distinct strategies illuminates the need for adaptation and change. Such a dynamic strategic plan also provides inherent mechanisms to sense the need for reacting to, as well as creating, change when necessary. The value of an "objective hierarchy" within a dynamic strategic plan is multifold and serves several purposes by collectively aligning strategy, processes, and metrics.

Goals and objectives can be derived from four primary perspectives:

1. A clear understanding of the essential purpose for which the system exists
2. The fundamental nature of the challenge being pursued
3. Authoritative institutional documents that prescribe desired capabilities
4. Benchmarks relevant to desired end states

Objectives can also be arrayed, left to right, to emphasize conditional dependence for systems or projects that exhibit "dependency chains" across a sequence of characteristics or attributes. Strategies must then be developed that relate means to these desired ends. More specifically, strategies associate implementation costs with results attained in terms of objectives being pursued. Strategies, which provide "ways" to relate "means" available to desired "ends," may consist of major programs, initiatives and new policies, procedures, or concepts. Finally, performance measures must be identified that capture and quantify the efficiency or effectiveness that has been achieved by adopting and implementing particular strategies.

Effective metrics help to communicate organizational strategy, thereby producing greater organizational cohesion and congruency in workforce tasks. These strategy-related metrics, or performance "measures of effectiveness" (MOEs), help to reinforce the pursuit of a common vision for the entire organization. And in contrast to companies or agencies that expend effort and energy trying to "measure everything"—a clear indication that they really do not know where they want to go—carefully selected metrics that relate meaningful performance to a well-developed strategy also provide insight into what an organization is truly willing to change.

Descriptors for "good" metrics—standards of measurement—are that they be specific; measurable (to drive the collection of objective data); relevant (to goals and objectives); and simple. In addition to defining performance, delineating accountability, monitoring progress toward strategic objectives, and providing means for management control, they also establish feedback mechanisms necessary to change a course of action when needed. Figure 60 illustrates the alignment of supporting MOEs to specific Logistics Transformation objectives, goals, and the ultimate purpose of this endeavor.

However, metrics can go beyond simply defining performance measures for various strategies. They also provide a quantitative mechanism for monitoring progress and providing responsive feedback on the efficiency, effectiveness, or productivity gains achieved by strategies that are in place. Ultimately these MOEs must relate directly to the goals and objectives of the effort undertaken. What is measured is a reflection of priorities and should have a powerful link to strategy. If this alignment has not been attained, then it becomes impossible to relate effects of particular

STRATEGIC MANAGEMENT CONCEPTS 237

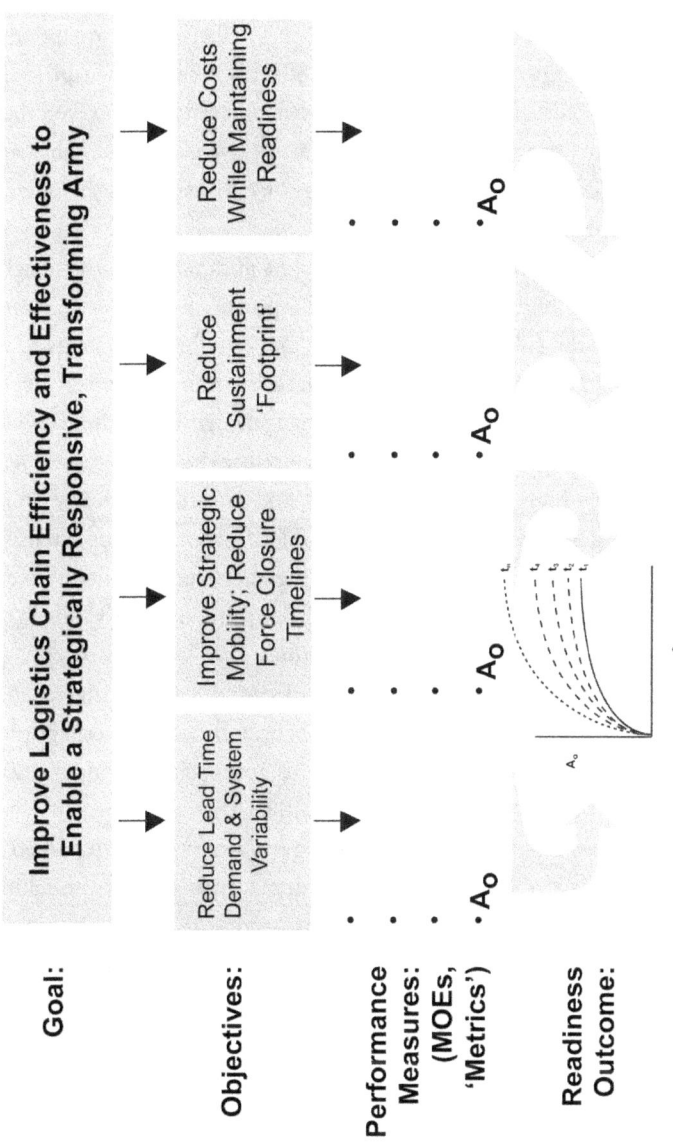

Figure 60. Objective hierarchy: Relating outcome (result) to goals and objectives (desired ends).

strategies to realized outcomes and overall purpose. Furthermore, any ability to identify and compare costs and benefits of strategies will be lost.

For enormously complex systems, mere intuition cannot be relied on to determine what is or is not important. Without the benefit of these analytical architectures, extra resources are more likely to be squandered than to have any discernable, productive effect. Once these empirically based hierarchies are developed, implemented, and refined, however, they can also help to identify metrics, strategies, or even objectives that are irrelevant to desired performance outcomes by focusing on the overall purpose for which the system exists.

Furthermore, metrics that rely on *average* values provide little insight into what is actually driving performance, especially in large-scale, complex supply chains subject to uncertainty and variability. Systems with interdependent components are characterized by information lags, feedback delays, and nonlinearities, where small changes can amplify with large effects. Averages mask variability in performance, yet those areas most afflicted by high variability, volatility, and uncertainty clearly point to directions for improved performance. Indeed, in the face of extensive systemic and structural variability, managing short-term results to average performance metrics is not only insufficient but also misleading and counterproductive. Results could be disastrous.

Ideally, then, metrics should be identified and selected that enable detection, segmentation, and exploitation of underlying and perhaps previously masked variability in outcomes. This approach can guide action and innovation conducive to learning processes that are linked to organizational strategy. This cycle of identifying key performance parameters and then detecting, understanding, explaining, learning from, and taking action based on *variability* in performance—rather than *average* performance—is portrayed at Figure 61. Effective measurement must be an integral part of the management process, grounded in the organization's strategic objectives and purpose. What is needed is not merely a measurement system but a management system to motivate improved performance and to ensure progress.

While aligning strategy to successful execution is essential, these objective hierarchies and supporting metrics should also be designed with the purpose of organizational learning in mind. Recent results from a comprehensive business strategy and management research effort indicate that

STRATEGIC MANAGEMENT CONCEPTS   239

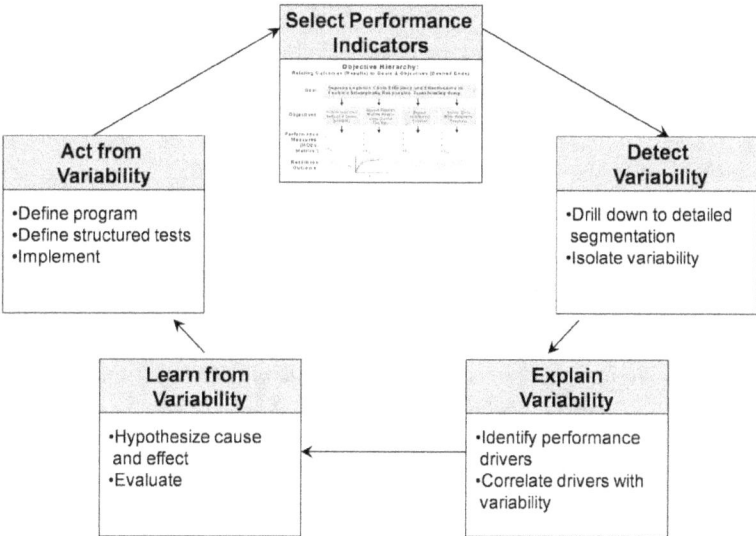

Figure 61. Aligning execution and strategy: Learning from performance variability.

executives today, inundated with heavy doses of both anecdotal information and average performance data, nevertheless have inadequate and inappropriate—even irrelevant—information at their disposal to fulfill their mandates of improving company performance in increasingly competitive environments. One supply chain expert has characterized this pervasive condition as "a plethora of data, but a dearth of information."[2] With only averages as a guide, it is not surprising that across-the-board, "salami slice" reductions are the result of organizational "reengineering" efforts.

Results from a recent investigation into supply chain process variability within the UK Ministry of Defence are directly relevant to Army Logistics Transformation. Conducted jointly by the UK Defence Procurement Agency and the Defence College of Management and Technology, this analysis revealed the "pernicious effects of an organizational dependence on the average as a performance metric." This research recommends that urgent consideration be given to the introduction of variance-based measures instead.[3]

In contrast, another recently completed long-term management research project indicates that companies that have adopted this process of detecting, explaining, and acting on sources of variability found the process provided an "important, and manageable, source of new knowledge"—a phenomenon otherwise known as "learning." Not only can meaningful progress and improvement be monitored with an appreciation for underlying cause-and-effect relationships but the feedback mechanism inherent in this cycle also leads to adaptation and experimentation. These methods can enable effective, positive, and responsive change, thereby "pushing the envelope" of continual operational and organizational improvement (refer to Figure 49).

If Logistics Transformation is to be successful, then the discovery process must be informed by a coherent set of experiments, empirical analysis, and lessons "learned" rather than mistakes merely "observed" and then errors repeated. Collectively, these resulting insights will provide the feedback necessary to build momentum for continuous improvement through innovation. This approach will keep the effort aligned, on track, and progressing while simultaneously linking execution with strategy. In summary, analytical architectures can enable, guide, and coordinate transformational change by doing the following

1. Translating strategy into operational goals
2. Aligning organizational effort (and design) to these operational objectives
3. Coordinating implementation using an empirically driven continual improvement process for strategic management

The Center for Innovation in Logistics Systems (CILS) concept, introduced earlier, can also fulfill a crucial relationship between strategy development and implementation through the use of appropriate management control systems. In his book *Levers of Control: How Managers Use Innovative Control Systems to Drive Strategic Renewal*, Harvard management professor and business consultant Robert Simons distinguishes between a top-down, "induced" strategy process and a bottom-up emergent, "autonomous" process. Induced strategic behavior, created persuasively or coerced by direction, focuses on fitting an organization's existing competencies to the environment through administrative mechanisms such as planning, organizational goals, and reference to critical performance variables.

These administrative mechanisms are typically embedded in diagnostic control systems (e.g., statistical process control). In contrast, autonomous strategic behavior focuses on initiatives outside the scope of the current strategy, which can encourage senior managers to recognize that major changes may be necessary. In the induced strategy process, management's role is to pursue an intended strategy using familiar administrative controls and existing cultural mechanisms. This makes it possible for the organization to build on past successes and to exploit opportunities within its internal environment. In contrast, for the autonomous strategic process, management's role also emphasizes strategic recognition (e.g., threats and opportunities derived from new, external perspectives) rather than traditional strategic planning alone.[4]

In their landmark text on organization theory and human behavior, *Organizational Learning*, Argyris and Schon also differentiate between "single-loop" learning using diagnostic control systems and "double-loop" learning where interactive control systems help management to recognize that a new strategy may be needed with solutions and capabilities that the organization may not yet possess. Burgelman then demonstrates in his work that those organizations that have survived and successfully adapted learned how to manage induced strategic behavior and stimulate autonomous strategic behavior. This was achieved using interactive control systems to guide the experimentation and learning necessary for creative strategic initiatives to emerge and be tested in the organization. Single-loop learning involves learning from the consequences of previous behavior, whereas double-loop learning is associated with self-organizing systems and is essential for organizations that must internally adapt to new environments and external challenges.[5]

The Department of Defense has increasingly been challenged with growing—in many cases, exponentially growing—operations and support costs across all the armed services. This trend is further magnified as increasing numbers of major systems reach and even exceed their original design lives. These trends persist, in part, due to a persistent inability to understand the consequences of improperly designed logistics networks and supply chain inefficiencies caused by the interactions between lead time variability and demand uncertainty. As newly developed systems mature, achieve operational status, and begin to stress supporting repair operations and supply chains, the army has a unique opportunity to reverse this worrisome trend. The key to achieving such a feat is adopting STAAMP and creating a "double-loop" learning organization, enabled and empowered by a CILS, as described in chapter 19.

Former Army Vice Chief of Staff General Richard A. Cody, a highly decorated combat veteran and aviator with long experience in the army, once asserted, "We have the best pilots in the world. We have the best commanders, the best maintenance crews, and the best equipment." Depending on one's perspective (and branch of service), this could be interpreted as an incontrovertible fact, a proud boast, or perhaps arguable rhetoric. But General Cody did not, indeed could not, proclaim that a world-class logistics support and supply chain management enterprise backs up the army's aviation soldiers. The army is simply not there yet.

CHAPTER 26

Final Thoughts

[Major General George] Goethals' best work had been the Panama Canal . . . He took over a demoralized crew with seemingly insurmountable problems and molded them into a unified organization [where] he controlled supply organizations and used scientific management. [Then recalled from retirement to lead the Army's supply system in World War I] in 1917 he once again found confusion but could never duplicate his earlier power to deal with it. He and his assistants worked hard to push the Army's supply organization toward a better, more rational operation suitable for the 20th century . . . [but] he could never succeed in centralizing the supply activities of the War Department . . . was not able to effect any substantial permanent reforms . . . [and] could not conquer the supply bureau.

—Phyllis A. Zimmerman, from *The Neck of the Bottle: George W. Goethals and the Reorganization of the U.S. Army Supply System, 1917–1918*

Ideas fight a grinding battle with circumstances.

—A. P. Thornton, from *The Imperial Idea and Its Enemies*

The purpose of this project is to ensure Logistics Transformation for the army's materiel enterprise transitions toward a readiness-focused outcome that, averting Path D, ultimately follows a strategic trajectory along Path C (Figure 59).

The future is properly the temporal focus of "transformation." However, a major precept of any "learning organization," even more fundamental than the five disciplines that characterize one, is the ability to actually learn from—not merely observe—the past.[1] In essence, simply failing to repeat past mistakes represents the most basic form of human progress.[2] The study of history informs contemporary conceptual thought. Paradoxically, a look to the past can reinforce rather than retard innovation. Since people naturally tend to see their current problems as unique and overwhelming, historical analogies can be especially helpful. They stretch and broaden our thinking and allow contemporary challenges to come into better focus through the long lens of history. Emphasis on "outside the box" thinking today should also be tempered through understanding and appreciation by "looking into the box" of the past.

Accordingly, consider the following characterization:

> The system lacked a clear chain of command. Agencies all shared responsibility yet no one was responsible . . . It could not coordinate and standardize [data] to a common "language." Each bureau had raw data, analyzed for only its purposes, expressed in its terms, and responsive to its need . . . Reorganizations [were] a response to crises and created the illusion of progress while merely producing confusion, inefficiency, and, most seriously, personnel demoralization . . . Because of continual reorganizations, the bureaus had new difficulty furnishing data . . . The situation became more complicated when records in one division differed from those in another . . . [He] found the independent, loosely related bureau financial practices a "nearly insuperable barrier to consolidation" [and] varying interpretations of regulations caused confusion . . . He believed supply should conform to industrial and scientific principles yet lacked the authority . . . The Army was pushing an already strained supply system into a state of paralysis . . . An integrated supply system remained a myth . . . By the end of the war he feared the supply system would collapse . . . [After the war, congressional] hearings pinpointed the supply problem . . . Yet their Act did not unify the system. It institutionalized divided authority, providing enough checks and balances to paralyze action.[3]

This extract is from Phyllis Zimmerman's biography of Major General George W. Goethals, the famous army engineer who designed and managed construction of the Panama Canal.[4] Today, more than a century later, this achievement is still recognized as one of the greatest engineering and project management feats in modern history. At the beginning of America's entry into World War I, Goethals was recalled from retirement to head the army's supply organization. While his frustrations, expressed in 1918, may also sound as accurate now, nearly a century later, the long lens of history surely reveals one major advantage now compared to conditions nearly a century ago.

Turning to history then, rather than technology, to provide comparative insight into past and current conditions, one powerful observation becomes apparent: the "power of analysis"—operations research, systems analysis, and supply chain management science—did not exist then to help Goethals with the army's enormous supply and logistics challenges. This truly incredible power is, however, at our disposal today. *We must harness it now to full advantage for the army.*

The contrast between the methods we have been using and what we could and should use could not be more stark. The underlying logic of current practices must be directly challenged. If it is not, then we will surely continue to deceive only ourselves, perpetuating self-delusion and increasingly greater risk while opportunity knocks at our door. Significant organizational change has always provoked resistance, which should naturally be expected. However, as one of our most distinguished historians, Barbara Tuchman, observed, pursuing flawed and failed policies *knowing* that plausible alternatives and better options are available is truly "the march of folly."[5]

This endeavor should also be viewed from the perspective of our much larger strategic resource challenges: the quest for solvency in public policy. Current trends within our federal budget, both discretionary and entitlement programs, in addition to larger Department of Defense–wide cost growth forecasts, render current spending trajectories unsustainable and future programs unachievable. Within this larger fiscal framework for budget policy and defense planning,

> demands on the U.S. military are even more daunting—fighting a highly unpredictable global war on terrorism while implementing a largely undefined transformation in organization, equipment, and doctrine. Current defense budget projections ignore future costs of the former and understate the potential costs of the latter . . . Difficult choices are inescapable with regard to readiness, force levels, and procurement for both traditional and transformational modernization. The current debate over Army end-strength illustrates the dilemma . . . offsetting procurement cutbacks will be needed to hold defense budgets within politically realistic limits . . . Since the defense budgets likely to be in place over the next several years cannot accommodate higher force levels, improved readiness, and transformational modernization, there must inevitably be painful tradeoffs.[6]

To the extent that immense and ever-growing operations and support costs can be contained and tied to predictable readiness outcomes, these painful trade-offs can be better managed by defense policy officials, budget analysts, and future administrations. Indeed, nearly 4 years into the Global War on Terror, the army's FY2006-11 Program Objective Memorandum (POM), which is generated by the Total Army Analysis requirements generation process, contained validated *peacetime* requirements that exceeded programmed resources by over 20%.[7]

Of course, a broader national security perspective must also address the foreseeable geopolitical environment, domestic sociodemographic patterns and education challenges, growing national infrastructure challenges ranging from energy to transportation, sagging personal savings and national investment levels, and increasingly intractable social entitlement policies. Realistic projections of these converging trends illuminate enormous risk to the nation—a potentially catastrophic gap between future expectations and unfolding realities.[8] We must not continue to "mortgage the future" in such a strategically irresponsible way.

We hope this endeavor will serve as a catalyst for an intellectual and professional resurgence in military logistics systems analysis. We are certainly encouraged by our empirical research results that continue to corroborate and reinforce many of the concepts and ideas presented in this book. Nonetheless, the degree to which the significant changes proposed herein can impact institutional culture and practice remains to be seen. Consequently, we have engaged the larger military operations research and professional logistics communities and continue to encourage the participation of all those interested to collectively pursue this enormous challenge.

Finally, it is certainly appropriate and necessary to ask what the personnel impacts and practical benefits of this undertaking may be. Figure 62 offers a series of direct responses to this question. They are framed around the various perspectives of several key professional positions involved in focusing logistics to better support and sustain the army's most effective, flexible, and adaptable assets—America's soldiers. Now at the dawn of the 21st century, just as they did during the 20th century, American soldiers represent the single most powerful force for good in the history of the world.

- **Specialist Four Dalton**: AH-64 attack helicopter mechanic, 82nd Airborne Division Combat Aviation Battalion—Reduces his labor-intensive "work-arounds"; he no longer is the routine "bill-payer" and go-to guy who must compensate for inadequate supply support; a more satisfied customer—the one who matters most.
- **SFC Dalton**: Maintenance Production noncommissioned officer—Gains much greater trust in a supply support system that is more responsive and better anticipates his needs; a more satisfied customer with renewed confidence.
- **CW2 Dalton**: Aviation company maintenance tech—No longer wastes so much time scrounging for parts, making "deals," and placing his integrity at risk to achieve readiness goals for his unit and commander; a more satisfied customer who believes the army is now beginning to have a smoothly functioning supply system.
- **CW5 Dalton**: Aviation Classification Repair Activity Depot production officer—For this "crusty" Vietnam vet, a long-recognized need without any previous attempts at an honest solution; the fundamental flaw has always been organizational design, and Operation Iraqi Freedom yielded a very predictable disaster; now, finally retiring, with an "honest solution" actually appearing on the horizon, he is no longer so cynical but, true-to-form, still "crusty."
- **LTC Dalton**: AH-64 attack battalion commander—Eliminates "distorted behavior" in his command; he no longer must "game" the readiness reporting, supply, and financial management systems, resorting to twisted, convoluted, counterproductive actions needed to achieve equipment readiness (ER) goals that he alone has always been held responsible for. Now, working collaboratively with both his supporting Apache program manager and contract logistics provider, he gradually believes that the supply "system" becomes at least partially accountable for ER his unit achieves.

Figure 62. Potential project impacts.

- **Ms. Dalton**: Integrated Materiel Management Center "item" manager—Empowers her to become a weapon system "readiness" manager. Always hardworking and dedicated, she notices fewer episodes of "intense management" and ad hoc workarounds. She knows her decisions make a real difference now, and she can see the results.
- **COL Dalton**: Program manager—Can now actually do his job and make sensible trade-offs among cost, performance, schedule—and, unlike before, reliability, maintainability, tactical operational availability, and sustainment costs (operations and maintenance)—empowering and enabling him to manage his program to readiness goals and life-cycle cost for the first time. He works smarter, not harder.
- **MG Dalton**: G-8, director, Program Analysis and Evaluation—Can now relate HQDA program investment inputs to future readiness (Ao) outcomes and recommend PPBS/PPBES-related PB decisions and trade-offs across RDTE, PA, and OMA accounts with much greater clarity and confidence. He can now provide compelling programmatic arguments, since he has the analytic foundation for determining a multiyear resource program that matches resources necessary to meet readiness demands for a "capabilities-based" force prescribed in the DPG.
- **LTG Dalton**: CG, CJTF—Is assured that he'll receive operations-based, mission-focused log support; neither "just-in-case" (too burdensome) nor "just-in-time" (too risky), he will have both the package appropriate for his mission and responsive resupply.
- **Dr. Dalton**: ASA (ALT)—Can now report to the Secretary of the Army that army complies with DRRS for Title X logistics function; he is now empowered with insight from a new "Logistics Early Warning System."

Figure 62. Potential project impacts (continued).

- **GEN Dalton**: CSA—Has greater confidence that his HQDA investment decisions can now be related to readiness-oriented results; unlike his predecessor, he no longer feels compelled to ask in frustration, "Why am I still throwing billions down this 'black hole' called 'spares'?"
- **Congressman Dalton**: HASC—Gains much greater confidence in credibility of both budget submissions and requirements presented for army logistics. He supports full funding because he understands implications for national security. He concurs with his colleagues that GAO should now remove army "inventory management" from its "high-risk" list of government programs, where it has been for over two decades.
- **Joe Dalton (the American taxpayer and SP4 Dalton's father)**: Gets a better return on his tax dollar; feels assured that his young, 82nd paratrooper son will be OK—Airborne Hooah!

Figure 62. Potential project impacts (continued).

We shall not cease from exploration
And the end of all our exploring
Will be to arrive where we started
And know the place for the first time.

—T. S. Eliot, *Four Quartets*, 1943

Knowledge is power.

—Sir Francis Bacon, 1597

The point . . . is not so much to *predict* the future as to *prepare* for it.

—John Lewis Gaddis, professor of history, Yale University

APPENDIX A

Acronyms

Ao–Operational Availability
AAR–After Action Review
ADMRU–(Army National Guard) Aviation Depot Maintenance Roundout Unit
AIT–Automatic Identification Technologies
ALMC–Army Logistics Management College
AMC–Army Materiel Command
AMCOM–(U.S. Army) Aviation and Missile Command
AMSAA–Army Materiel Systems Analysis Activity
ARFORGEN–Army Force Generation (force management model)
ASA(ALT)–Assistant Secretary of the Army (Acquisition, Logistics, and Technology)
ASC–Army Sustainment Command
ASL–Authorized Stock List
AVCRAD–Aviation Classification Repair Activity Depot
AVF–All-Volunteer Force
AWCF–Army Working Capital Fund
C3–Command, Control, and Communications
CBM–Condition Based Maintenance
CASCOM–(U.S. Army) Combined Arms Support Command
CCAD–Corpus Christi Army Depot
CCSS–Commodity Command Standard System
CDSN–Capability-Driven Supply Network
CENTCOM–U.S. Central Command
CER–Cost-Estimating Relationship
CILS–Center for Innovation in Logistics Systems
CJTF–Commander, Joint Task Force
CKO–Chief Knowledge Officer

CLS–Contract Logistics Support
CONUS–Continental United States
CSA–Chief of Staff, Army
CTL–(MIT) Center for Transportation and Logistics
CWT–Customer Wait Time
DAU–Defense Acquisition University
DBOF–Defense Business Operating Fund
DDOC–(Theater Joint) Deployment and Distribution Operations Center
DEPTEMPO–Deployment Tempo
DHS–Department of Homeland Security
DLA–Defense Logistics Agency
DLR–Depot-Level Reparable
DMSMS–Diminishing Manufacturing Sources and Material Shortages
DoD–Department of Defense
DP–Dynamic Programming
DPG–Defense Planning Guidance
DRB–Division Ready Brigade
DRF–Division Ready Force
DRP–Distribution Requirements Planning
DRRS–Defense Readiness Reporting System
DSLP–Dynamic Strategic Logistics Planning
DSS–Decision Support System
ERP–Enterprise Resource Planning
EUCOM–U.S. European Command
FAA–Federal Aviation Administration
FCS–Future Combat System
FFRDC–Federally Funded Research and Development Center
FMC–Fully Mission Capable
FORSCOM–(U.S. Army) Forces Command
GAO–Government Accountability Office
GWOT–Global War on Terror
HASC–House Armed Services Committee
HQDA–Headquarters, Department of the Army
HUMS–Health and Usage Monitoring System
IDA–Institute for Defense Analyses

IMMC–Integrated Materiel Management Center
INFORMS–Institute for Operations Research and Management Science
IRO–(U.S. Army) Inventory Research Office
IT–Information Technology
ITV–In-Transit Visibility
IRC–Initial Ready Company
ISR–Intelligence, Surveillance, and Reconnaissance
JROC–Joint Requirements Oversight Council
LCC–Life-Cycle Cost
LCMC–Life Cycle Management Command
LIA–(U.S. Army) Logistics Innovation Agency
LMI–Logistics Management Institute
LMP–(U.S. Army) Logistics Modernization Plan
LOGSA–(U.S. Army) Logistics Support Activity
LRU–Line Replaceable Unit
MAMSC–Mobile Aircraft Maintenance Sustainment Capability
MC–Mission Capable
MDA–Missile Defense Agency
MEF–Marine Expeditionary Force
METRIC–Multiechelon Technique for Recoverable Item Control
MIST–Management Innovation as a Strategic Technology
MIT–Massachusetts Institute of Technology
MLDT–Mean Logistics Delay Time
MOE–Measure of Effectiveness
MORS–Military Operations Research Society
MRP–Materials Requirements Planning
MTBF–Mean Time Between Failure
MTBUR–Mean Time Between Unit Replacement
MTTR–Mean Time To Repair
NASA–National Aeronautics and Space Administration
NEO–Noncombatant Evacuation Operation
NICP–National Inventory Control Point
NMC–Non-Mission Capable
NMCM–Non-Mission-Capable Maintenance
NMCS–Non-Mission-Capable Supply
NORTHCOM–U.S. Northern Command

OEF–Operation Enduring Freedom (Afghanistan)
OEM–Original Equipment Manufacturer
OFT–(OSD) Office of Force Transformation
OIF–Operation Iraqi Freedom
O&M–Operations and Maintenance
OMA–Operations and Maintenance, Army
OPTEMPO–Operations Tempo
OR–Operations Research
OR/MS–Operations Research/Management Science
ORSA–Operations Research/Systems Analysis
OSD–Office of the Secretary of Defense
PACOM–U.S. Pacific Command
PAE–Program Analysis and Evaluation
PBL–Performance-Based Logistics
PDM–Program Depot Maintenance
PEO–Program Executive Office
PMC–Partially Mission Capable
PMRM–Partitioned Multiobjective Risk Method
PNNL–(Department of Energy) Pacific Northwest National Laboratory
RBS–Readiness-Based Sparing
RDES–Requirements Determination and Execution System
RDSN–Readiness-Driven Supply Network
RDTE–Research, Development, Test, and Evaluation
RECAP–(U.S. Army) Recapitalization Program
RFID–Radio Frequency Identification
RFRM–Risk Filtering, Ranking, and Management
RL–Reverse Logistics
RMA–Revolution in Military Affairs
RO–Requirement Objective
ROP–Reorder Point
SA–Secretary of the Army
SALE–Single Army Logistics Enterprise
SAMS–Standard Army Maintenance System
SARSS–Standard Army Retail Supply System
SCM–Supply Chain Management
SLEP–Service Life Extension Program

SNL–(Department of Energy) Sandia National Laboratory
SOUTHCOM–U.S. Southern Command
S&RL–Sense and Respond Logistics
SSA–Supply Support Activity
SSF–Single Stock Fund
STA–Sparing to Availability
STAAMP–Strategic Architectures for Analysis, Management, and Planning
TAA–Total Army Analysis
TAT–Turnaround Time
TAV–Total Asset Visibility
TOC–Theory of Constraints
TRADOC–(U.S. Army) Training and Doctrine Command
TRANSCOM–U.S. Transportation Command
TRT–Total Retrograde Time
UAH–University of Alabama in Huntsville
UCG–(AWCF) Unit Cost Goal
UFR–Unfinanced Requirement
ULLS–Unit-Level Logistics System
ULLS-A–Unit-Level Logistics System–Aviation
ULLS-A(E)–Unit-Level Logistics System–Aviation (Enhanced)
USAREC–U.S. Army Recruiting Command

APPENDIX B
Additional Reading

Anupindi, R., Chopra, S., Deshmukh, S. D., Van Meighem, J. A., & Zemel, E. (1999). *Managing business process flows.* Upper Saddle River, NJ: Prentice-Hall.

Blanchard, B. S. (1981). *Logistics engineering and management.* Prentice-Hall.

Brownlee, L., & Schoomaker, P. J. (2004). Serving a nation at war: A campaign quality army with joint and expeditionary capabilities. *Parameters,* U.S. Army War College, *34,* 4–23.

Buede, D. (2000). *The engineering design of systems: Models and methods.* Wiley Interscience.

Chang, Y. S. et al. (Eds.) (2004). *Evolution of supply chain management: Symbiosis of adaptive value networks and ICT.* Kluwer.

Chopr, S., & Meindl, P. (2004). *Supply chain management: Strategy, planning, and operations.* Prentice Hall.

Christopher, M. (2004). *Logistics and supply chain management: Strategies for reducing cost and improving service.* Prentice Hall.

Cohen, M. A. et al. (2006). Achieving breakthrough service delivery through dynamic asset deployment strategies. *Interfaces, 36*(3), 259–271.

Cohen, S., & Roussel, J. (2005). *Strategic supply chain management: The five disciplines for top performance.* McGraw-Hill.

Damaskopoulos, P. (2005). Toward a network topology of enterprise transformation and innovation. In W. H. Dutton et al. (Eds.), *Transforming enterprise: The economic and social implications of information technology.* Cambridge, MA: MIT Press.

Davila, T., Epstein, M. J., & Shelton, R. (2006). *Making innovation work: How to manage it, measure it, and profit from it.* Wharton School Publishing.

Fabrie, R. (2005). *Evaluating, managing, and forecasting army equipment readiness: The army logistics system for aviation spares* (draft). Alexandria, VA: IDA.

Fullan, M. (2001). *Leading in a culture of change.* Jossey-Bass.

Geunes, J., & Pardalos, P. M. (Eds.) (2005). *Supply chain optimization.* Springer.

Goldsby, T., & Martichenko, R. *Lean Six Sigma logistics: Strategic development to operational success.* J. Ross Publishing.

Goldsmith, M. et al. (2004). *Leading organizational change: Harnessing the power of knowledge.* Jossey-Bass.

Greenwald, B. E. (2000). "The anatomy of change: Why armies succeed or fail at transformation (Institute of Land Warfare Paper Number #35). AUSA.

Harrison, T. P. et al. (Eds.) (2003). *The practice of supply chain management: Where theory and application converge.* Kluwer.

Hatch, M. J. (1997). *Organization theory: Modern, symbolic, and postmodern perspectives.* New York, NY: Oxford University Press.

Holland, C. (2005). *Breakthrough business results with MVT.* Hoboken, NJ: John Wiley.

Huzurbazar, A. V. (2005). *Flowgraph models for multistate time-to-event data.* Wiley-Interscience.

Jack Mezirow and Associates. (2000). *Learning as transformation: Critical perspectives on a theory in progress.* Jossey-Bass.

Jackson, M. C. (2000). *Systems approaches to management.* Kluwer Academic/Plenum Publishers.

Jackson, M. C. (2003). *Systems thinking: Creative holism for managers.* John Wiley.

Kern, P. J. (n.d.). Got It? Some thoughts on future logistics. AMC Pamphlet.

Krolmayer, G. et al. (2002). *Supply chain management based on SAP systems.* Springer.

Kuhn, T. S. (1956). *The structure of scientific revolutions* (3rd ed). Chicago, IL: University of Chicago Press.

Lawler, E. E., III, & Worley, C. G. *Built to change: How to achieve sustained organizational effectiveness.* Hoboken, NJ: Jossey-Bass.

Lee, H. L. (2004, October). The Triple-A supply chain. *Harvard Business Review,* Oct 2004.

Lee, H. L., & Billington, C. (1992, Spring). Managing supply chain inventory: Pitfalls and opportunities. *MIT Sloan Management Review,* 65–73.

Levenbach, H., &. Cleary, J. P. (1984). *The modern forecaster: The forecasting process through data analysis.* Wadsworth.

Malone, T. W. et al. (Ed.) (2003). *Inventing the organizations of the 21st century.* Cambridge, MA: MIT Press.

Malone, T. W. et al. (Eds.) (2003). *Organizing business knowledge: The MIT process handbook.* Cambridge, MA: MIT Press.

Martin, J. W. (2007). *Lean Six Sigma for supply chain management: The 10-Step solution process.* McGraw Hill.

Mason, R. O., & Apte, U. (2005). Using knowledge to transform enterprises. In Dutton et al. (Eds.), *Transforming enterprise: The economic and social implications of information technology.* Cambridge, MA: MIT Press.

Mathaisel, D. F. X. (2007). *Sustaining the military enterprise.* Auerbach, Taylor & Francis Group.

Musmanno et al. (2004). *Introduction to logistics systems planning and control.* Hoboken, NJ: John Wiley.

Parlier, G. H. (2005). *Transforming U.S. Army logistics: A strategic supply chain approach for inventory management* (AUSA Land Warfare Paper Number 54).

Posner, R. A. (2004). *Catastrophe: Risks and responses.* New York, NY: Oxford University Press.

Pundoor, G., & Herrman, J. W. (2004). A hierarchical approach to supply chain simulation modeling using the SCOR model. Institute for Systems Research paper, University of Maryland, July 28, 2004.

Rubenstein, M. F., & Firstenberg, I. R. (1999). *The minding organization.* John Wiley.

Scotchmer, S. (2004). *Innovations and incentives.* Cambridge, MA: MIT Press.

Simchi-Levi, D. et al. (2004). *Managing the supply chain: The definitive guide for the business professional.* McGraw-Hill.

Simchi-Levi, D. et al. (Eds.) (2004). *Handbook of quantitative supply chain analysis: Modeling in the e-business era.* Kluwer.

Sodhi, M. J. (2005). How to do strategic supply chain planning. MIT *Sloan Management Review, 34*(1), 69–75.

Spector, P. E. (1981). *Research design.* Sage Publications.

Taylor, D. A. (2004). *Supply chain: A manager's guide.* Addison Wesley.

Tayur et al. (Eds.) (1999). *Quantitative models for supply chain management.* Kluwer.

Notes

Preface

1. This direct quote is an extract from Secretary of Defense Robert Gates's speech at the Eisenhower Library, May 8, 2010.

Chapter 1

1. Kern (2004), p. 72.
2. U.S. Government Accountability Office (GAO) report (2005), p. 66.
3. U.S. GAO (2003), pp. 1–4.
4. Association of the U.S. Army (AUSA) (2004).
5. Brown (2003).
6. Heinrich and Simchi-Levi (2010).
7. For technology-oriented proposals supporting Logistics Transformation see, for example, the 84 initiatives developed by the Army Logistics Transformation Task Force (LTTF); for management-oriented concepts see Army Logistics Transformation Task Force (LTTF), Army Logistics Transformation, HQDA G-4, January 2003.
8. The final presentation for the initial phase of this AMCOM project, with supporting analyses and recommendations, is available upon request. Additionally, several follow-on research reports, briefings, and articles have been published and are available in the public domain. Contact the author at gparlier@knology.net for assistance.
9. U.S. GAO (2003); Fontenot, Degen, and Tohn (2005); Peltz, Boren, Robbins, and Wolff (2005); Murdock (2005).

Chapter 2

1. Department of Defense Office of Inspector General (2003).

Chapter 3

1. Croson and Donohue (2002), pp. 74–82.

262 NOTES

Chapter 4

1. Lee, Padmanabhan, and Whang (1997a); Chen, Drezner, Ryan, and Simchi-Levi (2000), pp. 436–443; Naim (2004), pp. 109–132.
2. Fisher (1997), pp. 105–116.
3. Lee (2002), pp. 105–119.
4. Sterman (2000), pp. 663–755; Killingsworth (2004).
5. Goldberg and Kimko (2003).

Chapter 5

1. Winograd (2001), pp. 64–68.
2. Butler (2005), pp. 39–40.
3. Office of Inspector General of the Department of Defense (2003), p. 8.
4. Held (2005).
5. Peltz, Boren, Robbins, and Wolff (2002), p. 78.

Chapter 6

1. U.S. GAO (2003).
2. Kallock (2004), pp. 23, 46–53.
3. Rubenstein and Firstenberg (1999), p. 62.
4. Levy and Lemeshow (1999). From a statistical perspective, the advantage of stratified sampling is described in Figure 63.

LMI research has consistently shown that this stratified sampling concept, when applied to demand forecasting for aviation spares and repair parts—

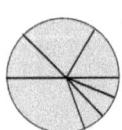

POPULATION OF SIZE **N** DIVIDED INTO **K** STRATA

RANDOM SAMPLING: $\hat{P}_{RSM} = \dfrac{X}{n}$

RANDOM SAMPLING: $P_k^1 = \dfrac{X_k}{n_k}$

THEN:

$$\hat{P}_{STRAT} = \dfrac{\sum_{l=1}^{k} N_k P_k^1}{N}$$

USUALLY:

$$Var(\hat{\Theta}_{STRAT}) \leq Var(\hat{\Theta}_{POP}) \leq Var(\hat{\Theta}_{RSM})$$

Figure 63. Stratified sampling.

mission-based forecasting—yields an order of magnitude improvement over existing methods in forecasting accuracy across a range of platforms, missions, and operational environments. Kuhn and Harleston (2009); Kuhn (2010a); Kuhn (2010b), pp. 35–39.

5. Biddle (2002); Biddle (2004).

6. Kuhn (1992).

7. Henderson and Kwinn, (2005); AHS International (2008).

8. Gavirneni (1999), p. 444.

9. For a theoretical perspective on Bayesian statistics, see McGee (1971); for applications using revised estimates, see section 15.3, "Revisions of Estimates," in de Neufville (1990b), pp. 279–285; and for practical applications of Bayesian statistics to spare parts forecasting, see Sherbrooke (1992), pp. 71–94.

Chapter 7

1. Office of the Deputy Under Secretary of Defense for Logistics and Materiel Readiness (2003); Department of the Army (2005a).

2. Slay et al. (1996), p. 2-2.

3. Sherbrooke (1992).

4. Kotkin (2003).

5. Sherbrooke (1992), p. 213.

Chapter 8

1. Daniel, Guide, and Van Wassenhove (2003).

2. Van De Vegte (1986).

3. Dreiner, Peltz, Lackey, Blake, and Vasidyanathan (2004); Folkeson & Brauner (2005).

4. Parlier (2003).

5. Wang (2004).

6. Pint, Brauner, Bondanella, Relles, and Steinberg (2002), p. 60; also in the Army's Commodity Command Standard System (CCSS), unserviceable return rates are inexplicably "capped" at 100% according to AMSAA Report TR-2006-17, p. 21.

7. Hall (2004); Wang (2005).

8. U.S. TRANSCOM DPO Update (2005).

9. Muckstadt (2005).

10. Callioni et al. (2005), pp. 135–141.

Chapter 9

1. Hammer (2002).
2. Hugos (2003), pp. 110–115; Fredendall and Hill (2001).
3. "Theory of Constraints and Lean Thinking," briefing to DUSD (L&MR) by USMC Maintenance Center, Albany, GA, undated (2003).
4. Calderwood et al. (2002).
5. Doneen and McQuerry (2002).
6. Department of Defense Office of Inspector General (2003), pp. 5–9.
7. Peltz, Collabella, Williams, and Boren (2004).
8. Cranwell, Haupt, and Haupt (2004).
9. Distasio (2004), p. 44.
10. Extract from "Inside the Army," (2005); Department of the Army (2007); Griffin (2008), p. 30.
11. Bachman (2005, manuscript pending publication).

Chapter 10

1. U.S. GAO (2007), pp. 11–12.
2. Guay (2007).
3. Fabrie (2005), p. 2.
4. Bilczo et al. (2003).
5. Sullivan (2004).
6. Defense Industrial Base Panel (1980).
7. For these historical patterns and trends, and examples of previous "crises response" solutions, I am indebted to IDA Adjunct Research Staff member Robert Fabrie who has been special assistant for contracting to the commander, Air Force Systems Command, and director for industrial support at the Defense Logistics Agency. Personal communication, March 2005.
8. Among those commercial suppliers that have developed, refined, and incorporated STA and RBS algorithms into complex, large-scale multiechelon inventory optimization decision support systems and are now marketing their software capabilities are TFD Group; MCA Solutions; Manugistics (recently bought by JDA); Xelus; Caterpillar Logistics; Servigistics; Demand Management; and Opus, which is a Swedish firm used extensively throughout Europe by both aircraft manufacturers and NATO air forces. Typically, these software applications have the capability to apply multi-item, multi-indenture, multiechelon RBS to optimize availability goals globally; by site or location; and by equipment type, model, and series.
9. Tyson, Horowitz, Evanovich, McBride, and Robinson (1990); Goldberg and Tyson (1991); Kelley (2004).
10. Eaton (2002), pp. 1–3.
11. Eaton (2002), pp. 1–3.

Chapter 12

1. Lee (2003).
2. Slay et al. (1996); Sherbrooke (1992); Muckstadt (2005).
3. Simchi-Levi et al. (2003); Simchi-Levi, Chen, and Bramel (2005).

Chapter 13

1. Army Logistics White Paper (2003).
2. Office of Force Transformation (OFT) of the Department of Defense (2004).
3. OFT of DoD (2004), p. 6.
4. Kaufmann (1993); Kaufmann (1995).
5. Kotkin (2003); Muckstadt (2005), pp. 150–160.
6. Cranfield University School of Management (2003); Christopher and Peck; Christopher and Towill; Tang (2006), pp. 33; Muckstadt (2005), p.45; Peck (2006), pp. 127–142; for "resilience" applied to disaster relief planning, see Lodree and Taskin (2007); for "resilience" applied to U.S. energy security policy, see Yergin (2006), pp. 75–76.

Chapter 14

1. Hundley (1999).
2. Maccagnan (2005), pp. 1–2.
3. Valikangas and Gibbert (2005), pp. 58–64.
4. Hill, Fancher, and Parlier (1999), pp. 6–7; Parlier (1999); Hauk and Parlier (2000), pp. 73–80; Knowles et al. (2002), pp. 78–92; Parlier (2002), pp. 13, 33–34.

Chapter 15

1. Bellman (1957); Phillips, Ravindran, and Solberg (1976), pp. 419–472; Denardo (1982); Powell (2007).

Chapter 16

1. de Neufville (1990a), pp. 320–323; de Neufville (2000), pp. 4–5.
2. Ignizio (1998); Ignizio (1999), pp. 6–8, 27.
3. Simon (1957), p. 198.
4. Sterman (1992).

5. Ideas, including examples of successful implementations, for these large-scale, complex systems "simulators" are illustrated in Senge and Sterman (2000).

6. For example, see the following pertaining to the theory of constraints (TOC) as a business process reengineering philosophy: Goldratt and Cox (1985); Dettmer (1996); Schragenheim (1998); Chase, Jacobs, and Aquilano (2001).

7. Sterman (2000).

8. de Neufville (2002); de Neufville (2004); Wang and de Neufville; http://ardent.mit.edu

9. Parlier et al. (1997); Parlier (1997) Parlier (1998).

10. Easterly (2006), pp. 373–374.

11. Box, Hunter, and Hunter (1978).

12. Spector (1981).

13. Holland (2005).

14. Blackett and Burman (1946), pp. 305–325.

Chapter 17

1. Haimes (2004); *http://www.sys.virginia.edu/risk.html*

2. Chopra and Sodhi (2004), pp. 53–61.

3. Cranfield University School of Management (2003).

4. Garvey (2009).

5. For an excellent vulnerability analysis from a Homeland Security perspective, and corresponding recommendations, see Flynn (2004).

6. MIT Center for Transportation and Logistics (2003); Rice and Caniatio (2003); *http://web.mit.edu/scresponse*

Chapter 18

1. Department of Defense (2002), pp. 2, 5.

2. For a general overview of the systems approach see Tillson, Burns, Freeman, Morton, and Rothmann (2003); for an application of the systems approach to "readiness-generating functions" within DoD see Tillson, Burns, Freeman, Morton, and Rothmann (2003), p. I–11 and Appendix F; and for a specific application of the systems approach using "theory of constraints" to U.S. Marine Corps aviation logistics see Baletreri and McDoniel (2002).

3. Congdon (2003), pp. 210–214.

4. Email dialogue among the author, Don Graham, Shoumen Datta, and Stan Horowitz, August 8 and 31, 2005.

5. Datta and Granger (2006); Datta et al. (2004), pp. 5–67; Datta (n.d.); Datta (2003).

NOTES 267

6. Levine (2007); Levine and Horowitz (2004); Horowitz (2005); Levine, Fabrie, and Horowitz (2006).

7. For an existing example of an econometric-based "readiness and early warning system" that is supporting USAREC (the Army's recruiting command), part of the Title 10 function for "manning," see Goldberg and Kimko (2003).

Chapter 19

1. There is a growing literature on military innovation, although it has been characterized as "underdeveloped, discursive, atheoretical, and unsystematic." Nonetheless, the foundational concept of "creative destruction" as a basis for innovation, economic and otherwise, is attributed to the great Austrian economist Joseph Schumpeter. See McGraw (2007).

2. Project participants have included the Logistics Management Institute (LMI); RAND's Arroyo Center; AMC's Army Materiel Systems Analysis Activity (AMSAA) and Logistics Support Activity (LOGSA); Institute for Defense Analysis (IDA); MIT's Forum for Supply Chain Innovation (FSCI); the University of Alabama in Huntsville (UAH); and SAIC. Funding support was provided by AMCOM, AMRDEC, and AMC G3.

3. These organizations include LOGSA; LAISO; AMCOM IMMC, G-3 CAD, and G-8; AMRDEC; PEOs Aviation and Missile; ALMC; DAU-South; and also the Huntsville-area corporate knowledge in simulation technology development and applications.

4. Department of the Army (2007), p. 34.

5. Birkenshaw and Mol (2006), pp. 81–88; Anthony et al. (2008), pp. 45–53.

Chapter 20

1. Coyle (2004).
2. Department of the Army (2007), pp. 4–34.
3. Memorandum (2004); Pillsbury (2005), pp. 32–36.
4. Thurow (2003).

Chapter 21

1. Shapiro (2001).
2. Hugos (2003), p. 127. For an overview of supply chain management system components see Simchi-Levi et al. (2003), pp. 283–292.
3. Shapiro (2007), p. 35.
4. Carr (2004); Hammer (2002), p. 28.
5. Fisher, Shoemaker, and Hoard (2005); Nye (2004); Her Majesty's Stationery Office (1963).

6. Fortun and Schweber (1993), p. 598.
7. Kirby (1970), p. 3.
8. Pringle.
9. Simchi-Levi (2010), pp. 103–130; Simchi-Levi, Kaminski, and Simchi-Levi (2003b).
10. Chin and Lucyshyn (2004), pp. 211–228.
11. Davenport and Harris (2007); Ferguson et al. (2005), pp. 51–58.
12. Hamel (2007), p. 40.

Chapter 22

1. Key PBL "alignment" challenges and concepts in this section, including the three charts that are used, are derived primarily from extensive dialogue with Robert Butler, the CEO of Tools For Decision Group (TFDG) Inc., and especially TFDG Chief Scientist John Millhouse; see also syllabi for "Spares Management and Modeling" and "PBL Solutions: Issues, Concepts, and Methods for Logisticians and Managers," TFDG short courses sponsored by Systems Exchange Seminars, 70 Garden Court, Suite 300, Monterey, CA.
2. Tuttle (2005), p. 177.
3. Bryson (2004), p. 10.
4. Hamel (2007), p. 261.

Chapter 23

1. U.S. GAO (1997), p. 23.
2. Hanks (2005); U.S. GAO (1997), p. 2.
3. Brauner et al. (1997).
4. Parlier (1989).
5. From material published by the history office of the Military Airlift Command, U.S. Air Force; quoted in Hanks (2005), p. 12.
6. From testimony by the Assistant DoD Inspector General, Robert Lieberman, before the Congress on DoD financial management, July 2000; see Hanks (2005), p. 10.
7. Hanks (2005), p. 3.
8. Cooper (2007).
9. Hanks (n.d.), p. 4.
10. Tuttle (2005).
11. Camm et al.(2007).
12. Tuttle (2005), p. 166,
13. Tuttle (2005), p. 161.
14. Hanks (n.d.), p. 15; Hanks (2008).

15. Hanks (n.d.), pp. 19–20.
16. Tuttle (2005), pp. 219–220.
17. Hanks (n.d.), p. 37.
18. Hanks (2009), pp. 181–196; Hanks (n.d.), p. 7.
19. Department of Defense Office of the Under Secretary of Defense (2010), pp. 28–55.
20. Pint, Brauner, Bondanella, Relles, and Steinberg (2002).
21. Tuttle (2005), p. 217.
22. Tuttle (2005), pp. 223–225.
23. U.S. GAO (2007). Congressional dissatisfaction with the LSI concept and lack of capacity across all the services (not just the army FCS program), including the Coast Guard's Deepwater Program, is now reflected in law, the 2008 Defense Authorization Act (Section 802), which severely limits further use of LSIs after October 1, 2010.
24. Comments at the Annual Department of Transportation Conference, January 17, 2008, recorded and heard on C-SPAN.
25. Goldsmith (2008), pp. 94–99.
26. Guttman (2000); Guttman (2004).
27. Verkuil (2007).
28. Wysocki (2007), p. A-1.
29. Hanks (n.d.), pp. 49–50.
30. Hanks et al. (2005), p. 56.
31. Kappmeier's comments during a conference presentation hosted by the Wharton School of Business, University of Pennsylvania, February 8, 2007.
32. Hanks (2005), pp. 6–7.
33. Tuttle (2005), pp. 223–225.
34. U.S. GAO (2007).

Chapter 24

1. Thomas (2004), pp. 33–41.
2. Roberto and Levesque (2005), pp. 53–60.
3. The Army developed a "management matrix" for Logistics Transformation and acknowledged that the "matrix is heavily dependent on modeling transformation initiatives." See Office of the Deputy Chief of Staff (2003), p. 11. Nonetheless, neither this comprehensive modeling capability nor an enabling "analytical architecture" as suggested herein has yet been developed. This transformation management matrix came to be referred to as the "bureaucratic weave."
4. Henderson (2004).
5. Association of the U.S. Army Institute of Land Warfare (2001).
6. Boot (2005), p. 106.
7. Metz (2007), p. 22.

8. Record (2006), p. 6.

9. Scales (2005), p. 25; Scales (2003).

10. Quinlivan (2003); Quinlivan (1995), pp. 56–69; Mockaitis (2007).

11. These intriguing (but worrisome) ideas are illustrated using recent examples and evidence addressing trends that suggest increasing potential for technological, engineering, and even social system failures. Failure causes are attributed to system interactions with inadequate or misaligned human decision support constructs and organizational designs, especially in tightly coupled systems that stress human cognitive abilities. Homer-Dixon (2000); Homer-Dixon (2006); Perrow (1984); Demchak (1991); Wesensten et al. (2005), pp. 94–105.

12. Maccagnan (2005), pp. 18–19.

13. Bonder (2002), pp. 25–34, emphasis added.

14. Melcher and Ferrari (2004), pp. 2–6.

15. Schrady (2004).

16. From several conversations with both civilian and military faculty at the Naval Postgraduate School (NPS), Air Force Institute of Technology (AFIT), and Army Logistics Management Center (ALMC) including the chair, systems engineering department; and dean, school of logistics sciences. For the Army, ALMC developed the POI for its very first SCM course in spring 2005.

17. Eaton (2002).

18. For example, the 2002 Defense Acquisition University (DAU) catalog listing of course descriptions and requirements for professional acquisition certification does not include inventory management and specifies "supply chain management" as a subject in only one course in the acquisition logistics career field. Yet this course is neither "required" nor "desired" for even the highest level of certification (level III) under DoD Directive 5000.52. In the 2005 catalog, for the new life-cycle logistics career field, "supply chain management" is treated as one of several introductory subjects in a level I nonresidence, self-paced, distance learning course. There are no other requirements for SCM at any level, including level III, although graduate level classes and SCM certificate programs are considered "desirable" at level II.

19. Biddle (2004), p. 203. Also, for an exposition of the enduring nature and character of war that argues that the "United States may be committed to a process of military transformation that is keyed to an inappropriately narrow vision of future war," see Gray (2005), pp. 14–26.

20. Courses would include both engineering and management subjects, including RAM-D, inventory theory, operations research and quantitative methods, systems dynamics and simulation, supply chain design and management, ERP, management of technological change, strategic management, organizational design, and leadership. Educational programs could be tailored to offer several options: MS in Logistics Engineering; MBA with concentration in SCM; MAPP with concentration in policy planning; and even dual-degree programs. Training

and certification programs would also incorporate DAU courses, especially in the acquisition logistics (AL), systems planning, RD&E (SPRDE), and test and evaluation (T&E) career fields, thereby promoting DAU's "strategic alliance" (with colleges and universities) and "communities of practice" (professionals in the same discipline) initiatives. Seminars could also be tailored to meet specific or sustained customer needs. Delivery means would include existing local programs but also other courses imported either to serve as gap-fillers in existing educational capacity or because of special stature or unique demand. Examples include Georgia Tech's Logistics Institute, MIT's seminar on "Supply Chain Strategy and Management," and courses available through Systems Exchange Inc. on "Spares Management and Modeling" and "Performance-Based Logistics." A professional development "clearinghouse" and central coordination office that provides one-stop customer shopping would be needed to effectively develop and manage such an ambitious, collaborative program.

21. These paragraphs on the evolution of organizational concepts and form draw primarily from the following sources: for a summary on organizational design in social systems, Davis (1982); for the development of bureaucracy in government organizations, Wilson (1989); for a comparative summary and historical perspective of organizational paradigms, Guillen (1989); and for the emerging collaborative enterprise, Heckscher (2007).

22. Ancona and Bresman (2007), pp. 25–34; Gloor (2006).
23. Rothstein (2006), pp. 76–77.
24. Hatch (1997), pp. 53–54.
25. Greiner (1972), pp. 173–176.
26. Bracken (2007), pp. 71–80.

Chapter 25

1. Blanco, (2004); Bessant (2004), pp. 165–190.
2. Hax and Wilde (2001), pp. 192–224.
3. Chappell and Peck (2006), pp. 253–267.
4. Simons (1995), p. 107.
5. Hatch (1997), pp. 371–372; Burgelman (1991).

Chapter 26

1. Senge (1990).
2. Using this definition of "human progress" as a guide—simply failing to repeat past mistakes—the recent public record of army logistics as a "learning" organization suggests significant "observations" but, regrettably and inexplicably,

few lessons "learned." See U.S. GAO (2003); U.S. GAO (1992); Department of Defense (1992); Department of Defense (2000).

3. Zimmerman (1992).

4. I am indebted to the late Dr. Benson D. Adams, then–AMC special assistant to the commanding general for transformation integration, for suggesting the relevance and timeliness of this biography.

5. Tuchman (1984). Historian Arthur Schlesinger Jr. has described the "enemies of progress" as gravity, custom, and fear: Gravity represents the inertia of tradition; custom represents known ways of doing things; and fear represents resistance to that which is new or different.

6. Ippolito (2005), pp. 34–35.

7. Letter from the Assistant Secretary of the Army (Acquisition, Logistics and Technology) (2005), p. 2, paragraph b.(5).

8. Peterson (2004); Boren (2008). And to cite just a few specifics collected from other sources on the trends mentioned: While health care costs are exploding, 72 million Americans (30%) now suffer obesity, which has become the biggest health problem of our time, doubling among adults in the last 25 years (more than 50% of middle-aged Black and Hispanic females are now obese) and tripling among children and still growing. We now invest $28 billion annually on research at the National Institutes of Health yet spend only $260 million—less than 1% of that amount—on R&D for education. In 2003 the United States accounted for 21% of global energy consumption with only 6% of world population; in 2005 the cost of congestion and highway delays alone was estimated to be $78 billion; over the last 25 years federal spending per capita has grown 40%; the debt-to-income ratio for the U.S. middle class is now nearly 150%; across the nation the debt-to-GDP ratio is 350% with taxpayers currently on the hook for nearly $60 trillion in liabilities equating to over half a million dollars per household in addition to their current average debt of $112,000 for mortgages, car loans, credit cards, and other debt combined; and every day foreigners invest about $3 billion in the U.S. economy. If these trends are not reversed, then the rising "millennial generation" will be the first in American history to earn *less* disposable income over their lifetimes than their parents. We are on an unsustainable path doing great disservice to future generations.

References

AHS International. (2008). Conference proceedings from CBM Specialists' Meeting. Retrieved February 13, 2008, from AHS Redstone Chapter Web site: http://www.ahsredstone.org

Ancona, D., & Bresman, H. (2007). *X-Teams: How to build teams that lead, innovate, and succeed*. Boston, MA: Harvard Business School Press.

Anthony, S. D. et al. (2008, Winter). Institutionalizing innovation. *MIT Sloan Management Review*, 45–53.

Argyris, C., & Schon, D. (1978). *Organizational learning*. Reading, MA: Addison-Wesley.

Army Materiel Systems Analysis Activity (AMSAA) Report TR-2006-17, *Aberdeen proving ground, MD*, p. 21.

Association of the U.S. Army (AUSA). (2004, March). The new paradigm: Bringing U.S. army logistics in to the 21st century. *Torchbearer National Security Report*.

Association of the U.S. Army Institute of Land Warfare. (2001). *Department of the Army Civilians: A "crises in human capital"* (Report Number DR 01-3). Arlington, VA: Author.

Bachman, T. (2005). *Reducing aircraft down for lack of parts with sporadic demand*. Briefing presented in WG 19 at 73rd Military Operations Research Symposium (MORSS), June 21, 2005.

Baletreri, W. G., & McDoniel, P. S. (2002). *Measuring success: Metrics that link supply chain management to aircraft readiness*. Naval Postgraduate School Master's Thesis.

Bellman, R. (1957). *Dynamic programming*. Princeton, NJ: Princeton University Press.

Bessant, J. (2004). Supply chain learning. In S. New & R. Westbrook (Eds.), *Understanding supply chains: Concepts, critiques, and futures* (pp. 165–190). New York, NY: Oxford University Press.

Biddle, S. (2002). *Afghanistan and the future of warfare: Implications for army and defense policy*. Carlisle, PA: AWC Strategic Studies Institute.

Biddle, S. (2004). *Military power: Explaining victory and defeat in modern battle*. Princeton, NJ: Princeton University Press.

Bilczo, D., Bugby, L., Fitzhugh, J., Gilbert, D., Halladin, S., & Rubert, J. (2003). Aerospace supply chain dynamics. In T. P. Harrison, H. Lee, & J. J. Neale, *The practice of supply chain management: Where theory and application converge*. Kluwer Academic Publishers.

Birkenshaw, J., & Mol, M. (2006, Summer). How management innovation happens. *MIT Sloan Management Review*, 81–88.

Blackett, R. L., & Burman, J. P. (1946, June). The design of optimum multifactorial experiments. *Biometrika, 33*(4), 305–325.

Blanco, H. (2004). *Towards an integrated management science.* Briefing presented at INFORMS Annual Meeting, October 27, 2004.

Bonder, S. (2002). Army operations research—Historical perspectives and lessons learned. *Operations Research, 50*(1), 25–34.

Boot, M. (2005). The struggle to transform the military. *Foreign Affairs, 84*(2), 106.

Boren, D. (2008). *A Letter to America.* Norman, OK: University of Oklahoma Press.

Box, G. E. P., Hunter, W. G., & Hunter, J. S. (1978). *Statistics for experimenters: An introduction to design, data analysis, and model building.* Hoboken, NJ: John Wiley.

Bracken, P. (2007). Managing to fail: Why strategy is disjointed. *The American Interest, 3*(1), 71–80.

Brauner, M. et al. (1997). *ISM-X evaluation and policy implications.* (Report Number MR-829-A). Santa Monica, CA: RAND Corporation.

Brown, G. G. (2003). *Has IT made OR obsolete?* Briefing presented at the Annual INFORMS Conference on OR/MS Practice, "Creating Value in the Extended Enterprise," May 4–6, 2003.

Bryson, J. M. (2004). *Strategic planning for public and nonprofit organizations.* Hoboken, NJ: Jossey-Bass.

Burgelman, R. (1991). Intraorganizational ecology of strategy making and organizational adaptation: Theory and field research. *Organization Science, 2*(3), 239–262.

Butler, R. A. (2005, April). Autonomic logistic analysis. Course notes from *PBL Solutions: Issues, Concepts and Methods for Logisticians and Managers* (pp. 39–40). Monterey, CA: TFD Group.

Calderwood, D. A. et al. (2002). *Intelligent collaborative aging aircraft parts support (ICAAPS)* (Report Number DL1221T1). McLean, VA: LMI.

Callioni, G. et al. (2005). Inventory-driven costs. *Harvard Business Review*, 135–141.

Camm, F. et al. (2007). *What the army needs to know to align its operational and institutional activities* (Report Number MG-530-A). Santa Monica, CA: RAND Corporation.

Cardin, M-A. et al. *Extracting value from uncertainty: A methodology for engineering systems design.* International Council on Systems Engineering.

Carr, N. (2004). *Does IT matter? Information technology and the corrosion of competitive advantage.* Boston, MA: Harvard Business School Publishing.

Chappell, A., & Peck, H. (2006). Risk management in military supply chains: Is there a role for Six Sigma? *International Journal of Logistics, 9*(3), 253–267.

Chase, R. B., Jacobs, R. F., & Aquilano, N. J. (2001). Synchronous manufacturing and the theory of constraints. In *Operations Management for Competitive Advantage*. McGraw-Hill.

Chen, F., Drezner, Z., Ryan, J. K., & Simchi-Levi, D. (2000). Quantifying the bullwhip effect in a simple supply chain: The impact of forecasting, lead times, and information. *Management Science, 46*(3), 436–443.

Chin, D., & Lucyshyn, W. (2004). Defense medical logistics standard support: The new DoD medical logistics supply chain. In J. S. Gansler & R. E. Luby (Eds.), *Transforming government supply chain management* (pp. 211–228). Lanham, MD: Rowman & Littlefield.

Chopra, S., & Sodhi, M. S. (2004). Managing risk to avoid supply chain breakdown. *MIT Sloan Management Review, 46*(1), 53–61.

Christopher, M., & Peck, H. *Building the resilient supply chain*. Retrieved from Cranfied University School of Management Web site: http://www.cranfied.ac.uk/som/scr

Christopher, M., & Towill, D. *An integrated model for the design of agile supply chains*. Retrieved from Cranfied University School of Management Web site: http://www.cranfied.ac.uk/som/scr

Congdon, P. (2003). Stochastic variances and stochastic volatility. In *Applied Bayesian Modelling* (pp. 210–214). Hoboken, NJ: John Wiley.

Cooper, W. (2007). *O&S trends and current issues*. Briefing presented at OSD PA&E/CAIG, May 7, 2007.

Coyle, J. J. (2004). *Transforming the supply chain: The challenge for change and supply chain management*. Briefing presented at LTA/Smeal College of Business Conference, Penn State University, June 22, 2004.

Cranfield University School of Management. (2003). *Creating resilient supply chains: A practical guide*. Bedford, England: Author.

Croson, R., & Donohue, K. (2002). Experimental economics and supply chain management. *Interfaces, 32*(5), 74–82.

Daniel, V., Guide, R., Jr., & Van Wassenhove, L. N. (Eds.). (2003). *Business aspects of closed-loop supply chains: Exploring the issues*. International Management Series 2. Pittsburgh, PA: Carnegie Bosch Institute.

Datta, S. (2003). *STARCH—A flight of ideas: Can econometric tools model real-time RFID data?* Cambridge, MA: MIT FSCI.

Datta, S. (n.d.). *A sense of the future (version 4.05)*. Cambridge, MA: MIT Forum for Supply Chain Innovation (FSCI).

Datta, S., Betts, R., Dinning, M., Erhun, F., Gibbs, T., Keskinocak, P., … Samuels, M. (2004). Adaptive value networks. In Y. S. Chang et al. (Eds.), *Evolution of supply chain management: Symbiosis of adaptive value networks and ICT*, (pp. 5–67). Boston, MA: Kluwer Academic Publishers.

Datta, S., & Granger, C. (2006). *Advances in supply chain management: Potential to improve forecasting accuracy* (Report Number ESD-WP-2006-11). Cambridge, MA: MIT ESD Working Paper Series.

Davenport, T. H., & Harris, J. G. (2007). *Competing on analytics: The new science of winning*. Boston, MA: Harvard Business School Press.

Davis, L. E. (1982). Organizational design. In G. Salvendy (Ed.), *Handbook for industrial engineering*. Hoboken, NJ: John Wiley.

Defense Industrial Base Panel. (1980). *The ailing defense industrial base: Unready for crises* (Report Number 96-29). Washington, DC: U.S. Government Printing Office.

Demchak, C. C. (1991). *Military organizations, complex machines: Modernization in the U.S. armed services*. Ithaca, NY: Cornell University Press.

Denardo, E. V. (2003). *Dynamic programming: Models and applications*. Mineola, NY: Dover.

de Neufville, R. (1990a). Decision analysis as strategy. In *Applied systems analysis: Engineering planning and echnology management* (pp. 320–323). New York, NY: McGraw-Hill.

de Neufville, R. (1990b). Revisions of estimates. In *Applied systems analysis: Engineering planning and technology management* (pp. 279–285). New York, NY: McGraw-Hill

de Neufville, R. (2000). *Dynamic strategic planning for technology policy.* Retrieved from http://ardent.mit.edu/real_options

de Neufville, R. (2002). *Architecting/designing engineering systems using real options* (Report Number ESD-WP-2003-01.09). Cambridge, MA: MIT Working Paper Series.

de Neufville, R. (2004). *Uncertainty management for engineering systems planning and design*. Cambridge, MA: MIT Engineering Systems Monograph.

Department of Defense. (1992). *Conduct of the Persian Gulf War: Final report to Congress*. Arlington, VA: Author.

Department of Defense. (2000). *Kosovo/Operation Allied Force After Action Report: Final report to Congress*. Arlington, VA: Author.

Department of the Army. (2005a). *Centralized inventory management of the army supply system* (Report Number AR 710-1). Washington, DC: Author.

Department of the Army. (2005b). *Inventory management: Supply policy below the national level* (Report Number AR 710–2). Washington, DC: Author.

Department of the Army. (2007). *2007 Army modernization plan*. Washington, DC: Government Printing Office.

Deputy Secretary of Defense. (2002). *Defense readiness reporting system* (Report Number 7730.65). Arlington, VA: Department of Defense.

Dettmer, H. W. (1996). *Goldratt's theory of constraints: A systems approach to continuous improvement.* Quality Press.

Distasio, F. A., Jr. (2004). *Fiscal year 2005 army budget: An analysis.* Arlington, VA: Association of the U.S. Army, Institute of Land Warfare.

Doneen, D. D., & McQuerry, D. D. (2002, February 2). Visualization of logistics data and systems health monitoring. Pacific Northwest National Laboratory, U.S. Department of Energy Lab.

Dreiner, D., Peltz, E., Lackey, A., Blake, D. J., & Vasidyanathan, K. (2004). *Value recovery from the reverse logistics pipeline* (Report Number MG-238). Santa Monica, CA: RAND Corporation.

Easterly, W. (2006). *The white man's burden.* New York, NY: Penguin Press.

Eaton, D. R. (2002a). Improving the management of reliability: Availability isn't everything, it's the only thing. *Our Aerospace Newsletter, 9*(B), 1–3.

Eaton, D. R. (2002b). Revolution in logistics affairs: A new strategy of cultural change. Naval Postgraduate School, May 1, 2002.

Fabrie, R. (2005). Aerospace supplier base. In *Evaluating, managing and forecasting readiness for army aviation.* Alexandria, VA: IDA.

Ferguson, G. et al. (2005). Evolving from Information to Insight. *MIT Sloan Management Review, 46*(2), 51–58.

Fisher, D. E. (2005). *A summer bright and shining.* Shoemaker and Hoard.

Fisher, M. L. (1997). What is the right supply chain for your product? *Harvard Business Review, 25*(2), 105–116.

Flynn, S. (2004). *America the vulnerable.* New York, NY: HarperCollins.

Folkeson, J. R., & Brauner, M. K. *Improving the army's management of reparable spare parts* (Report Number MG-205-A). Santa Monica, CA: RAND Corporation.

Fontenot, G., Degen, E. J., & Tohn, D. (2005). *On point: The U.S. Army in Operation Iraqi Freedom.* Annapolis, MD: Naval Institute Press.

Fortun, M., & Schweber, S. S. (1993). Scientists and the legacy of World War II: The case of operations research (OR). *Social Studies of Science, 23,* 595–642.

Fredendall, L. D., & Hill, E. (2001). *Basics of supply chain management.* Boca Raton, FL: St. Lucie Press.

Garvey, P. (2009). *Analytical methods for risk management: A systems engineering perspective.* Boca Raton, FL: Chapman and Hall/CRC.

Gavirneni, S. (1999). Value of information sharing and comparison with delayed differentiation. In S. Tayur et al. (Eds.), *Quantitative Models for Supply Chain Management* (p. 444). Boston, MA: Kluwer.

Gloor, P. (2006). *Swarm creativity: Competitive advantage through collaborative innovative networks.* New York, NY: Oxford University Press.

Goldberg, L., & Kimko, D. (2003). *An enlistment early warning system to prevent the next recruiting crises* (Report Number D-2720). Alexandria, VA: IDA.

Goldberg, M. S., & Tyson, K. W. (1991). *The costs and benefits of aircraft availability.* (IDA Paper P-2462). Alexandria, VA: IDA.

Goldratt, E. M., & Cox, J. (1985). *The goal.* Great Barrington, MA: North River Press.

Goldsmith, S. (2008). What's left for government to do? *The American,* 94–99.

Gray, C. S. (2005). How has war changed since the end of the Cold War? *Parameters, 35*(1), 14–26.

Greiner, L. (1972). Evolution and revolution as organizations grow. *Harvard Business Review, 50,* 173–176.

Griffin, B. S. (2008). Supplying the warfighter. *Army, 58*(3), 30.

Guay, T. R. (2007). *Globalization and its implications for the defense industrial base.* Carlisle, PA: AWC Strategic Studies Institute.

Guillen, M. F. (1989). *Models of management: Work, authority, and organization in a comparative perspective.* Chicago, IL: University of Chicago Press.

Guttman, D. (2004). Inherently governmental functions and the new millennium. In T. H. Stanton & B. Ginsberg (Eds.), *Making government manageable: Executive organization and management in the twenty-first Century* (chap. 3, pp. 40–65). Baltimore, MD: Johns Hopkins University Press.

Guttman, G. (2000). Public purpose and the private sector. 52 *Administrative Law Review* 859.

Haimes, Y. Y. (2004). *Risk modeling, assessment, and management.* Hoboken, NJ: Wiley-Interscience.

Hall, J. (2004). *LOGSA retrograde metric development (draft).* Briefing presented to Army Material Command, May 24, 2004.

Hamel, G. (2007). *The future of management.* Boston, MA: Harvard Business School Press.

Hammer, M. (2002, January 15). Process management and the future of Six Sigma. *MIT Sloan Management Review, 43*(2).

Hanks, C. H. (2005). *A critical examination of the DoD's business management modernization program (BMMP).* Presented at 2nd Annual Acquisition Symposium, Naval Postgraduate School.

Hanks, C. H. (2008). Advice and dissent: Viewpoint business sense. Retrieved May 1, 2008, from Government Executive Web site: http://www.govexec.com

Hanks, C. H. (2009). Financial accountability at the DoD: Reviewing the bidding. *Defense Acquisition Review Journal, 16*(2), 181–196.

Hanks, C. H. (n.d.). *Financing spares in the air force (FSAF).* Unpublished manuscript.

Hanks, C. H. et al. (2005). *Reexamining military acquisition reform: Are we there yet?* (Report Number MG-291). Santa Monica, CA: RAND Corporation.

Hatch, M. J. (1997). *Organization theory: Modern, symbolic, and postmodern perspectives.* New York, NY: Oxford University Press.

Hauk, K. B., & Parlier, G. H. (2000). Recruiting: Crises and cures. *Military Review*, 73–80.

Haupt, R. L., & Haupt, S. E. (2004). *Practical genetic algorithms*. Hoboken, NJ: Wiley-Interscience.

Hax, A. C., & Wilde, D. L., II. (2001). *The Delta Project: Discovering new sources of profitability in a networked economy*. New York, NY: Palgrave.

Heckscher, C. (2007). *The collaborative enterprise: Managing speed and complexity in knowledge-based businesses*. New Haven, CT: Yale University Press.

Heinrich, C. E., & Simchi-Levi, D. (2005). Do IT Investments Really Change Financial Performance? *Supply Chain Management Review*.

Held, T. (2005). *Assessing assumptions for linking logistics to aviation readiness*. RAND Arroyo briefing, January 19, 2005.

Henderson, R. (2004). *Developing and managing a successful technology and product strategy*. Course Briefing presented at MIT Sloan School of Management, September 23, 2004.

Henderson, S., & Kwinn, M. J. (2005). *A data warehouse to support condition based maintenance (CBM)*. Retrieved from U.S. Military Academy Operations Research Center, Department of Systems Engineering Web site: http://portal.dean.usma.edu

Her Majesty's Stationery Office. (1963). *The origins and development of operational research in the Royal Air Force* (Air Ministry Publication 3368). London, England.

Hill, C. H., Fancher, R., & Parlier, G. H. (1999). Recruiting America's army at the millennium: Challenges ahead. *Phalanx: The Bulletin of Military Operations Research, 31*(3), 6–7.

Holland, C. (2005). *Breakthrough business results with MVT*. Hoboken, NJ: John Wiley.

Homer-Dixon, T. (2000). *The ingenuity gap: How can we solve the problems of the future*. New York, NY: Alfred A. Knopf.

Homer-Dixon, T. (2006). *The upside of down: Catastrophe, creativity, and the renewal of civilization*. Washington, DC: Island Press.

Horowitz, S. (2005). *Evaluating, managing and forecasting readiness for army aviation*. Briefing presented to IDA, February 24, 2005.

Hugos, M. (2003). *Essentials of supply chain management*. Hoboken, NJ: John Wiley.

Hundley, R. O. (1999). *Past revolutions: Future transformations* (Report Number MR-1029-DARPA). Santa Monica, CA: RAND Corporation.

Ignizio, J. P. (1998). *Illusions of optimality*. Briefing presented at INFORMS MAS Conference, May 21, 1998.

Ignizio, J. P. (1999). System stability: A proxy for graceful degradation. *Phalanx: The Bulletin of Military Operations Research, 32*(1), 6–8, 27.

Ippolito, D. S. (2005). *Budget policy, deficits, and defense: A fiscal framework for defense planning*. Carlisle, PA: AWC Strategic Studies Institute.

Joint Staff Objective Assessment of Logistics in Iraq. (2004). Science Applications International Corporation Report for the Deputy Under Secretary of Defense (Logistics and Materiel Readiness) and Joint Staff J-4.

Kallock, R. W. (2004, May/June). From factory to foxhole. *Supply Chain Management Review, 23*, 46–53.

Kaufmann, A. (1993). *The origins of order: Self-organization and selection in evolution*. New York, NY: Oxford University Press.

Kaufmann, S. A. (1995). *At home in the universe: The search for laws of self-organization and complexity*, New York, NY: Oxford University Press.

Kelley, C. T. (2004). *The impact of equipment availability and reliability on mission outcomes* (Report Number DB-423-A). Santa Monica, CA: RAND Corporation.

Kern, P. J. (2004, October). Getting soldiers what they need when and where they need it. *Army, 54*(10), 72.

Killingsworth, W. R. (2004). *An integrated analysis of the supply chain for Army Aviation spares*. Briefing presented to Office of Economic Development, UAH, March 9, 2004.

Kirby, M. W. (2003). *Operational research in war and peace: The British experience from the 1930s to 1970*. London, England: Imperial College Press.

Knowles, J. A., Parlier, G. H., Hoscheit, G. C., Ayer, R., Lyman, K., & Fancher, R. (2002). Reinventing army recruiting. *Interfaces, 32*(1), 78–92.

Kotkin, Meyer. (2003). *III Corps stock positioning (Demonstration of stock optimization model)*. AMSAA briefing, March 17, 2003.

Kuhn, W. S. (1992). *Ground force battle casualty rate patterns: Uses in casualty estimation and simulation evaluation* LMI Report presented at the 60th annual Military Operations Research Symposium. McLean, VA: LMI.

Kuhn, W. S. (2010a). *Higher-resolution support planning: Patterns of operations basis*. LMI briefing, May 26, 2010.

Kuhn, W. S. (2010b). When will support planning finally escape its "mass-logistics" past? *Phalanx: The Bulletin of Military Operations Research, 43*(1), 35–39.

Kuhn, W. S., & Harleston, E. (2009). *Planning forecasts in terms of patterns of operations*. LMI briefing, April 7, 2009.

Lee, C. B. (2003). Multi-echelon inventory optimization. Evant White Paper Series.

Lee, H. L. (2002). Aligning supply chain strategy with product uncertainty. *California Management Review, 44*(3), 105–119.

Lee, H. L., Padmanabhan, V., & Whang, S. (1997a). The bullwhip effect in supply chains. *MIT Sloan Management Review, 38*(3), 93–102.

Lee, H. L., Padmanabhan, V., & Whang, S. (1997b). Information distortion in a supply chain: The bullwhip effect. *Management Science, 43*(4), 546–558.

Levine, D. (2007). *Enhancing the readiness of army helicopters* (Report Number P-4245). Alexandria, VA: IDA.

Levine, D., Fabrie, B., & Horowitz, S. (2006). *Army equipment readiness: Status report*. Briefing presented to IDA, March 20, 2006.

Levine, D., & Horowitz, S. (2004). *Predictive relationships for army aircraft readiness (IDA preliminary draft)*. Alexandria, VA: IDA.

Levy, P. S., & Lemeshow, S. (1999). *Sampling of populations: Methods and applications*. Hoboken, NJ: John Wiley.

Lodree, E. J., & Taskin, S. (2007). An insurance risk management framework for disaster relief and supply chain disruption inventory planning. *Journal of the Operational Research Society*.

Maccagnan, V., Jr. (2005). *Logistics transformation: Restarting a stalled process*. Carlisle, PA: AWC Strategic Studies Institute.

McGee, V. E. (1971). *Principles of statistics: Traditional and Bayesian*. New York, NY: Prentice-Hall.

McGraw, T. K. (2007). *Prophet of innovation: Joseph Schumpeter and creative destruction*. Boston, MA: Harvard Business School Press.

Melcher, D. F., & Ferrari, J. G. (2004). A view from the FA49 foxhole: Operational research and systems analysis. *Military Review*, 2–6.

Metz, S. (2007). *Learning from Iraq: Counterinsurgency in American strategy*. Carlisle, PA: AWC Strategic Studies Institute.

MIT Center for Transportation and Logistics. (2003). *Supply chain response to terrorism: Creating resilient and secure supply chains*. Cambridge, MA: Author.

Mockaitis, T. R. (2007). *The Iraqi War: Learning from the past, adapting to the present, and planning for the future*. Carlisle, PA: AWC Strategic Studies Institute.

Muckstadt, J. A. (2005). *Analysis and algorithms for service parts supply chains*. New York, NY: Springer.

Murdock, C. A., Flournoy, M. A., Campbell, K. M., Chao, P. A., Smith, J., Witkowsky, A. A., & Wormuth, C. E. (2005). Organizing for logistics support. In *Beyond Goldwater-Nichols: U.S. government and defense reform for a new strategic era–Phase 2 report* (pp. 99–103). Washington, DC: Center for Strategic and International Studies (CSS).

Naim, M. (2004). Supply chain dynamics. In S. New & R. Westbrook (Eds.), *Understanding supply chains: Concepts, critiques, and futures* (pp. 109–132). New York, NY: Oxford University Press.

Nye, M. J. (2004). *Blackett: Physics, war, and politics in the twentieth century*. Cambridge, MA: Harvard University Press.

Office of Force Transformation of the Department of Defense. (2004). *Operational sense and respond logistics: Coevolution of an adaptive enterprise capability.* Arlington, VA: Department of Defense.

Office of the Deputy Chief of Staff. (2003). *Army logistics transformation: Management, synchronization, and integration to achieve full spectrum capabilities.* G-4, HQDA.

Office of the Deputy Under Secretary of Defense for Logistics and Materiel Readiness. (2003). *DoD supply chain materiel management regulation* (Report Number DoD 4140.1-R). Ft. Belvoir, VA: Department of Defense.

Office of the Inspector General of the Department of Defense (2003). *Financial reporting of deferred maintenance information on army weapons systems for FY2002* (Report Number D-2003-054). Arlington, VA: Department of Defense.

Office of the Under Secretary of Defense (Comptroller). (2010). *Financial Management Regulation 7000.14-R.* Arlington, VA: Department of Defense. Retrieved from http://comptroller.defense.gov/fmr

Parlier, G. H. (1989). *The Goldwater-Nichols Act of 1986: Resurgence in defense reform and the legacy of Eisenhower.* USMC Command and Staff College, War in the Modern Era Seminar, May 15, 1989.

Parlier, G. H. (1997a). *Dynamic strategic resource planning: Toward properly resourcing the army in an uncertain environment* (RPAD Tech Report 97-03). Washington, DC: PAE, OCSA.

Parlier, G. H. (1997b). *The long-term implications for analysis of the quadrennial defense review.* Briefing presented at 65th MORS Symposium, June 10–12, 1997.

Parlier, G. H. (1998). *Resourcing the United States Army in an era of strategic uncertainty.* Briefing presented at INFORMS MAS Conference, UAH, May 21, 1998.

Parlier, G. H. (1999). *Manning the army of the future* (Audiovisual tape #A0515-00-B035). USAREC briefing presented at Fort Knox, KY, November 22, 1999.

Parlier, G. H. (2002). Award presented to USAREC's PAE. *Phalanx: The Bulletin of Military Operations Research, 35*(4), 13, 33–34.

Parlier, G. H. (2003, May 22). *AMCOM Deployment Support Observations (CG Update).* AMCOM Memorandum for Record.

Peck, H. (2006). Reconciling supply chain vulnerability, risk, and supply chain management. *International Journal of Logistics, 9*(1), 127–142.

Peltz, E., Boren, P., Robbins, M., & Wolff, M. (2002). *Diagnosing the army's equipment readiness* (Report Number MR-1481). Santa Monica, CA: RAND Corporation.

Peltz, E., Collabella, L. P., Williams, B., & Boren, P. (2004). *The effects of equipment age on mission-critical failure rates* (Report Number MR-1789). Santa Monica, CA: RAND Corporation.

Peltz, E., Robbins, M. L., Girardini, K. J., Eden, R., Halliday, J. M., & Angers, J. (2005). *Sustainment of army forces in Operation Iraqi Freedom: Major findings and recommendations* (Report Number MG-342). Santa Monica, CA: RAND Corporation.

Perrow, C. (1984). *Normal accidents: Living with high-risk technologies*, New York, NY: Basic Books.

Peterson, P. G. (2004). *Running on empty*. New York, NY: Farrar, Straus & Giroux.

Phillips, D., Ravindran, A., & Solberg, J. J. (1976). Dynamic programming. In *Operations Research: Principles and Practice* (pp. 419–472). Hoboken, NJ: John Wiley.

Pillsbury, J. H. (2006, January). Support of the soldier: Life cycle management at Redstone Arsenal. *Army Magazine, 55*(1), 32–36.

Pint, E. M., Brauner, M. K., Bondanella, J. R., Relles, D. A., & Steinberg, P. (2002). *Right price, fair credit: Criteria to improve financial incentives for army logistics decisions* (Report Number MR1150-A). Santa Monica, CA: RAND Corporation.

Powell, W. B. (2007). *Approximate dynamic programming: Solving the curses of dimensionality*. Hoboken, NJ: John Wiley.

Pringle, L. *Operations research: The productivity engine*. Retrieved from Institute for Operations Research and the Management Sciences (INFORMS) Website: http://www.scienceofbetter.org

Quinlivan, J. T. (1995). Force requirements in stability operations. *Parameters, 25*(4), 56–69.

Quinlivan, J. T. (2003). Burden of victory: The painful arithmetic of stability operations. *RAND Review*.

Record, J. (2006). *The American way of war: Cultural barriers to successful counterinsurgency*. Maxwell AFB, AL: USAF Air War College.

Rice, J. B., & Caniatio, F. (2003, September/October). Building a secure and resilient supply network. *Supply Chain Management Review*.

Roberto, M. A., & Levesque, L. C. (2005). The art of making change initiatives tick. *MIT Sloan Management Review, 46*(4), 53–60.

Rothstein, H. (2006). *Afghanistan and the troubled future of unconventional warfare*. Annapolis, MD: Naval Institute Press.

Rubenstein, M. F., & Firstenberg, I. B. (1999). *The minding organization*. New York, NY: John Wiley.

Scales, R. H. (2003). *Yellow smoke: The future of land warfare for America's military*. Lanham, MD: Rowman & Littlefield.

Scales, R. H. (2005). The lost art of land war. *The American Legion, 159*(4), 25.

Schrady, D. (2004). Military logistics modeling tutorial. Briefing presented at 72nd MORSS, June 2004.

Schragenheim, E. (1998). *The theory of constraints*. Marietta, GA: Lionhart Publishing.

Senge, P. M. (1990). *The fifth discipline: The art and science of the learning organization*. New York, NY: Currency Doubleday.

Senge, P. M., & Sterman, J. D. (2000). Systems thinking and organizational learning. In J. D. W. Morecroft & J. D. Sterman (Eds.), *Modeling for learning organizations* (chap. 8, pp. 195–216). Portland, OR: Productivity Press.

Shapiro, J. F. (2001). *Modeling the supply chain*. Pacific Grove, CA: Duxbury Press.

Shapiro, J. F. (2007). *Modeling the supply chain* (2nd ed.). Duxbury.

Sherbrooke, C. C. (1992). *Optimal inventory modeling of systems: Multi-echelon techniques*. Hoboken, NJ: John Wiley.

Simchi-Levi, D. (2010). Rethinking the role of information technology. In *Operations rules: Delivering customer value through flexible operations* (Chap. 6, pp. 103–130). Cambridge, WA: MIT Press.

Simchi-Levi, D., Chen, X., & Bramel, J. (2005). *The logic of logistics: Theory, algorithms and applications for logistics and supply chain management*. New York, NY: Springer.

Simchi-Levi, D., Kaminsky, P., & Simchi-Levi, E. (2003a). *Designing and managing the supply chain: Concepts, strategies and case studies*. New York, NY: McGraw-Hill Irwin.

Simchi-Levi, D., Kaminski, P., & Simchi-Levi, E. (2003b). Information technology for supply chain management. In *Designing and managing the supply chain* (pp. 283–292). New York, NY: McGraw-Hill Irwin.

Simon, H. (1957). *Models of man*. Hoboken, NJ: John Wiley.

Simons, R. (1995). *Levers of control: How managers use innovative control systems to drive strategic renewal*. Boston, MA: Harvard Business School Press.

Slay, M., Bachman, T. C., Kline, R. C., O'Malley, T. J., Eichorn, F., & King, R. M. (1996). *Optimizing spares support: The aircraft sustainability model* (LMI Report Number AF501MR1). McLean, VA: LMI.

Spector, P. E. (1981). *Research designs*. Thousand Oaks, CA: Sage Publications.

Sterman, J. D. (1992). *System dynamics modeling for project management*. MIT Sloan System Dynamics Group.

Sterman, J. D. (2000). *Business dynamics: Systems thinking and modeling for a complex world*. New York, NY: McGraw-Hill.

Sullivan, K. (2004). *Lean enterprise initiative status briefing*. Briefing presented at Office for Economic Development, UAH, October 22, 2004.

Systems Exchange Seminars. Syllabi for Spares Management and Modeling and PBL Solutions: Issues, Concepts, and Methods for Logisticians and Managers. Monterey, CA: Author.

Tang, C. C. (2006). Robust strategies for mitigating supply chain disruptions.
Theory of constraints and lean thinking. (2003). Briefing presented to Deputy Under Secretary of Defense (Logistics and Materiel Readiness) by U.S. marine Corps Maintenance Center.
Thomas, M. U. (2004). Assessing the reliability of a contingency logistics network. *Journal of Military Operations Research, 9*(1), 33–41.
Thurow, L. C. (2003). Help wanted: A chief knowledge office. In *Fortune favors the bold.* (pp. 261–295). New York, NY: HarperCollins.
Tillson, J. C. F. (2003). *Transforming DoD management: The systems approach.* Alexandria, VA: IDA.
Tillson, J. C. F., Burns, W., Freeman, W., Morton, L., & Rothmann, H. (2003). *Improving readiness reporting: Thoughts on content and design of the DRRS* (Draft Report D-2841). Alexandria, VA: IDA.
Tuchman, B. (1984). *The march of folly: From Troy to Vietnam.* New York, NY: Random House.
Tuttle, W. G. T., Jr. (2005). *Defense logistics for the 21st century.* Annapolis, MD: Naval Institute Press.
Tyson, K. W., Horowitz, S., Evanovich, P., McBride, D. G., & Robinson, M. A. (1990). *Support costs and reliability in weapons acquisition: Approaches for evaluating new systems* (IDA Paper P-2421) Alexandria, VA: IDA.
U.S. Army, 101st Airborne Division (Air Assault). (2003). *Operation Iraqi Freedom Safety Lessons Learned.* Ft. Stewart, GA: U.S. Army. http://www.globalsecurity.org/military/ops/oif-lessons-learned.htm
U.S. Army, Third Infantry Division (Mechanized). *Operation Iraqi Freedom Third Infantry Division (Mechanized) "Rock of the Marne" After Action Report, (Final Draft).* Ft. Stewart, GA: U.S. Army. http://www.globalsecurity.org/military/ops/oif-lessons-learned.htm
U.S. Army, 32nd Army Air and Missile Defense Command. (2003). *Operation Iraqi Freedom: Theater Air and Missile Defense History.* Fort Bliss, TX: Headquarters, 32nd AMDC.
U.S. Government Accountability Office (GAO). (1992). *Failure to apply "lessons learned" from prior operations and "Operation Desert Storm"* (Report Number GAO/NSIAD-92-258). Washington, DC: Government Printing Office.
U.S. GAO. (1997). *Defense financial management* (Report Number HR-97-3) Washington, DC: Government Printing Office.
U.S. GAO. (2003a). *The army needs a plan to overcome critical spare parts shortages* (Report Number 03–705). Washington, DC: Government Printing Office.
U.S. GAO. (2003b). *Defense logistics: Preliminary observations on logistics effectiveness in OIF* (Report Number 04-305R). Washington, DC: Government Printing Office.

U.S. GAO. (2003c). *Preliminary observations on the effectiveness of logistics activities during Operation Iraqi Freedom* (Report Number 04–305R). Washington, DC: Government Printing Office.

U.S. GAO. (2005). *High risk series: An update*. Washington, DC: Government Printing Office.

U.S. GAO. (2007a). *Defense inventory: Opportunities exist to improve the management of DoD's acquisition lead time for spare parts* (Report Number 07-281). Washington, DC: Government Printing Office.

U.S. GAO. (2007b). *Progress made implementing supply chain recommendations but full extent of improvement unknown* (Report Number GAO-07-234). Washington, DC: Government Printing Office.

U.S. GAO. (2007c). *Role of lead systems integrator on future combat systems program poses oversight challenges* (Report Number GAO-07-380). Washington, DC: Government Printing Office.

University of Virginia Center for Risk Management in Engineering Systems. http://www.sys.virginia.edu/risk.html

Valikangas, L., & Gibbert, M. (2005). Boundary-setting strategies for escaping innovation traps. *MIT Sloan Management Review, 46*(3), 58–64.

Van De Vegte, J. (1986). *Feedback control systems*. New York, NY: Prentice-Hall.

Verkuil, P. R. (2007). *Outsourcing sovereignty*. New York, NY: Cambridge University Press.

Wang, M. (2004). *OIF value recovery*. Briefing presented at RAND Conference on Distribution Management and OIF Logistics Research Review, July 23, 2004.

Wang, M. (2005). *Retrograde distribution management operations study (draft)*. RAND Corporation briefing to CASCOM, April 28, 2005.

Wang, T., & de Neufville, R. Identification of real options in projects.

Wesensten, N. J. et al. (2005). Cognitive readiness in network-centric operations. *Parameters, 35*(1), 94–105.

Wilson, J. Q. (1989). *Bureaucracy: What government agencies do and why they do it*. New York, NY: Basic Books.

Winograd, E. Q. (2001, July). What about Army Aviation? *Air Force, 84*(7), 64–68.

Wysocki, B., Jr. (2007, March). Is government "outsourcing its brain"? *Wall Street Journal*, p. A-1.

Yergin, D. (2006). Ensuring energy security. *Foreign Policy, 85*(2), 75–76.

Zimmerman, P. A. (1992). *The neck of the bottle: George W. Goethals and the reorganization of the U.S. Army supply system, 1917–1918*. College Station, TX: Texas A&M University Press.

Index

The *italicized f* following page numbers refers to figures.

A
accelerating transformation, 157–66
Ackoff, Russell, 101
acquisition stage, 13, 85–94, 85*f*
adaptive logistics network concepts, 111–17
after action reports (AARs), 4
analyses, 2
analytical architecture, 6, 125–27
arborescence, 56, 112, 112*f*, 116
Argyris, C., 241
Army Force Generation (ARFORGEN), 5, 175–76, 177*f*
Army Working Capital Fund (AWCF), 10, 64–65, 205–7, 210, 217
authorized stock lists (ASLs), 51, 53–57
availability improvement analysis, 80*f*
AWCF hardware (aviation) resource trends, 10*f*

B
bathtub curve, 78*f*
Bayes' Theorem, 93
Bracken, Paul, 230–31
bullwhip effect, 18, 20*f*, 21, 27, 35, 71, 81, 88, 96–97, 104, 106, 138, 152, 176
Burgelman, R., 241
business modernization, 215

C
capabilities-based planning, 193–99
capacity, inventory, and knowledge, 38*f*
Center for Innovation in Logistics Systems (CILS), 157–66, 160*f*, 169, 180, 181, 240, 242
challenges, 3–5
change reality, 221*f*
Chief Financial Officer (CFO) Act of 1990, 203, 215
civilian ORSA strength in AMC, 174*f*
Cody, Richard A., 242
Cold War, 5, 39, 66, 88, 90, 109, 123, 171–72, 180, 208
condition-based maintenance (CBM), 34–36, 37*f*, 48–50
contract logistics support (CLS), 90, 196–97
conventional linear regression models (CLRMs), 152–53

D
Davenport, Thomas, 189
Defense Management Report Decision (DMRD), 203
Defense Readiness Reporting System (DRRS), 151–55, 248*f*
demand
  forecasting, 40
  information latency, 35
  volatility in supply chains, 20*f*
de Neufville, Richard, 139, 145
depot-level reparables (DLRs), 13, 24, 56, 60–66, 70–71, 76–79, 84, 96, 99, 107, 109, 114, 116, 208, 209, 214–16
Deputy Under Secretary of Defense, 4
design and evaluation, 2

design of experiments (DOE), 139–43
dollar cost banding (DCB), 52
dynamic strategic planning (DSP), 133–34, 138–39, 143, 146

E
effectiveness improvement, 119–24
efficiency achievement, 103–10
efficiency in cost-availability trade space, 120f, 121f
efficient frontier, 11f
end items, 52, 69, 74, 76, 85
enhanced class IX planning, 41f
enterprise resource planning (ERP), 4, 152, 154, 183–84, 189, 190, 191
evolution of insight, 190f
execution and strategy, 239f
extended enterprise, 16

F
fill rate, 52–54, 82, 84, 178, 196, 197, 198f
financial management challenges, 201–18
Fisher, D. E., 21

G
Global War on Terror, 1, 79, 149, 172, 222, 245–46
Goethals, George W., 243–45
Government Accountability Office (GAO), 3, 4, 86, 87, 201, 208, 217, 249
Greiner, Larry, 229

H
Haimes, Yacov, 147
Hamel, Gary, 190
Harris, Jeanne, 189
Hewlett Packard, 63
human capital investment, 219–32

I
Institute for Operations Research and the Management Sciences (INFORMS), 185–86
integration, 2
Intelligent Collaborative Aging Aircraft Spare Parts Support (ICAAPS), 74–76, 75f
inventory-driven cost (IDC), 63–64
inventory pooling, 56, 97

L
Lean, 71, 72f, 73, 88, 111–12, 142–43, 193, 235
Lee, H. L., 21, 24
logistics
  model, 14f
  readiness and early warning system, 155
  structure, 13–15
  system readiness and program development, 151–55
  transformation framework, 168f
Logistics Management Institute (LMI), 17, 82–84

M
management innovation for improved decision-making, 192f
Metcalfe's Law, 230
mission-based forecasting (MBF), 34, 46f–47f, 48–50, 57
mission demand stage, 39f
MITRE Corporation, 148
model, 2
multiechelon integration, 105f
multistage optimization advantages, 107f–108f
multistage supply chain optimization, 129–32
multivariable testing (MVT), 139–43

N
non-mission-capable (NMC) aircraft, 29–30

O
objective hierarchy, 237f
officer ORSA strength in AMC, 173f
operational and organizational risk evaluation, 145–49

operational availability components, 92*f*
operational mission and training demand stage, 39–50
Operation Enduring Freedom (OEF), 4, 7, 10, 77, 81
Operation Iraqi Freedom (OIF), 4, 7, 9, 10, 77, 81
operations research (OR), 183–92, 223–24
optimizing the system, 131*f*
organizational redesign for Army force generation, 171–82
organizational risk reduction, 148*f*, 153*f*
original equipment manufacturers (OEMs), 6, 61, 65, 85, 88, 90, 91, 216

P
Panama Canal, 244
part demand, 45*f*
performance-based logistics (PBL), 6, 7, 23, 24, 55, 90, 158, 193–99, 197*f*, 210, 214
performance-based logistics planning, 193–99
principle of bounded rationality, 134
production function for readiness, 31*f*, 33*f*, 80*f*, 91*f*
Program Objective Memorandum (POM), 246

R
readiness-based sparing (RBS), 24, 34, 53–54, 55*f*, 56–57, 79, 81, 84, 107, 109–10, 114, 116, 130, 132, 143, 158, 175–76, 177*f*, 178
readiness-driven supply network, 115*f*
readiness equation, 14, 24, 31
readiness production stage, 29–38
reduced transformation risk, 162*f*
resilience design, 111–17
retail stage, 51–57, 51*f*
retrograde efficiency, 64*f*, 67*f*
return on investment (ROI), 24
reverse logistics, 14
stage, 59–67
structure, 62*f*
risk pooling, 56
Rubinstein, Moshe, 42, 214

S
Schon, D., 241
segmented logistics, 15*f*
sense and respond logistics (S&RL), 113, 116
service supply chains, 23
Shapiro, Jeremy, 184
Simon, Herbert, 134
Simons, Robert, 240
Single Army Logistics Enterprise (SALE), 4
Six Sigma, 71, 72*f*, 73, 142–43, 193, 235
stock management structure, 137*f*
strategic management concepts, 233–42
supply chain
 concepts, 17–25
 flows, 18*f*
 integration, 15*f*
 strategies, 22*f*
supply-chain management (SCM), 17
system dynamics modeling, 133–44
system efficiency improvement, 98*f*
system life-cycle failure rate pattern, 78*f*

T
tactical units, 29–38
 stage, 29*f*
templates, 18
theory of constraints, 71–73, 72*f*, 136, 235
transactional information system technology, 183–92
transformation, 243
Tuchman, Barbara, 245
Tuttle, William, 216

U
uncertainty framework, 21, 21*f*
unfunded requirements (UFRs), 9
unit-level logistics system (ULLS), 35

U.S. Army, 1
U.S. Army Aviation and Missile Command (AMCOM), 11, 172, 181
U.S. Army Forces Command (FORSCOM), 9
U.S. Army Logistics Transformation, 1–2, 5–6, 24, 96, 102, 110, 122, 125–29, 133, 136, 138, 146–47, 157–58
U.S. Army Material Command (AMC), 103, 158, 172, 173*f*, 176, 181, 209, 210, 216
U.S. Army Recapitalization Program (RECAP), 34, 78–81, 89, 175
U.S. Department of Defense (DoD), 3, 6, 17, 22–23, 62, 85–86, 107, 109, 151, 154–55, 171, 245

V

value recovery, 14
Verkuil, Paul R., 213
Visualization of Logistics Data (VLD), 76

W

Weber, Max, 226
wholesale stage, 13, 69–84, 69*f*, 106, 109
work-arounds, 11*f*, 31–32, 34, 53, 82, 91, 96, 167, 193, 205, 206, 220, 247*f*

Z

Zimmerman, Phyllis, 244

Announcing the Business Expert Press Digital Library

Concise E-books Business Students Need for Classroom and Research

This book can also be purchased in an e-book collection by your library as

- a one-time purchase,
- that is owned forever,
- allows for simultaneous readers,
- has no restrictions on printing, and
- can be downloaded as PDFs from within the library community.

Our digital library collections are a great solution to beat the rising cost of textbooks. e-books can be loaded into their course management systems or onto student's e-book readers.

The **Business Expert Press** digital libraries are very affordable, with no obligation to buy in future years.

For more information, please visit **www.businessexpert.com/libraries**. To set up a trial in the United States, please contact **Sheri Allen** at *sheri.allen@globalepress.com*; for all other regions, contact **Nicole Lee** at *nicole.lee@igroupnet.com*.

OTHER TITLES IN OUR SUPPLY AND OPERATIONS MANAGEMENT COLLECTION

Series Editor: **Steven Nahmias**, *Georgia Tech*

A Primer on Negotiating Corporate Purchase Contracts
by Patrick Penfield

Production Line Efficiency: A Comprehensive Guide for Managers
by Sabry Shaaban and Sarah Hudson

Orchestrating Supply Chain Opportunities: Achieving Stretch Goals Efficiently
by Ananth Iyer and Alex Zelikovsky

Design, Analysis and Optimization of Supply Chains: A System Dynamics Approach
by William R. Killingsworth

www.ingramcontent.com/pod-product-compliance
Lightning Source LLC
Chambersburg PA
CBHW071956220426
43662CB00009B/1155